高职高专"十三五"规划教材
21世纪高职高专能力本位型系列规划教材

财经英语阅读（第2版）

主　编　朱　琳
副主编　张小曼　向　梅
主　审　杨秀玉　黎　瑛

内 容 简 介

本书共 12 章，内容涉及经济合作与发展、金融市场、国际贸易、财务管理、企业管理、投资与理财、银行业、保险、市场营销、新经济与新业务、跨国企业和会计。每章含有学习目标、导入、课文、阅读技巧、扩展阅读、注释、专业词汇表和习题。教材内容新颖，编排合理，生词量及习题难易程度适中。

本书可作为全国高职高专院校财经管理类专业的教材，也可作为在职人员培训学习的参考用书。

图书在版编目（CIP）数据

财经英语阅读/朱琳主编. —2 版. —北京：北京大学出版社，2018.1
（21 世纪高职高专能力本位型系列规划教材）
ISBN 978-7-301-28943-3

Ⅰ. ①财… Ⅱ. ①朱… Ⅲ. ①经济—英语—阅读教学—高等职业教育—教材 Ⅳ. ①F0

中国版本图书馆 CIP 数据核字（2017）第 266914 号

书　　　名	财经英语阅读（第 2 版） CAIJING YINGYU YUEDU
著作责任者	朱　琳　主编
策 划 编 辑	吴　迪
责 任 编 辑	翟　源
标 准 书 号	ISBN 978-7-301-28943-3
出 版 发 行	北京大学出版社
地　　　址	北京市海淀区成府路 205 号　100871
网　　　址	http://www.pup.cn　新浪微博：@北京大学出版社
电 子 信 箱	pup_6@163.com
电　　　话	邮购部 62752015　发行部 62750672　编辑部 62750667
印 刷 者	北京溢漾印刷有限公司
经 销 者	新华书店
	787 毫米×1092 毫米　16 开本　17 印张　393 千字 2010 年 1 月第 1 版 2018 年 1 月第 2 版　2018 年 1 月第 1 次印刷
定　　　价	42.00 元

未经许可，不得以任何方式复制或抄袭本书之部分或全部内容。
版权所有，侵权必究
举报电话：010-62752024　电子信箱：fd@pup.pku.edu.cn
图书如有印装质量问题，请与出版部联系，电话：010-62756370

第 2 版前言

随着经济全球化进程不断加快，国际经济以及亚太经济合作进一步加强。在"一带一路"倡议下，亚投行、金砖银行、丝路基金纷纷设立，将中国的国际化进程推向了新的高度。这些都对高职院校国际化人才培养，特别是国际化财务金融人才的培养提出了更高要求。当今社会是一个信息社会，如何快速地获取所需信息显得越来越重要，这对于财经类专业的学生来说也不例外。提高英语阅读能力，掌握英语阅读技巧是获取信息的一种重要方法。

本教材根据高等院校财经专业特点，以帮助学生了解、掌握财经专业的基础知识为主线，以扩大学生专业词汇量为驱动，以提高学生阅读能力为目的，组织设计教学内容。教材内容涉及财经专业的主要方面，分为 12 章，紧紧围绕当今社会的热点财经类话题，选材于国内外的相关资料，选材独特、时代感强、语言地道、趣味性强。通过每章的专业知识编排，帮助学生掌握财经专业的相关基础知识、专业词汇、日常用语，为进一步学习专业英语打下基础。教材结合阅读材料的特点，将阅读技巧穿插于每章之中，并配合练习供学生进行技能训练与检测，帮助学生有效地提高财经英语阅读技巧及能力，提升学生的专业知识与英语水平。

本教材在前版教材的基础上，对内容做了以下编排，使其在同类教材中更具有竞争力和吸引力：

1. 夯实基础，突出知识性和实用性。 本教材根据财经专业特点，以帮助学生了解、掌握财经专业的基础知识为主线，以扩大学生专业词汇量为驱动，以提高学生英语阅读能力为目的，组织设计符合高职学生水平的教材内容。教材通过每章的专业知识的编排，提供丰富有趣的阅读材料，帮助学生掌握财经专业的相关基础知识、专业词汇、日常用语，为进一步学习专业英语打下基础。

2. 选材新颖，时代感强。 教材内容涉及财经专业的主要方面，对原有章节内容做了调整，精心选取安排 12 章内容，并更新教材内容，选材上突出一个"新"字。内容紧紧围绕当今社会的热点财经类话题，选材于我国和英美等国最新出版的书籍、报纸杂志，财经新闻报道及国外著名网站，内容丰富、涉及面广、时代感强、语言地道、趣味性强。

3. 彰显高职特色，讲练结合，难度适中。 本教材以《高职高专教育英语课程教学基本要求(试行)》为依据，以培养高级应用型人才为教学目标，在英语教学中，贯彻"实用为主，够用为度"的方针，无论是精读，还是泛读文章都经过反复筛选，具有较强的实用性，力求符合高职学生的阅读水平。阅读文章后包括形式多样的阅读练习题，并配有课文的中文译文和词汇表，便于学生课后自主学习。

本教材在原教材基础上对章节设计上做如下调整：

Highlights 每个单元新增 **Highlights**。每章的第一页都详细列出本章节各个栏目的内容摘要(Outline)以及各篇文章的导读(Preview)，有助于学生在学习之前了解整个章节的主体内容。

Starter 每章都设置一个导入栏目，选取与本章话题相关的材料。导入形式多样，如图片讨论、财经图表分析、典型案例分析、财经新闻导读、全球财经热点话题讨论等。教师可利用此栏目引导学生进行热身练习，激发学生对章节话题的学习兴趣，启发思考，活跃课堂气氛。

Text 每章选取一篇来自国内外财经书刊、杂志或网站的全新前沿资料，作为精读课文，供学生进行深入学习，选材新颖独特、时效性强、语言规范。每篇课文都搭配相应的阅读练习以帮助学生更好地掌握阅读技巧，提高阅读水平。

Words and Terms 在课文后设置词汇表，对课文中出现的生词及专业术语做注释，解决学生阅读时所遇到的专业词汇难的问题，帮助学生扫除阅读时的词汇障碍。

Reading Skills 结合阅读材料的特点，每章介绍一种实用的阅读技巧，帮助学生进一步提高阅读理解能力。

Further Development 为了训练学生阅读财经英语资料的技能，每章设置两篇泛读文章(Passage I & Passage II)，并设置相应的阅读练习题，供学生进行实训，掌握阅读技巧，提高阅读能力。

Special Terms 每章设有专业词汇表，这些词汇均选自本章节的各篇文章，既有助于学生复习，也能帮助其积累专业术语及词汇。

本教材在编写过程中为了能更好地符合教学需求，编者大量地查阅和参考了相关的资料，同时，为了让学生能够阅读到原汁原味的英文，书中部分文章或章节选自国内外的财经报道、专业刊物和网站。由于所选用的教材涉及面较广，在此不一一注明，谨向所有被选文章或章节的原作者和单位机构表示诚挚的谢意。此外，为了改变传统专业教材枯燥乏味的设计，本教材在每章开头增加了一副小插图，在此一并向被采用插图的原作者表示衷心的感谢。

本教材由海南经贸职业技术学院的教师集体编写，朱琳副教授担任主编，由杨秀玉、黎瑛担任主审，编写分工如下：朱琳编写第 1 章；张小曼编写第 11、12 章；向梅编写第 6、9 章；韩望编写第 2、7 章；钟素静编写第 3、5 章；林贞编写第 8 章；李春怡编写第 4、10 章。

为了方便教学，本书提供习题答案、电子课件以及电子教案，用书老师可以发邮件到 7264280@qq.com 获取相关资料。

由于编者水平有限，加之时间仓促，书中不当之处在所难免，恳请广大读者批评指正。

编 者
2017 年 8 月

Contents

Chapter One Globalized Economic Cooperation 1
  Text The Asia-Pacific Economic Cooperation 2
  Reading Skills (1) Reading & Reading Abilities 8
  Further Development 10
    Passage I The Belt and Road 10
    Passage II The Belt and Road Initiative—Idea from China but Belongs to the Whole World 15
    Special Terms 19

Chapter Two Financial Markets 20
  Text Financial Markets 21
  Reading Skills (2) Establish Good Reading Habits 27
  Further Development 28
    Passage I The Chinese Stock Market 28
    Passage II China's Bond Market Is Showing Signs of Distress—The Situation Has Spooked Investors 32
    Special Terms 35

Chapter Three International Trade 37
  Text International Trade—The Eternal Topic of the World 38
  Reading Skills (3) Recognizing the Signal Words 43
  Further Development 45
    Passage I Trade in the Balance—Can Globalization Make Everyone Better off ? 45
    Passage II Protectionism Doesn't Pay 49
    Special Terms 53

Chapter Four Financial Management 54
  Text Introduction to Financial Management 55
  Reading Skills (4) Guessing the Meanings from the Context 60
  Further Development 61
    Passage I 2016: A Big Year for Shanghai's Financial Sector 61
    Passage II Top Ten Financial Aid Tips for Parents 67
    Special Terms 70

Chapter Five Business Management 71
  Text Managers and Management—The Eternal Topic of the Workplace 72
  Reading Skills (5) Drawing Conclusions 78
  Further Development 78

    Passage I   Workplaces' Skills 78

    Passage II   Job Interview— 7 Rules for Meetings with Top Execs 82

    Special Terms 85

Chapter Six   Investment and Financing 86

  Text   Five Really Dumb Money Moves You've Got to Avoid 87

  Reading Skills (6)   Skimming 93

  Further Development 94

    Passage I   Companies' Investment Plans 94

    Passage II   Student Finance: Top 10 Student Money Saving Tips 98

    Special Terms 102

Chapter Seven   Banking 103

  Text   Banking in China 104

  Reading Skills (7)   Guessing the Meanings from the Context 110

  Further Development 110

    Passage I   Mobile Banking—A Platform for Engagement 110

    Passage II   China Traditional Banks Strike Back Against Threat from Internet Finance 114

    Special Terms 118

Chapter Eight   Insurance 119

  Text   Social Insurance 120

  Reading Skills (8)   Using Word Part Clues for Word Meanings 125

  Further Development 127

    Passage I   Life Insurance 127

    Passage II   Auto Insurance Market 130

    Special Terms 134

Chapter Nine   Marketing 135

  Text   Marketing 136

  Reading Skills (9)   Note-taking and Thinking 143

  Further Development 146

    Passage I   Marketing in the Digital Age——A Brand-new Game 146

    Passage II   Classic Cases of SWOT Analysis 151

    Special Terms 155

Chapter Ten   New Economy and New Business 156

  Text   Introduction to E-business Technology and E-business 157

  Reading Skills (10)   Recognizing Important Facts or Details 163

  Further Development 164

    Passage I   Alipay to Launch in Europe as Alibaba Steps Up Payments Game 164

Passage II It's So Hard to Get Cash in India That Some People Are Ordering It Online 168
  Special Terms 170

Chapter Eleven Multinational Companies 171
 Text The US-based Multinational Company Wal-Mart 172
 Reading Skills (11) Note-taking and Thinking 178
 Further Development 180
  Passage I An American Hamburger and Fast Food Restaurant Chain—McDonald's 180
  Passage II Toyota-Suzuki Alliance Marks Auto Industry Fight for Survival 184
  Special Terms 188

Chapter Twelve Accounting 189
 Text What is Accounting? 190
 Reading Skills (12) Drawing a Conclusion 196
 Further Development 196
  Passage I Management Accounting Information 196
  Passage II Could an Accounting Change Destroy Jobs? 200
  Special Terms 204

参考译文 205
 第一章 全球化的经济合作 205
 第二章 金融市场 209
 第三章 国际贸易 214
 第四章 财务管理 218
 第五章 企业管理 223
 第六章 投资与理财 227
 第七章 银行业 232
 第八章 保险 237
 第九章 市场营销 240
 第十章 新经济和新业务 247
 第十一章 跨国企业 250
 第十二章 会计 255

参考文献 260

Chapter One

Globalized Economic Cooperation

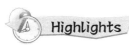

Highlights

Text

The Asia-Pacific Economic Cooperation

Reading Skills (1)

Reading & Reading Abilities

Further Development

Passage I

The Belt and Road

Passage II

The Belt and Road Initiative

— Idea from China but Belongs to the Whole World

This is the first chapter of the book. In the first section, you will learn a Text, and you will have some information about globalized economic cooperation. In the second section, you will learn reading skills and have a deeper understanding about reading. In the third section, you will learn two passages and it will help you have a further development on mastering reading skill and gain more information about globalized economic cooperation.

Starter

A globalized economy calls for globalized cooperation. What do you think?

(The Logo of the Economic Cooperation Organization)

Text

The Asia-Pacific Economic Cooperation

Asia-Pacific Economic Cooperation (APEC) is a forum for 21 Pacific Rim member economies that promotes free trade throughout the Asia-Pacific region. It was established in 1989 in response to the growing interdependence of Asia-Pacific economies and the advent of regional trade blocs in other parts of the world; to defuse fears that highly industrialised Japan would come to dominate economic activity in the Asia-Pacific region; and to establish new markets for agricultural products and raw materials beyond Europe.

History

In January 1989, Australian Prime Minister Bob Hawke called for more effective economic cooperation across the Pacific Rim region. This led to the first meeting of APEC in the Australian capital of Canberra in November, chaired by Australian Foreign Affairs Minister Gareth Evans. Attended by ministers from twelve countries, the meeting concluded with commitments for future annual meetings in Singapore and Korea.

The first APEC Economic Leaders' Meeting occurred in 1993 when U.S. President Bill Clinton,

Chapter One Globalized Economic Cooperation

after discussions with Australian Prime Minister Paul Keating, invited the heads of government from member economies to a summit on Blake Island. He believed it would help bring the stalled Uruguay Round of trade talks back on track. At the meeting, some leaders called for continued reduction of barriers to trade and investment, envisioning a community in the Asia-Pacific region that might promote prosperity through cooperation. The APEC Secretariat, based in Singapore, was established to coordinate the activities of the organization.

APEC currently has 21 members, including most countries with a coastline on the Pacific Ocean. However, the criterion for membership is that the member is a separate economy, rather than a state. As a result, APEC uses the term "member economies" rather than "member countries" to refer to its members. One result of this criterion is that membership of the forum includes Taipei China, as well as Hong Kong, China which entered APEC as a British colony but it is now a Special Administrative Region of the People's Republic of China.

Free Trade Area of the Asia-Pacific

APEC first formally started discussing the concept of a Free Trade Area of the Asia-Pacific (FTAAP) at its summit in 2006 in Hanoi. However, the proposal for such an area has been around since at least 1966 and Japanese economist Kiyoshi Kojima 's proposal for a Pacific Free Trade agreement proposal. While it gained little traction, the idea led to the formation of Pacific Trade and Development Conference and then the Pacific Economic Cooperation Council in 1980 and then APEC in 1989.

In the wake of the 2006 summit, economist C. Fred Bergsten advocated a Free Trade Agreement of Asia-Pacific. His ideas convinced the APEC Business Advisory Council to support this concept. Relatedly, ASEAN and existing Free Trade Agreement (FTA) partners are negotiating as Regional Comprehensive Economic Partnership (RCEP), not officially including Russia. The Trans-Pacific Partnership (TPP) without China or Russia involved has become the US-promoted trade negotiation in the region. At the APEC summit in Beijing in 2014, the three plans were all in discussion. President Obama hosted a TPP meeting at the US Embassy in Beijing in advance of the APEC gathering.

At the 2014 APEC summit in Beijing, APEC leaders agreed to launch "a collective strategic study" on the FTAAP and instruct officials to undertake the study, consult stakeholders and report the result by the end of 2016. APEC Executive Director Alan Bollard revealed in the Elite Talk show that FTAAP will be APEC's big goal out into the future.

Annual APEC Economic Leaders' Meetings

Since its formation in 1989, APEC has held annual meetings with representatives from all member economies. The first four annual meetings were attended by ministerial-level officials. Beginning in 1993, the annual meetings are named APEC Economic Leaders' Meetings and are attended by the heads of government from all member economies except Taiwan, China, which is represented by a ministerial-level official. The annual Leaders' Meetings are not called summits.

At the 2001 Leaders' Meeting in Shanghai, APEC leaders pushed for a new round of trade negotiations and support for a program of trade capacity-building assistance, leading to the launch of the Doha Development Agenda a few weeks later. The meeting also endorsed the Shanghai Accord proposed by the United States, emphasising the implementation of open markets, structural reform, and capacity building. As part of the accord, the meeting committed to develop and implement APEC transparency standards, reduce trade transaction costs in the Asia-Pacific region by 5 percent over 5 years, and pursue trade liberalisation policies relating to information technology goods and services.

Words and Terms

forum [fɔːrəm]	n.	论坛，讨论会
interdependence [ˌɪntədjˈpendəns]	n.	互相依赖
advent [ˈdvent]	n.	出现；到来
bloc [blɔk]	n.	集团，联盟
regional [ˈriːdʒənl]	adj.	地区的，区域的
defuse [ˌdiːˈfjuːz]	vt.	拆除；平息
dominate [ˈdɒmjneɪt]	v.	支配，影响
establish [jˈstæblɪʃ]	vt.	建立，创建
chair [tʃeə]	vt.	主持
commitment [kəˈmɪtmənt]	n.	承诺；致力；承担义务
summit [ˈsʌmɪt]	n.	高层会议；峰会
stall [stɔːl]	vi. & vt.	拖延；搁置
barrier [ˈbæriə]	n.	障碍；分界线
secretariat [ˌsekrɪˈteərɪət]	n.	秘书处；秘书；书记处
criterion [kraɪˈtɪərɪən]	n.	规范；标准，准则
Bogor [ˈbəugɔː]	n.	茂物(印度尼西亚爪哇岛西部城市)(音译博果尔)
colony [ˈkɔləni]	n.	殖民地；群体；聚居地
traction [ˈtrækʃn]	n.	牵引力；附着摩擦力
advocate [ˈædvəkeɪt]	vt.& n.	提倡；提倡者
undertake [ˌʌndəˈteɪk]	vt.	承担，从事；承诺
consult [kənˈsʌlt]	vi.&vt.	商议；咨询；请教
reveal [rɪˈviːl]	vt.	揭露
agenda [əˈdʒendə]	n.	日常工作事项；议程
endorse [ɪnˈdɔːs]	vt.	背书，签名；开证明文件
implementation [ˌɪmplɪmenˈteɪʃn]	n.	成就；贯彻
transparency [trænˈspærənsɪ]	n.	透明；透明度
Hanoi [hæˈnɔɪ]		河内(越南首都)
Canberra [ˈkænbərə]		堪培拉(澳大利亚首都)

Pacific Rim   太平洋地区；环太平洋
trade blocs   贸易集团，贸易联盟
free trade agreement   自由贸易协定
Asia-Pacific region   亚太地区
Pacific Islands Forum   太平洋岛屿论坛
Australian Foreign Affairs Minister   澳大利亚外交部长
Free Trade Area of the Asia-Pacific (FTAAP)   亚太自由贸易区
Pacific Economic Cooperation Council   太平洋经济合作委员会
Asia-Pacific Economic Cooperation   亚太经济合作组织
Regional Comprehensive Economic Partnership (RCEP)   区域全面经济伙伴关系
APEC Business Advisory Council(ABAC)   工商咨询理事会
ASEAN['æsiæn] (Association of Southeast Asian Nations) 东盟(东南亚国家联盟)

Notes

1. Asia-Pacific Economic Cooperation (APEC) is a forum for 21 Pacific Rim member economies that promotes free trade throughout the Asia-Pacific region.
亚太经济合作组织(APEC)是一个经济体论坛，由太平洋地区21个经济体成员组成，旨在促进整个亚太地区的自由贸易。

2. It was established in 1989 in response to the growing interdependence of Asia-Pacific economies and the advent of regional trade blocs in other parts of the world; to defuse fears that highly industrialised Japan would come to dominate economic activity in the Asia-Pacific region; and to establish new markets for agricultural products and raw materials beyond Europe. 它成立于1989年，以应对日益增长并相互依存的亚太经济和在世界的其他地方出现的区域贸易集团，化解因高度工业化的日本将在亚太地区主宰经济活动的担忧，并建立欧洲以外国家的农产品和原材料的新市场。

　　in response to 对……做出反应
　　e. g: The meeting was called in response to a request from consumer. 这次会议是应消费者的要求而召开的。
　　the advent of ……的到来
　　e. g: the advent of new technology 新技术的出现
　　The advent of the Euro will redefine Europe. 欧元的出现将重新定义欧洲。

3. In January 1989, Australian Prime Minister Bob Hawke called for more effective economic cooperation across the Pacific Rim region. 1989年1月，澳大利亚总理鲍勃·霍克呼吁更有效的环太平洋地区的经济合作。

　　call for 呼吁
　　e.g: The French government today called for an end to the violence. 如今,法国政府呼吁结束暴力行为。

Opposition leaders had called for a boycott of the vote. 反对党领袖已号召人们拒绝投票。

4. As a result, APEC uses the term "member economies" rather than "member countries" to refer to its members. 因此，亚太经合组织对于其成员使用的术语是"成员经济体"而非"成员国"。

as a result 结果，因此

e.g: As a result, the number has gone up. 因此，报告出来的人数就上升了。

As a result, quality that cannot be guaranteed. 因此，质量也无法保证了。

rather than… 而不……，与其……倒不如……；instead of sb. /sth. 代替；

e. g: We'll have the meeting in the classroom rather than in the auditorium. 我们与其在礼堂里开会，不如在教室开会。

5. He believed it would help bring the stalled Uruguay Round of trade talks back on track. 他相信这将帮助陷入僵局的乌拉圭回合贸易谈判重回正轨。

bring back 带回(某人或某物)；回忆；使(某人)恢复(某状态)

e. g: Your article brought back sad memories for me. 你的文章使我想起了伤心的往事。

Talking about it brought it all back. 谈到这个让人想起了整件事。

6. At the meeting, some leaders called for continued reduction of barriers to trade and investment, envisioning a community in the Asia-Pacific region that might promote prosperity through cooperation.

在会议上，一些领导人呼吁继续减少贸易和投资壁垒，在亚太地区构想一个共同体，通过合作促进繁荣。

7. In the wake of the 2006 summit, economist C. Fred Bergsten advocated a Free Trade Agreement of Asia-Pacific. 在2006年峰会之后，经济学家弗雷德·伯格斯腾倡导亚太地区的自由贸易协定。

in the wake of 紧跟，仿效；随着；跟着

e. g: Social problems cropped up in the wake of natural disasters. 自然灾害之后，出现了许多社会问题。

8. At the 2001 Leaders' Meeting in Shanghai, APEC leaders pushed for a new round of trade negotiations and support for a program of trade capacity-building assistance, leading to the launch of the Doha Development Agenda a few weeks later.

在2001年上海举行的领导人会议上，亚太组合组织领导人推动新一轮贸易谈判和支持贸易能力建设援助的计划，导致几周后多哈发展议程的开始。

push for 急切地要求，为……奋力争取

e. g: People living near the airport are pushing for new rules about night flight. 住在机场附近的人们正强烈要求制订夜航班机的新规。

He pushed me for an answer. 他催我作出答复。

We were pushed for time and had to quit some place to visit. 由于时间紧迫,我们只好放弃一些地方不去参观了。

Chapter One　Globalized Economic Cooperation

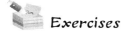 *Exercises*

I. Answer the following questions according to the text.

1. What is Asia-Pacific Economic Cooperation (APEC)?
2. Why was Asia-Pacific Economic Cooperation (APEC) established?
3. When was the first APEC Economic Leaders' Meeting held?
4. How many members does APEC have currently?
5. What did APEC leaders agree to do at the 2014 APEC summit in Beijing?

II. Identify the key words or main ideas of the following parts.

Part 1	_____ is a forum for 21 Pacific Rim member economies that promotes _____ throughout the Asia-Pacific region.
Part 2	The first APEC Economic Leaders' Meeting occurred in _____. It currently has _____ members, including most countries with a coastline on the Pacific Ocean.
Part 3	APEC first formally started discussing the concept of _____ at its summit in 2006 in Hanoi.
Part 4	Since its formation in 1989, APEC has held _____ with representatives from all _____.

III. Match the words or phrases in Column A to the words or phrases in Column B.

A   B

1. _____ forum   A. 高层会议；政府首脑的
2. _____ commitment   B. 总经理；行政部门
3. _____ summit   C. 从事；承担
4. _____ executive   D. 亚太经济合作组织
5. _____ undertake   E. 自由贸易协定
6. _____ agenda   F. 承诺；委任；承担义务
7. _____ consult   G. 经济合作
8. _____ Asia-Pacific Economic Cooperation   H. 商量；咨询；请教
9. _____ economic cooperation   I. 论坛，讨论会
10. _____ Free Trade Agreement   J. 日常工作事项；议程

IV. Choose the best translation.

1. As a result, APEC uses the term "member economies" rather than "member countries" to refer to its members. (　　)

  A. 因此，亚太经合组织对于其成员使用的术语是"成员经济体"而非"成员国"。
  B. 因此，亚太经合组织对于其成员使用的术语是"成员国"而非"成员经济体"。

7

C. 因此，亚太经合组织对于其他成员国使用的术语是"成员经济体"。

D. 因此，亚太经合组织对于其他成经济体使用的术语是"成员国"。

2. It was established in 1989 in response to the growing interdependence of Asia-Pacific economies and the advent of regional trade blocs in other parts of the world. (　　)

A. 它成立于 1989 年，以应对日益增长并相互依存的亚太经济和在世界的其他地方出现的区域贸易集团。

B. 它成立于 1989 年，来解决日益增长并相互依存的亚太经济和在世界的其他地方出现的区域贸易集团。

C. 它成立于 1989 年，来回答日益增长并相互依存的亚太经济和在世界的其他地方出现的区域贸易集团。

D. 它成立于 1989 年，以应对相互依存的亚太经济和在世界的其他地方出现的区域贸易集团。

3. At the meeting, some leaders called for continued reduction of barriers to trade and investment. (　　)

A. 在会议上，一些领导人打电话要求继续减少贸易和投资壁垒。

B. 在会议上，一些领导人呼吁继续增加贸易和投资壁垒。

C. 在会议上，一些领导人呼吁继续增加贸易和减少投资壁垒。

D. 在会议上，一些领导人呼吁继续减少贸易和投资壁垒。

4. In the wake of the 2006 summit, economist C. Fred Bergsten advocated a Free Trade Agreement of Asia-Pacific. (　　)

A. 峰会于 2006 年举行，经济学家弗雷德·伯格斯腾倡导亚太地区的自由贸易协定。

B. 在 2006 年峰会之后，经济学家弗雷德·伯格斯腾倡导太平洋地区的自由贸易协定。

C. 在 2006 年峰会之后，经济学家弗雷德·伯格斯腾倡导亚太地区的自由贸易协定。

D. 在 2006 年峰会之前，经济学家弗雷德·伯格斯腾倡导亚太地区的自由贸易协定。

5. Since its formation in 1989, APEC has held annual meetings with representatives from all member economies. (　　)

A. 自 1989 年以来，亚太经合组织与所有成员经济体的代表举行了年度会议。

B. 自 1989 年以来，亚太经合组织与所有成员国的代表举行了年度会议。

C. 自 1989 年成立以来，亚太经合组织与所有成员经济体的代表举行了年度会议。

D. 自 1989 年成立以来，亚太经合组织与所有成员经济体的代表经常举行会议。

Reading Skills (1)
Reading & Reading Abilities

What Is Reading?

Most of us think of reading as a simple, passive(被动的；消极的) process that involves reading words in a linear fashion (线性方式；直线性方式)and internalizing(使内在化) their meaning one at a time. But reading is actually a very complex process that requires a great deal of active participation on the part of the reader.

To get a better sense of the complexity (复杂性)of reading, read what some experts in the field have said about the reading process:

What do we read? The message is not something given in advance-or given at all — but something created by interaction between writers and readers as participants in a particular communicative situation. — Roy Harris in Rethinking Writing (2000)

Reading is asking questions of printed text. And reading with comprehension becomes a matter of getting your questions answered. — Frank Smith in Reading Without Nonsense (1997)

Reading is a psycholinguistic guessing game. It involves an interaction between thought and language. Efficient reading does not result from precise perception and identification of all elements, but from skill in selecting the fewest, most productive cues necessary to produce guesses which are right the first time. The ability to anticipate that which has not been seen, of course, is vital in reading, just as the ability to anticipate what has not yet been heard is vital in listening.

—Kenneth Goodman in Journal of the Reading Specialist (1967)

Literacy practices are almost always fully integrated with, interwoven into, constituted as part of, the very texture of wider practices that involve talk, interaction, values, and beliefs.

—James Gee in Social Linguistics and Literacies (社会语言学与素养)(1996)

As you can see, reading involves many complex skills that have to come together in order for the reader to be successful. For example:

Proficient readers recognize the purpose for reading, approach the reading with that purpose in mind, use strategies that have proven successful to them in the past when reading similar texts for similar purposes, monitor their comprehension of the text in light of the purpose for reading, and if needed adjust their strategy use.

Proficient readers know when unknown words will interfere with achieving their purpose for reading, and when they won't. When unknown words arise and their meaning is needed for comprehension, proficient readers have a number of word attack strategies available to them that will allow them to decipher the meaning of the words to the extent that they are needed to achieve the purpose for reading. Reading is also a complex process in that proficient readers give to the text as much as they take. They make meaning from the text by using their own prior knowledge and experiences.

Proficient readers are constantly making predictions while reading. They are continuously anticipating what will come next. Their prior knowledge and experiences with texts as well as with the world around them allow them to do this. It is this continuous interaction with the text that allows readers to make sense of what they are reading.

Further Development

Passage I

The Belt and Road

The Silk Road Economic Belt and the 21st-century Maritime Silk Road are also known as the Belt and Road. Belt and Road Initiative is a development strategy and framework, proposed by Chinese leader Xi Jinping that focuses on connectivity and cooperation among countries primarily between the People's Republic of China and the rest of Eurasia, which consists of two main components, the land-based "Silk Road Economic Belt" and oceangoing "Maritime Silk Road". The strategy underlines China's push to take a bigger role in global affairs.

The coverage area of the initiative is primarily Asia and Europe, encompassing around 60 countries. Oceania and East Africa are also included. The Belt and Road has been contrasted with the two US-centric trading arrangements, the Trans-Pacific Partnership and the Transatlantic Trade and Investment Partnership.

Silk Road Economic Belt

When Chinese leader Xi Jinping visited Central Asia and Southeast Asia in September and October 2013, he raised the initiative of jointly building the Silk Road Economic Belt and the 21st-Century Maritime Silk Road. Essentially, the "belt" includes countries situated on the original Silk Road through Central Asia, West Asia, the Middle East, and Europe. The initiative calls for the integration of the region into a cohesive economic area through building infrastructure, increasing cultural exchanges, and broadening trade.

Apart from this zone, which is largely analogous to the historical Silk Road, another area that is said to be included in the extension of this "belt" is South Asia and Southeast Asia. Many of the countries that are part of this belt are also members of the China-led Asian Infrastructure Investment Bank (AIIB). North, central and south belts are proposed. The North belt goes through Central Asia, Russia to Europe. The Central belt goes through Central Asia, West Asia to the Persian Gulf and the Mediterranean. The South belt starts from China to Southeast Asia, South Asia, the Indian Ocean.

Maritime Silk Road

The Maritime Silk Road, also known as the "the 21st-Century Maritime Silk Road" is a complementary initiative aimed at investing and fostering collaboration in Southeast Asia, Oceania, and North Africa, through several contiguous bodies of water — the South China Sea, the South Pacific Ocean, and the wider Indian Ocean area.

The 21st-Century Maritime Silk Road initiative was first proposed by Xi Jinping during a speech to the Indonesian Parliament in October 2013. Like its sister initiative the Silk Road

Economic Belt, most countries in this area have joined the China-led Asian Infrastructure Investment Bank.

East Africa

East Africa, including Zanzibar in particular, will form an important part of the Maritime Silk Road after improvements to local ports and construction of a modern standard-gauge rail link between Nairobi and Kampala is completed.

In May 2014, Premier Li Keqiang visited Kenya to sign a cooperation agreement with the Kenyan government. Under this agreement, a railroad line will be constructed connecting Mombasa to Nairobi. When completed, the railroad will stretch approximately 2,700 kilometers costing around 250 million USD.

In September 2015, China's Sinomach signed a strategic, cooperative memorandum of understanding with General Electric. The memorandum of understanding set goals to build wind turbines, to promote clean energy programs and to increase the number of energy consumers in sub-Saharan Africa.

Financial institutions

AIIB

The Asian Infrastructure Investment Bank, first proposed by China in October 2013, is a development bank dedicated to lending for projects regarding infrastructure. As of 2015, China announced that over one trillion yuan (US$160 billion) of infrastructure projects were in planning or construction.

On 29 June 2015, the Articles of Agreement of the Asian Infrastructure Investment Bank (AIIB), the legal framework was signed in Beijing. The proposed multilateral bank has an authorized capital of US$100 billion, 75% of which will come from Asian and Oceanian countries. China will be the single largest stakeholder, holding 26% of voting rights. The bank plans to start operation by year end.

Silk Road Fund

In November 2014, Xi Jinping announced plans to create a 40 billion USD development fund, which will be distinguished from the banks created for the initiative. As a fund its role will be to invest in businesses rather than lend money for projects. The Karot Hydropower Station in Pakistan is the first investment project of the Silk Road Fund.

In January 2016, Sanxia Construction Corporation began work on the Karot Hydropower Station 50 kilometers from Islamabad. This is the Silk Road Fund's first foreign investment project. The Chinese government has already promised to provide Pakistan with at least 350 million USD by 2030 to finance the hydropower station.

Oversight

The Leading Group for Advancing the Development of the Belt and Road and formed sometime in late 2014, and its leadership line-up publicized on February 1, 2015. This steering committee reports directly into the State Council of the People's Republic of China and is composed of several political heavyweights, evidence of the importance of the program to the government. Vice-Premier Zhang Gaoli, who is also a member of the 7-man Politburo Standing Committee, was named leader of the group, with Wang Huning, Wang Yang, Yang Jing, and Yang Jiechi being named deputy leaders.

In March 2014, Chinese Premier Li Keqiang called for accelerating the "Belt and Road" initiative along with the Bangladesh-China-India-Myanmar Economic Corridor and the China-Pakistan Economic Corridor in his government work report presented to the annual meeting of the country's legislature.

Words and Terms

initiative [ɪˈnɪʃətɪv]	n. & adj.	倡议；主动权；自发的
Eurasia [juəˈreɪʃə]	n.	欧亚大陆
encompass [ɪnˈkʌmpəs]	vt.	围绕，包围；完成
integration [ˌɪntɪˈɡreɪʃn]	n.	整合；一体化
cohesive [kəʊˈhiːsɪv]	adj.	有黏着力的；紧密结合的
analogous [əˈnæləɡəs]	adj.	相似的，可比拟的
foster [ˈfɒstə]	v.	培养；促进
Politburo [pəlɪtbjuərəʊ]	n.	政治局
collaboration [kəlæbəˈreɪʃn]	n.	合作，协作
standard-gauge [sˈtændədɡˈeɪdʒ]		标准轨距
memorandum [meməˈrændəm]	n.	备忘录；记录
stakeholder [ˈsteɪkhəʊldə(r)]	n.	股东；利益相关者
hydropower [ˈhaɪdrəpaʊə]	n.	水力发电；水电
oversight [ˈəʊvəsaɪt]	n.	监督；负责
heavyweight [ˈhevɪweɪt]	n. & adj.	重要的人物；重量级的
Vice-Premier		副总理，副首相
Zanzibar [ˌzænziˈbɑː]		桑给巴尔岛(坦桑尼亚东北部)
Mombasa [mɔmˈbæsə]		蒙巴萨岛(肯尼亚)
Nairobi [ˌnaɪəˈrəʊbi]		内罗毕
in contrast with		对比
consist of		由……组成；包括
US-centric trading		以美国为中心的贸易
dedicate to		献(身)于……；把(时间、精力等)投入到……；
Asian Infrastructure Investment Bank (AIIB)		亚洲基础设施投资银行

Chapter One   Globalized Economic Cooperation

 Notes

1. The Initiative is a development strategy and framework, proposed by Chinese paramount leader Xi Jinping that focuses on connectivity and cooperation among countries between the People's Republic of China and the rest of Eurasia, which consists of two main components, the land-based "Silk Road Economic Belt" and oceangoing "Maritime Silk Road". "一带一路" 是由中国最高领导人习近平提出的关于发展战略和框架的倡议，关注中华人民共和国和欧亚大陆其他国家紧密的连接和合作，主要包括两大部分，陆上"丝绸之路"的经济带和远洋"海上丝绸之路"。

the rest of 其余的；剩下的

e. g: He wolfed down the rest of the biscuit and cheese. 他把剩下的饼干和奶酪一扫而光。

The price of oil should remain stable for the rest of 2017. 油价会在 2017 年剩下的时间里保持稳定。

consist of 由……组成；由……组成；包括

e. g: A healthy diet should consist of wholefood. 健康饮食应由全天然食物构成。

The book consists of nineteen chapters. 这本书共分 19 章。

A chair consists of a seat with a back. 椅子是由椅座和椅背构成的。

2. East Africa, including Zanzibar, will form an important part of the MSR Maritime Silk Road after improvements to local ports and construction of a modern standard-gauge rail link between Nairobi and Kampala is completed. 东非，包括桑给巴尔岛，在经过对当地港口的改进，以及内罗毕和坎帕拉之间的现代标准轨距铁路建设的完成，将形成海上丝绸之路一个重要组成部分。

Nairobi: 内罗毕是东非国家肯尼亚的首都，人口超过 200 万，是一座国际化大都市，是非洲最大、最时尚、最现代化的城市之一。内罗毕于 1899 年建城，一开始是乌干达铁路的补给站，负责肯尼亚南方城市蒙巴萨和乌干达之间的补给。19 世纪 90 年代时，在突然爆发的瘟疫之后开始重建，当时英属东非殖民地开始兴建，内罗毕就变成了殖民者的重镇，1907 年英属东非殖民地将内罗毕设为首都。1963 年肯尼亚独立后继续将这里作为首都。联合国人类居住规划署(UNHABITAT)与环境署(UNEP)的总部皆设在内罗毕。国际民用航空组织(ICAO)的非洲东部、南部办事处设于此市。

3. As of 2015, China announced that over one trillion yuan (US$160 billion) of infrastructure projects were in planning or construction. 自 2015 年起，中国宣布正在计划或建设超过 10000 亿元(1600 亿美元)的基础设施项目。

as of 自……起，从……时起

e. g: The event was regarded as of such insignificance that not one major newspaper carried a report. 该事件被认为无足轻重，以至于没有一家主流报纸发文报道。

As of now we don't know much about Mars. 目前我们对火星还知之甚少。

The regulations come into force as of today. 本条例自即日起施行。

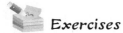

Exercises

I. Read the following statements and decide whether they are True (T) or False (F).

1. The Belt and Road Initiative was proposed by Chinese paramount leader Xi Jinping. ( )

2. The coverage area of the initiative is primarily Asia and Europe, encompassing around 30 countries. ( )

3. When Chinese leader Xi Jinping visited Central Asia and Southeast Asia in September and October 2015, he raised the initiative of jointly building the Silk Road Economic Belt and the 21st-Century Maritime Silk Road . ( )

4. The Asian Infrastructure Investment Bank, first proposed by America in October 2013, is a development bank dedicated to lending for projects regarding infrastructure. ( )

5. The Leading Group for Advancing the Development of the Belt and Road was formed sometime in late 2014, vice-Premier Zhang Gaoli, was named leader of the group, and Yang Jiechi being named deputy leaders. ( )

II. Choose the correct answer according to Passage I.

1. _____ , also known as The Belt and Road. ( )

A. the Asia-Pacific region

B. Southeast Asia, South Asia,

C. the Indian Ocean

D. the Silk Road Economic Belt and the 21st-century Maritime Silk Road

2. The strategy of the Belt and Road underlines China's push to take _____ role in global affairs. ( )

A. A bigger   B. a smaller

C. no   D. less important

3. In September and October 2013, _____ raised the initiative of jointly building the Silk Road Economic Belt and the 21st-Century Maritime Silk Road. ( )

A. Chinese President Xi Jinping   B. American leader Obama

C. Chinese Premier Li Keqiang   D. Russian leader Putin

4. On 29 June 2015, the _____, the legal framework was signed in Beijing. ( )

A. Asian Infrastructure Investment Bank (AIIB)

B. memorandum

C. US-centric trading

D. The belt and road

5. The _____ is the first investment project of the Silk Road Fund. ( )

A. Sanxia Construction Corporation   B. AIIB

C. Karot Hydropower Station   D. Maritime Silk Road initiative

III. Fill in the missing information according to Passage I.

Chinese leader Xi Jinping visited _____ and _____ (Central Asia and Southeast Asia) in September and October 2013, he raised the _____ of _____ building the Silk Road Economic Belt and the 21st-Century Maritime Silk Road. The initiative aimed at _____ and _____ collaboration in Southeast Asia, Oceania, and North Africa. _____ first proposed by China in October 2013, is a development bank dedicated to lending for projects regarding infrastructure. On 29 June 2015, the Articles of _____, the legal framework was signed in Beijing.

Passage II

The Belt and Road Initiative
—Idea from China but Belongs to the Whole World

BEIJING — The Belt and Road Initiative has become the most popular public goods and platform for international cooperation with the brightest prospects in the world amid rising protectionism and unilateralism, Chinese Foreign Minister Wang Yi said on the sideline of the recently concluded China's two sessions.

Proposed in 2013 by Chinese President Xi Jinping, the initiative has witnessed continuous expansion of its "friend circle", and yield tangible benefits for countries along its routes.

It will provide unprecedented opportunities for the economic and social development of countries involved, as "it is the way leading to the community of shared future for mankind," said Gerrishon K. Ikiara, a senior lecturer at the University of Nairobi.

Ideal of Openness, Inclusiveness

With its guiding principles of extensive consultation, joint contribution and shared benefits, the initiative has become a chorus instead of a solo.

Inspired by the ancient major trading route that linked China with Asia, Europe and Africa for a long time, the initiative aims to modernize the ancient trade route while aspiring to create common prosperity within those areas.

While the trends of protectionism and unilateralism are rising, the Belt and Road Initiative has become the common cause of the world which will help rebalance the economic globalization by making it more universally-beneficial and inclusive, said Wang Yi.

"The Belt and Road Initiative is against narrow-minded protectionism and isolationism," said Sergei Luzyanin, director of the Far Eastern Studies Institute under the Russian Academy of Sciences. "We only had the Western European-American option of integration and economic development in the 1990s, now there is a new option from China."

Global Growth Stimulator

The construction of the Belt and Road Initiative benefits not only China itself, but also countries along the routes. Against the backdrop of insufficient global demand, the blueprint will make contribution to the world economic growth.

A report issued by China's Renmin University said China has already begun the coordination of its signature initiative with the development strategies of many countries along the route, such as Kazakhstan's Bright Road program as well as the Sustainable Development Strategy of Kyrgyzstan.

So far, Chinese enterprises have established 56 economic and trade cooperative areas in more than 20 countries along the routes, invested accumulatively more than US$18 billion, and created US$1 billion revenue and 160,000 jobs.

Last year, China's direct investment in 53 countries along the routes reached US$14.53 billion and the total value of contracts China signed with 61 related countries reached over US$126 billion.

This year, the construction of the Belt and Road Initiative will continue to be a growth point of the global economy, and the further expanding of trade exchange, infrastructure connectivity and financial intermediation will drive the development of production capacity cooperation, cross border e-commerce and other fields.

New Engine for Globalization

Globalization currently is facing various problems and challenges, and the China-proposed Belt and Road Initiative will become the engine for the future of globalization, said Pascal Lamy, former chief of the World Trade Organization, while addressing a public session recently in Jakarta.

Globalization in the past was basically driven by the West and now the new globalization will be motivated more by the East than the West, Amitav Acharya, writer of the popular book told Xinhua in a recent interview.

When the West moves backward by erecting "walls", the East is building its gateway to the outside world, embracing globalization via China-proposed Belt and Road Initiative, Malaysia's New Straits Times said in an article published on its website.

Proposed in 2013, the initiative has so far gained the support of over 100 countries and international organizations, and more than 40 of them have signed cooperation agreements with China.

"China's initiative to jointly build the Belt and Road, embracing the trend towards a multipolar world, economic globalization, cultural diversity and greater IT application, aims at being highly efficient in terms of the allocation of resources, and at achieving a deep integration of markets among the countries concerned," said Keith Bennett, vice chair of the London-based 48 Club Group.

"It will thereby jointly create an open, inclusive and balanced regional economic cooperation architecture that benefits all," the British business leader told Xinhua.

(From http://www.chinadaily.com.cn/business/2017-03/17/content_28596217.htm)

Chapter One Globalized Economic Cooperation

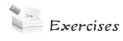 Exercises

I. Choose the correct answer according to Passage II.

1. _____ has become the most popular public goods and platform for international cooperation with the brightest prospects in the world amid rising protectionism and unilateralism. ( )

A. The ancient major trading route

B. Friend circle

C. World Trade Organization

D. The Belt and Road Initiative

2. Inspired by _____ that linked China with Asia, Europe and Africa for a long time, the initiative aims to modernize the ancient trade route while aspiring to create common prosperity within those areas. ( )

A. the ancient major trading route

B. the modern major trading route

C. the American international business trade

D. the British international business trade

3. The construction of the Belt and Road Initiative benefits _____. ( )

A. only China

B. only Africa

C. not only China but also Africa

D. not only China itself, but also countries along the routes

4. _____ has become the common cause of the world which will help rebalance the economic globalization. ( )

A. The Belt and Road Initiative

B. China

C. Asia

D. Africa

5. Proposed in 2013, the initiative has so far gained the support of over _____ countries and international organizations, and more than _____ of them have signed cooperation agreements with China. ( )

A. 100, 40

B. 100, 100

C. 40, 100

D. 50, 40

II. Choose the best translation.

1. "一带一路"的倡议已经成为最受欢迎的公益事业和有着光明前景的国际合作平台。( )

A. The Belt and Road Initiative has become the most popular public goods and platform for international cooperation.

B. The Belt and Road Initiative will become the most popular public goods and platform for international cooperation.

C. The Belt and Road suggestion has become the most popular public goods and platform for cooperation.

D. The Belt and Road Initiative has become more and more popular public goods and platform for international cooperation.

2. "我们曾经只有九十年代的西方欧美经济一体化发展的选择，现在有一个来自中国的新选择。"（   ）

A. "We only had the Western European-American option of integration and economic development in the 1990, now there is a new option from China."

B. "We only had the Western European-American option of integration and economic development in the 1990s, now there is a new option from China."

C. "We only had the Western European-American option of integration and economic development in the 1990, now there is another option from China."

D. "We had the Western European-American option of integration and economic development in the 1990, now there is a new option from China."

3. 全球化目前正面临各种问题和挑战，中国提出的一带一路倡议将成为未来全球化引擎。
（   ）

A. Globalization currently is facing various problems and challenges, and the China-proposed Belt and Road Initiative will become the machine for the future of globalization

B. Globalization is facing various problems and challenges, and the China-proposed Belt and Road Initiative will become the engine for the future of globalization

C. Globalization currently is facing various problems and challenges, and the American-proposed Belt and Road Initiative will become the engine for the future of globalization

D. Globalization currently is facing various problems and challenges, and the China-proposed Belt and Road Initiative will become the engine for the future of globalization

4. 过去的全球化基本上是由西方驱动，而现在新的全球化将更多地由东方而非西方推动。
（   ）

A. Globalization in the past was basically driven by the West and now the new globalization will be motivated more by the East than the West.

B. Globalization in the past was basically driven by the East and now the new globalization will be motivated more by the West than the East.

C. Globalization in the past was driven by the West and now the new globalization will be motivated more by the East than the West.

D. Globalization in the past was basically driven by the West and now the new globalization will be motivated more by the East.

5. 迄今为止，中国企业已经在20多个沿线国家建立了56个经贸合作区。（　　）

A. Now, Chinese enterprises have established 56 economic and trade cooperative areas in more than 20 countries along the routes.

B. So far, Chinese enterprises have established 56 economic and trade cooperative areas in more than 20 countries along the routes.

C. So far, Chinese enterprises have established 20 economic and trade cooperative areas in more than 56 countries along the routes.

D. So far, China has established 56 economic and trade cooperative areas in more than 20 countries along the routes.

Special Terms

stakeholder	股东；利益相关者
Free Trade Area	自由贸易区
Free Trade Agreement	自由贸易协定
The Belt and Road	一带一路
Vice-Premier	副总理，副首相
Foreign Affairs Minister	外交部长
Asia-Pacific Economic Cooperation	亚太经济合作组织
Asian Infrastructure Investment Bank (AIIB)	亚洲基础设施投资银行

Chapter Two

Financial Markets

Text
Financial Market
Reading Skills (2)
Establish Good Reading Habits
Further Development
Passage I
The Chinese Stock Market
Passage II
China's Bond Market Is Showing Signs of Distress—The Situation Has Spooked Investors

　　This is the 2rd chapter of the book. In the first section, you will learn a text, and you will have some information about the financial market. In the second section, you will have a deeper understanding about Financial Markets. In this section, you will learn two passages about the Chinese stock market and China's bond market. And in this chapter you will master a reading skill of how to establish good reading habits.

Chapter Two　Financial Markets

Starter

"If you want one year of prosperity, grow grain. If you want ten years of prosperity, grow trees. If you want 100 years of prosperity, grow people." How do you understand this sentence?

Text

Financial Markets

A financial market is a market in which people trade financial securities, commodities, and other fungible items of value at low transaction costs and at prices that reflect supply and demand. Securities include stocks and bonds, and commodities include precious metals or agricultural products.

Within the financial sector, the term "financial markets" is often used to refer to the markets that are used to raise finance: for long term finance — the Capital markets; for short term finance — the Money markets. Financial markets attract funds from investors and channel them to corporations — they thus allow corporations to finance their operations and achieve growth. Money markets allow firms to borrow funds on a short-term basis, while capital markets allow corporations to gain long-term funding to support expansion.

Basic Functions of Financial Markets

Financial markets serve six basic functions. These functions are briefly listed below:

① Borrowing and Lending: Financial markets permit the transfer of funds (purchasing power) from one agent to another for either investment or consumption purposes.

② Determination of Price: Prices of the new assets as well as the existing stocks of financial assets are set in financial markets. Determination of prices is the major function of financial market.

③ Information Aggregation and Coordination: Financial markets act as collectors and aggregators of information about financial asset values and the flow of funds from lenders to borrowers.

④ Risk Sharing: Financial markets allow a transfer of risk from those who undertake investments to those who provide funds for those investments.

⑤ Liquidity: Financial markets provide the holders of financial assets with a chance to resell or liquidate these assets.

⑥ Efficiency: Financial markets reduce the cost of transaction and acquiring information. It helps to increase efficiency in financial market.

Categories of Financial Markets

The financial market can be classified into several sub-categories. The components are listed below.

① Commodity market. It facilitates the trading of commodities.

② Money market. It provides short term debt financing and investment. The main vehicle for acquiring short-term finance is through a bank loan or overdraft, or through trade or treasury bills of exchange.

③ Derivatives market. It provides instruments for the management of financial risk.

④ Future market. It is an auction market in which participants buy and sell commodity and futures contracts for delivery on a specified future date.

⑤ Foreign exchange market. It facilitates the trading of foreign exchange and international currencies.

⑥ Spot market. It is the market which commodities, foreign exchange and securities are traded immediately or on the spot and goods are sold for cash payment and delivered immediately (7 business days for commodities and securities, 2 business days for foreign exchange).

⑦ Interbank market. It is the financial system of trading currencies among banks and financial institutions, excluding retail investors and smaller trading parties.

⑧ Capital market. It consists of stock market and bond market. Stock market provides financing through the issuance of shares or common stock. Bond market provides financing through the issuance of bonds.

The capital markets may also be divided into primary markets and secondary markets. Primary markets are securities markets in which newly formed (issued) securities are offered for sale to buyers. Financial products, including the supply of credit, mortgages, company shares and insurance, are bought and sold in primary and secondary financial markets. Secondary markets are securities markets in which existing securities that have previously been issued are resold, existing to enable buyers and sellers to resell their products and existing securities to a third party. The initial issuer raises funds only through the primary market. The transactions in primary markets exist between issuers and investors, while secondary market transactions exist among investors. The most

Chapter Two Financial Markets

well-known secondary financial market is the stock exchange, which allows trading in company shares that have been issued in the past.

Liquidity is a crucial aspect of securities that are traded in secondary markets. Liquidity refers to the ease with which a security can be sold without a loss of value. Investors benefit from liquid securities because they can sell their assets whenever they want; an illiquid security may force the seller to get rid of their asset at a large discount.

How to Choose a Stock

A good example of a financial market is a stock exchange. A company can raise money by selling shares to investors and its existing shares can be bought or sold. As investors, how to choose a stock? With so many options, selecting stocks can be a challenge for the average investor.

The first step in choosing stock is to determine your goals. Is your portfolio intended to generate income? Consider low-growth firms in industries like utilities, or REITs or master limited partnerships. Do you want to preserve capital? Stable blue-chip companies tend to appeal to investors with low risk tolerance. Do you want your capital to grow? Target a range of market caps and cycle stages. A combination of these strategies can diversify a portfolio.

Investors need to keep their eyes open, which means keeping up to date with current events and opinions. Blogs, magazines and online financial news inform investors about important developments in the market, and prompt them to seek more information. Sometimes, a news article or blog post will form the foundation of the underlying investment thesis.

Next, investors need to find companies that interest them. Once you're sold on an industry, and know its major players, look for investor presentations that discuss how a company makes its money. Presentations should include balance sheet information, income and cash flow performance and growth opportunities.

Following these steps might uncover several stocks you like, or none. If it's the latter, you've avoid potentially bad investments.

 Words and Terms

security [sɪˈkjʊərətɪ]	n.	安全；有价证券
commodity [kəˈmɒdɪtɪ]	n.	商品；货物
fungible [ˈfʌndʒɪbl]	adj.	可互换的
transaction [trænˈzækʃn]	n.	交易；业务
stock [stɒk]	n.	股票；股份
bond [bɒnd]	n.	债券
finance [faɪˈnæns]	n.	资金；金融
capital [ˈkæpɪtl]	n.	资本
fund [fʌnd]	n.	基金；现款
agent [ˈeɪdʒənt]	n.	经纪人；代理人
consumption [kənˈsʌmpʃn]	n.	消费

asset [ˈæset]	n.	资产
aggregation [ˌægrɪˈgeɪʃn]	n.	聚集
liquidity [lɪˈkwɪdɪti]	n.	流动性；资产流动性
liquidate [ˈlɪkwɪdeɪt]	vt.	清算
efficiency [ɪˈfɪʃnsɪ]	n.	效率
share [ʃeə]	n.	股份
financing [faɪˈnænsɪŋ]	n.	融资；理财
overdraft [ˈəʊvədrɑːft]	v.	透支
derivative [dɪˈrɪvətɪv]	adj.	衍生的
spot [spɒt]	n.	现货
mortgage [ˈmɔːgɪdʒ]	n.	抵押
portfolio [pɔːtˈfəʊlɪəʊ]	n.	证券投资组合
utilities [juːˈtɪlɪtɪz]	n.	公用事业

financial asset	金融资产
treasury bills of exchange	国库券；国债
future market	期货市场
foreign exchange	外汇
interbank market	银行行间市场
financial institution	金融机构
stock exchange	证券交易所
REITs	房地产信托投资基金

 Notes

1. A financial market is a market in which people trade financial securities, commodities, and other fungible items of value at low transaction costs and at prices that reflect supply and demand. 金融市场是一个以低交易成本交易买卖金融证券、商品及其他有价值的可互换物品，所成交的价格反映金融市场供求关系的资金融通市场。

2. Financial markets attract funds from investors and channel them to corporations—they thus allow corporations to finance their operations and achieve growth. 金融市场吸引投资者投入资金，为企业提供融资渠道—它们以这种方式帮助企业为自己的运营筹措资金，实现增长。

3. Spot market, which commodities, foreign exchange and securities are traded immediately or on the spot and goods are sold for cash payment and delivered immediately. 现货市场是商品、外汇和有价证券即刻或现场交易，商品现金出售并立即交割。

Spot Markets 现货市场是指与期货、期权和互换等衍生工具市场相对的市场的一个统称。在外汇和债券市场，现货市场指期限为 12 个月左右的债务工具(如票据、债券、银行承兑汇票)的交易。

4. Secondary markets are securities markets in which existing securities that have previously

been issued are resold, existing to enable buyers and sellers to resell their products and existing securities to a third party. 二级市场是对已发行的现有证券进行转售，使得买卖方可以转售他们的产品和现有证券给第三方的有价证券市场。

5. Liquidity refers to the ease with which a security can be sold without a loss of value. 资产流动性指的是投资者可以轻松地出售其购买的证券而不会影响损失资产的价值。

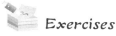

Exercises

I. Answer the following questions according to the text.

1. What is a financial market?
2. According to the text, how many basic functions of financial markets? What are they?
3. What are the categories of financial markets?
4. What is the difference between primary market and secondary market?
5. How to choose a stock?

II. Identify the key words or main ideas of the following paragraphs.

Part 1	the _____ of financial markets
Part 2	_____ functions of financial markets
Part 3	_____ of financial markets
Part 4	_____ to choose a stock

III. Match the words or phrases in Column A to the words or phrases in Column B.

	A		B
1. _____	capital	A.	股份
2. _____	security	B.	期货市场
3. _____	financial asset	C.	资本
4. _____	transaction	D.	债券
5. _____	share	E.	证券交易所
6. _____	bond	F.	金融资产
7. _____	future market	G.	融资
8. _____	financing	H.	有价证券
9. _____	financial market	I.	交易
10. _____	stock exchange	J.	金融市场

IV. Choose the best translation.

1. Future markets, which is an auction market in which participants buy and sell commodity and futures contracts for delivery on a specified future date. (   )

A. 期货市场是参与者在将来某一日期购买货物和交割期货合约的拍卖市场。

B. 期货市场是参与者在未来某一特定的日期买卖货物和交割期货合约的拍卖市场。

C. 期货市场是个拍卖市场，是参与者在未来某日期购买货物和期货合约的地方。

D. 期货市场是个拍卖市场，是参与者在将来某一特定日期买卖货物和期货合约的地方。

2. Financial markets attract funds from investors and channel them to corporations—they thus allow corporations to finance their operations and achieve growth. (　　)

A. 金融市场吸引投资者投入资金，为企业提供融资渠道—它们以这种方式帮助企业为自己的运营筹措资金，实现增长。

B. 金融市场吸引投资者投入资金，为企业提供资金—它们以这种方式帮助企业为自己筹措资金，以此实现增长。

C. 金融市场吸引投资者的资金，为企业提供渠道—它们允许企业为自己的运营筹款，实现增长。

D. 金融市场吸引投资者的资金，为企业提供资金渠道—它们允许企业为自己筹措资金，以此实现增长。

3. Investors need to keep their eyes open, which means keeping up to date with current events and opinions. (　　)

A. 投资者需要睁开眼睛，这意味着要及时了解事实和观点。

B. 投资者需要睁开双眼，这意思是要及时了解观点。

C. 投资者需要留心，这意味着要及时了解观点。

D. 投资者需要留心，这意味着要及时了解时事和观点。

4. Secondary markets are securities markets in which existing securities that have previously been issued are resold, existing to enable buyers and sellers to resell their products and existing securities to a third party. (　　)

A. 二级市场是对现有证券进行转售，使得买卖双方可以转售他们的产品和现有证券给第三方的有价证券市场。

B. 二级市场是对已发行的现有证券进行转售，使得买卖方可以转售他们的产品和现有证券给第三方的有价证券市场。

C. 二级市场是有价证券市场，是对现有证券进行转售，使得买方可以出售他们的产品和现有证券给第三者。

D. 二级市场是有价证券市场，是对现有证券进行买卖，使得买方可以出售他们的产品和现有证券。

5. The most well-known secondary financial market is the stock exchange, which allows trading in company shares that have been issued in the past. (　　)

A. 最让人熟悉的二级金融市场是股票交易所，它允许对过去的股份进行交易。

B. 最让人熟悉的的二级市场是股票交易所，它允许对过去的股份进行交易。

C. 众所周知的二级金融市场是证券交易所，允许对过去已发行的公司股份进行交易。

D. 众所周知的二级市场是证券交易所，允许对过去的公司股份进行交易。

Chapter Two　Financial Markets

Reading Skills (2)
Establish Good Reading Habits

Reading provides necessary survival skills. Good reading is a more important life skill than ever before, and the printed word continues to be the cornerstone of both higher education and better positions in the job market. Establishing good reading habits is very helpful for a person to become a successful reader.

Scanning: One good reading habit is scanning and get a good idea about the material. Before you really start reading the text, you can get a good idea about it by taking a few moments right away to read or scan the title, chapter headings, section titles and headlines of the material. Through this way you can get a quick understanding about what to expect from the reading, and you will know what you are reading as you go along. Maps, charts and pictures are clues that will help you to cue in on the content and organization of the material.

Reading Speed: Another good reading habit is reading fast. In fact, most people read much too slowly. Right now you are probably reading this slower than you need for good comprehension. Studies show that fast readers are the best readers, and that slow readers often lose their concentration and comprehension abilities because their minds will wander out of boredom. Remember, nothing hurts concentration more than reading too slowly. Your mind will keep up with your reading speed if you ask it to. By always reading at your top speed, you challenge your understanding and make it easier for your mind to concentrate on the material.

Vocabulary Building: For a person with good reading habits, a printed page contains not only words but also ideas, thoughts and feelings. But all these things are built on words. The more words you are familiar with, the less you are aware of reading words and the more you are aware of content and meaning. Expanding your vocabulary will help you to read more effectively and rapidly.

Many people simply skip over words they do not understand. This, naturally, hurts their overall comprehension. Other people stop at each new word and look it up in the dictionary, but this method can slow down the reading speed, affecting concentration and comprehension. But you can build your vocabulary without using a dictionary each time. When you meet with some unknown words while reading, remember to pause for a moment on each new word and let it register in your mind; or try to guess what the word means from context clues, from the words around it or the sentence before and after the word. With this method, you will see the word again and again. And then you will have a stronger impression of the meaning. Soon, the new word will be familiar and its meaning clear.

Finding the Main Idea: To pay attention to paragraph structure is also important in reading. Most paragraphs have a "topic sentence" which expresses the main idea. The main idea is the most important element of a paragraph. The remaining sentences contain sentences made up of detains that support and explain the main idea. Always pay attention to the first sentence of a paragraph, it is most likely to give you the main idea. Sometimes, the first sentence does not seem to give us enough new information to justify a paragraph. The next most likely place to look for the topic sentence is the last sentence of the paragraph.

Further Development

Passage I

The Chinese Stock Market

The Chinese stock market rout in recent weeks has prompted the country's government to act aggressively to stop the slide. If stocks continue to fall that could erode consumer confidence in China and slow further the country's already weakening economy, which would have painful implications for the global economy.

What has happened?

Chinese stocks have surged almost unimpeded, more than doubling in the 12 months ending June 12. Millions of working-class and middle-class Chinese families bet heavily on stocks, often borrowing money to do so and further spurring the rise.

But the rally defied fundamentals, prompting concerns of a bubble. Stocks rose even as the Chinese economy was slowing. While foreigners and domestic institutions bought shares in large companies with fairly stable businesses, working-class and middle-class families mainly bought inexpensive shares in small and medium-size companies, and kept buying these shares simply because they were rising. Weak balance sheets and chronic problems with corporate governance at many of these companies were swept aside.

In recent months, the Chinese stocks have experienced brief periods of weakness, as investors started to grow concerned that the market was getting overheated. The government, though, has regularly reassured investors, helping to steady the markets.

Now, investors are losing faith. After a drop of more than 7 percent in the Shanghai and Shenzhen markets on June 26, the Chinese central bank responded the next day with an interest rate cut, saying it was acting to shore up the economy. A broad slide in stocks continued, prompting the government to take aggressive action.

What is China doing about the sell-off?

Since June 25, the Chinese government has tried a series of policy measures to halt the slide. It has cut interest rates, made more loans available to buyers of stocks and promised to investigate anyone involved in market manipulation.

Chapter Two　Financial Markets

The government made its boldest move on July 4, orchestrating a plan for 21 brokerages to put US$19.4 billion in a fund to buy the shares of large companies. The Shanghai and Shenzhen stock exchanges suspended 28 pending initial public offerings and said that all deposits paid for shares would be returned to the would-be buyers, freeing up cash that could be invested in existing stocks. Government agencies announced on July 5 that they would lend money to brokerages so that the brokerages could lend the money to investors who wanted to buy shares.

Following the move, large company shares held most of their value on July 6. But the shares of small and medium-size companies, widely held by retail investors, kept falling.

How exposed are foreign investors?

The Chinese markets have only recently started to open up to outside investors, so overseas players are not heavily exposed to the downturn. Such investors own an estimated 4 percent of Chinese shares. And they have been heavily concentrated in large companies, which have not been as volatile as their smaller brethren.

But stock market routs can quickly spread. The Hong Kong market withstood previous bouts of selling, but fell on July 6 after the Chinese government's moves. And foreigners have invested heavily in the Hong Kong market, often as a proxy for mainland China.

Will China's stock market troubles affect the global economy?

Possibly.

China has the world's second-largest economy. It is the biggest importer of commodities, from countries like Australia and Brazil. China is also a huge buyer of factory equipment and other machinery in Germany and other places. If the Chinese stock market slide damages consumer confidence, it could lead to a slowdown in those purchases.

The stock market weakness, should it spread to the Chinese economy over the long term, could prompt Beijing to reassess its overseas loans and investments. Many countries, industries and companies have come to depend on Chinese money to fund their own growth. But Chinese outbound investment could still increase if companies and individuals seek safety overseas.

(From: http://www.kekenet.com/read/201507/385251.shtml)

Words and Terms

rout [raʊt]	v.	溃败；崩溃；搜寻
prompt [prɒmpt]	v.	促使；鼓励
slide [slaɪd]	n.	下跌；滑落
erode [ɪˈrəʊd]	v.	损害；削弱
surge [sɜːdʒ]	v.	飙升；汹涌；蜂拥而来
unimpeded [ˌʌnɪmˈpiːdɪd]	adj.	无阻挡的；畅通的
spur [spɜː]	vt. & vi.	刺激；急速前进
bubble [ˈbʌbl]	n.	泡沫；水泡

chronic ['krɒnɪk]	adj.	长期的；慢性的
reassure [ˌriːəˈʃɔː]	vt.	使安心；安抚
sell-off [ˈsel ˌɔːf]	n.	暴跌；下跌；廉价抛售
manipulation [məˌnɪpjʊˈleɪʃn]	n.	操控；控制
orchestrate [ˈɔːkɪstreɪt]	v.	精心策划；策动；谱写
suspend [səˈspend]	v.	暂停；延缓；中断
downturn [ˈdaʊntɜːn]	n.	衰退
volatile [ˈvɒlətaɪl]	adj.	不稳定的；易变的
reassess [ˌriːəˈses]	v.	重新审视；重新评估

balance sheet	资产负债表
interest rate cut	降息；降低利率
halt the slide	防止下跌；遏止衰退
would-be buyers	潜在购买者

1. But the rally defied fundamentals, prompting concerns of a bubble. 但上涨与经济基本面并不相符，催生了对于泡沫的担忧。

2. Weak balance sheets and chronic problems with corporate governance at many of these companies were swept aside. 许多公司脆弱的资产负债表和长期的公司管理问题被搁置一边。

3. The government made its boldest move on July 4, orchestrating a plan for 21 brokerages to put US$19.4 billion in a fund to buy the shares of large companies. 政府在7月4日采取了最勇敢的举措，策划了一项计划，21家证券公司将出资194亿美元(1200亿人民币)建立基金购买大型公司的股票。

4. The Shanghai and Shenzhen stock exchanges suspended 28 pending initial public offerings and said that all deposits paid for shares would be returned to the would-be buyers, freeing up cash that could be invested in existing stocks. 上海证券交易所和深圳证券交易所暂停了28只新股的发行计划，并称将向潜在购买者退还所有已支付的定金，以释放更多现金投入到现有的股票中。

5. The Hong Kong market withstood previous bouts of selling, but fell on July 6 after the Chinese government's moves. 香港股市抵挡住了此前的几轮抛售，但在7月6日中国政府行动之后下挫。

Exercises

I. Read the following statements and decide whether they are True (T) or False (F).

1. Chinese stocks have surged, more than doubling in the 12 months from June.　　　(　　)

Chapter Two　Financial Markets

2. Working-class and middle-class families kept buying inexpensive shares in and medium-size companies simply because they were rising.　　　　　　　　　　（　）
3. Since June 25, the Chinese government has done nothing to halt the slide.　（　）
4. Overseas investors are not heavily exposed to the downturn of Chinese stock market.（　）
5. China's stock market troubles won't affect the global economy.　　　　（　）

II. Choose the correct answer according to Passage I.

1. The Chinese stock market rout has prompted _____ to act aggressively to stop the slide.（　）
   A. stock agencies　　　　　　　　　B. the country's government
   C. investment institutions　　　　　D. investors

2. According to the passage, _____ bet heavily on stocks, often borrowing money to invest in stocks and further spurring the rise of stock in China. （　）
   A. thousands of working-class and middle-class Chinese families
   B. millions of affluent class Chinese families
   C. millions of working-class and middle-class Chinese families
   D. thousands of capital class and domestic institutions

3. What policy measures did the government try to halt the slide? （　）
   A. Made more loans available to buyers of stocks
   B. Cut interest rates
   C. Promised to investigate anyone involved in market manipulation
   D. All of above

4. Following the government's move of rescue package, the shares of _____ widely held by retail investors, kept falling. （　）
   A. small and medium-size companies
   B. small-size companies
   C. large companies
   D. medium and large-size companies

5. Which of the following statement is NOT true? （　）
   A. Chinese stocks still rose even as the Chinese economy was slowing.
   B. Chinese stocks have surged almost unimpeded, more than doubling in a year ending June 12.
   C. The government made its boldest move on July 4, planning a plan for 21 brokerages to put US$19.4 million in a fund to buy the shares of large companies.
   D. The Shanghai and Shenzhen stock exchanges said that all deposits paid for shares would be returned to the would-be buyers, freeing up cash that could be invested in existing stocks.

III. Fill in the missing information.

The Chinese stock market rout in recent weeks has prompted the country's government to act aggressively to _____. Now, _____ are losing faith. Since June 25, the Chinese government has tried _____ to halt the slide. It has cut interest rates, made more loans available to buyers of stocks and promised to _____. The government made its _____ on July 4, orchestrating a plan for 21 brokerages to put US$ _____ in a fund to buy the shares of large companies. Government agencies announced on July 5 that they would lend money to brokerages so that the brokerages could lend the money to _____. But _____ can quickly spread. China's stock market troubles will _____ affect the global economy.

Passage II

China's Bond Market Is Showing Signs of Distress
—The Situation Has Spooked Investors

Now another fast-growing part of China's vast and increasingly complicated financial market is showing signs of distress: its US$9 trillion bond market.

Prices for government and corporate bonds have tumbled over the past week, a sell-off that continued on Tuesday. The situation has alarmed investors, prompting the government to temporarily restrain some trading and to make emergency loans to struggling financial institutions.

The price drops have resulted in higher borrowing costs at a time when more Chinese companies need the money to cope with slowing economic growth. Yields reached new highs again on Tuesday.

In part, China is reacting to financial shifts across the globe. With the Federal Reserve raising short-term interest rates and many expecting the presidency of Donald J. Trump to lead to heavier government spending, investors worldwide are selling bonds.

But China is struggling with its own balancing act. The Chinese bond slump also stems from Beijing's efforts to wring excess money from its financial system and to stop potential bubbles that may lurk in shadowy, hard-to-track corners of its economy. Should it continue with those efforts, bonds could fall further?

At least 40 companies have said they would postpone or cancel bond offerings rather than risk being forced to pay high interest rates to sell the bonds—or being unable to sell them at all. Among them was the Jiangsu Sumec Group Corporation, an industrial trading house that exports items as varied as gardening tools and auto parts; the company said on Thursday that it would not go through with the sale of US$130 million in short-term bonds.

China has particular reason to worry. As the world's second-largest economy, after the United States, it relies on a rickety financial system that is mired in debt and susceptible to hidden stresses. Higher overseas interest rates could also prompt more Chinese investors to move their money out of the country, either to chase higher returns elsewhere or to avoid what some see as China's growing problems.

A healthy bond market is crucial to China's restructuring plans. The country has been counting on its fast-growing bond market as one way to bring market discipline to its traditionally state-directed—and wasteful—economy.

In the mature financial system of the United States, businesses have plenty of ways to get money. They can borrow from a bank, raise money selling stocks or bonds, or seek funds directly from any number of investors.

But in China, state-run banks are by far the main source of funding. That helped power the country's economic rise, but it also led to loans going to politically connected borrowers rather than to where the economy needed it most. That is one reason the Chinese economy is now stuck with more steel, glass, cement and auto factories than it needs.

Particularly in the past two years, China has taken steps to encourage the development of robust stock and bond markets as well as private lenders, needing a way to ensure the flow of money was being directed by profit-minded investors rather than politicians and their allies at state-owned banks.

The stock market crashed last year, and private lending has been slow to take off. But until this past week, the bond market had performed well. The investment arms of local governments and other large borrowers rushed in recent months to issue bonds at low interest rates and to pay off bank loans issued at higher rates—just as the government intended. Bond issuance jumped 47 percent in the first 11 months of this year from the same period last year.

What the government did not foresee was an explosion of speculative bond trading by Chinese banks.

Banks have increasingly raised money by selling wealth management products, investments that have the look and feel of dependable bank deposits and are usually sold to average investors. Banks rarely disclose what is behind those wealth management products and generally keep them off their books.

Still, it is becoming increasingly clear that many of them are backed by bonds. The bond holdings of wealth management products more than doubled over the 18-month period that ended in June. Adding to the risks, banks are also making large, leveraged bets on the direction of bond prices. Now the government is moving to rein it in.

On Tuesday, the yield on one-year government bonds rose to 3.11 percent, compared with 2.35 percent two weeks ago, a considerable jump for bonds. Yields go up when bond prices go down, and a higher yield makes it more expensive to issue bonds.

Corporate bond yields are also rising fast, as investors have begun demanding a better return from entrusting their money to China's frequently opaque companies. That reverses a trend from earlier this year, when investors were so enthusiastic for Chinese bonds that they bought corporate bonds as well, narrowing the natural spread between government and corporate bonds. Mr. Miao, of FXM Brothers, predicted that corporate bonds would continue to sell off until the spread between government corporate yields was wider again.

(From http://www.kekenet.com/read/201612/484964.shtml)

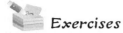

Exercises

I. Choose the correct answer according to Passage II.

1. Now in China's vast and increasingly complicated financial market, _____ is showing signs of distress.

   A. stock market   B. bond market

   C. money market   D. commodity market

2. In China, many of wealth management products are backed by _____.

   A. bonds   B. funds

   C. stocks   D. banks

3. When bond prices go down _____ go up, and a higher _____ makes it more expensive to issue bonds.

   A. yields, yield   B. yields, price

   C. yield, interest   D. yield, return

4. One reason that the Chinese economy is now stuck with more steel, glass, cement and auto factories than it needs is _____.

   A. state-run banks led to loans going to where the economy needed it

   B. state-run banks led to loans going to where the economy needed it most

   C. state-run banks led to loans going to investors

   D. state-run banks led to loans going to politically connected borrowers

5. According to the passage, businesses in United States have plenty of ways to get money except _____.

   A. borrowing from a bank

   B. raising money by selling stocks or bonds

   C. getting money from stock market

   D. seeking funds directly from any number of investors

II. Choose the best translation.

1. 中国债券下跌的另一个原因是北京力图从金融体系中挤压出超发的货币，防止潜在泡沫出现。( )

   A. The Chinese bond slump also stems from Beijing's efforts to wring excess money from its financial system and to stop potential bubbles

   B. The Chinese bond slump also stems from Beijing's efforts to wring money from its financial system and to stop economic bubbles

   C. The Chinese bond crashed stems from Beijing's efforts to wring excess money from its financial system and to stop from economic bubbles

   D. The Chinese bond crashed stems from Beijing's efforts to wring money from its financial system and to stop from economic bubbles

2. 银行越来越多地通过出售理财产品给普通投资者来筹集资金。(　　)
A. Banks raised money by selling wealth management products to investors.
B. Banks raised money by selling finance management products to average investor.
C. Banks have raised money by selling wealth management products to average investors.
D. Banks have increasingly raised money by selling wealth management products to average investors.

3. 海外利率升高也可能会促使更多的中国投资者将资金转移出国，以追求更高的回报。(　　)
A. Higher overseas interest rates could also force Chinese investors to move their money out of the country, to chase high returns elsewhere.
B. Higher overseas interest rates could also prompt more Chinese investors to move their money out of the country, to chase higher returns elsewhere.
C. Higher interest rates could also prompt more investors to move their money out of the country, to chase higher returns elsewhere.
D. High interest rates could also prompt more Chinese investors to move their money out, to chase high returns elsewhere.

4. 除了这种风险之外，银行还使用大规模杠杆押注债券价格的走向。(　　)
A. Adding to the risks, banks are also making large, leveraged bets on the direction of bond prices.
B. Adding the risks, banks are also making large, leveraged bets on the direction of bond prices.
C. Adding the risks, banks are also making large bets to the direction of bond prices.
D. Adding to the risks, banks are also making large bets to the direction of bond prices.

5. 企业债券的收益率也在快速上升，相比将资金注入信息不透明的中国公司，投资者已经开始要求获得更好的回报。(　　)
A. Corporate bond yields are rising fast, investors have begun demanding a better return from entrusting their money to China's opaque companies.
B. Corporate bond yields are also rising fast, as investors have begun demanding a better return from entrusting their money to China's frequently opaque companies.
C. Corporate bond yields are also rising fast, as investors have begun demanding return from entrusting their money to China's opaque companies.
D. Corporate bond yields are rising fast, investors have begun demanding return from entrusting their money to China's frequently opaque companies.

Special Terms

| financial asset | 金融资产 |
| treasury bills of exchange | 国库券；国债 |

future market	期货市场
foreign exchange	外汇
interest rate cut	降息
financial market	金融市场
money market	货币市场
bond market	债券市场
interbank market	银行行间市场
financial institution	金融机构
stock exchange	证券交易所

Chapter Three

International Trade

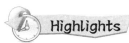

Text
International Trade—The Eternal Topic of the world
Reading Skills (3)
Recognizing the Signal Words
Further Development
Passage I
Trade in the Balance—Can Globalization Make Everyone Better off?
Passage II
Protectionism Doesn't Pay

This is the 3rd chapter of the book. In the first section, you will learn a text, and you will have some information about International Trade. In the second section, you will have a deeper understanding about world trade. In this section, you will learn two passages about trade in the balance and trade protectionism and they will help you have a further development on mastering reading skills of recognizing the signal words.

Starter

Trade makes the world a better place. What do you think?

Text

International Trade
—The Eternal Topic of the World

Trade, the exchange of goods and services, is the most basic social activity. Trade began to exist almost the same time as human being did. Without trade, there would have been no society.

As one of the most important economic activities in the world today, international trade plays a more and more important role in the development of a nation's economy and in the acceleration of globalization worldwide. But what is international trade? International trade, also known as world trade, foreign trade or oversea trade, is the exchange of goods and service between nations. International trade includes many types. Here are some of them as following.

From the direction of cargo flow, international trade can be classified into import trade, export trade, transit trade.

Export trade   It means to transport the goods which are produced and processed in domestic market to international market for sale.

Import trade   It refers to the transaction to transport the goods from foreign countries to domestic market for sale or use.

Chapter Three International Trade

Transit trade If goods are transported from the producing country to the consuming country via a third country's border, this is known as transit trade.

From the form of the goods, international trade can be classified into visible goods trade and invisible goods trade.

Visible goods trade Also known as tangible goods trade, visible goods trade refers to the exchange of physically tangible goods. Very often the things we buy are a "real" thing that we can touch or see and can make use of, such as cars, wines, shoes etc.

Invisible goods trade Sometimes we do not pay money for anything tangible. The goods we buy we "invisible", or they can not be "seen", for example, hotel services, postal service. In this case, we buy "services" instead of "goods". The purchase and sale of services are called "invisible trade". In international trade, likewise, we not only import and export goods, we also import and export services.

Reasons for International Trade

In today's complex economic world, neither individuals nor nations are self-sufficient. Nations have utilized different economic resources; people have developed different skills. This is the foundation of international trade and economic activities. It takes place for many reasons.

1. Resource Reasons

Climatic conditions and terrain are very important for agricultural products. The difference in these factors enables some countries to grow certain plants and leaves other countries with the only choice to import the products they consume. For example, Colombia and Brazil have the opportunity to export coffee beans to countries worldwide. Another example is that the US Great Plains states have the ideal climate and terrain for raising wheat. This has made the US a big wheat exporter.

2. Economic Reasons

In addition to getting the products they need, countries also want to gain economically by trading with each other. It is made possible by varied prices for the same commodity around the world, reflecting the differences in the cost of production. For example, Country A and Country B may have the same capability in producing card and computers, but the cost for the production of them will decrease if the goods are produced on a large scale. Both countries would find it advantageous if each were to specialize completely in the production of one and import the other.

3. Political Reasons

Political objectives can sometimes outweigh economic considerations between countries. One country might trade with another country in order to support the latter's government which upholds the same political doctrine. Or trade with some countries is banned or restricted just not to benefit a government with political disagreements.

Benefits of International Trade

It seems that most countries of the world have a strong desire to mutually expand their trade. At first sight, different nations appear to have many different economic political and social reasons for wanting to trade. Under the surface, however, there is a common financial advantage enabling all countries to make a profit through international trade.

1. Cheaper Goods

For one thing, countries trade because there is a cost advantage. This has been explained in the section of "economic reason" for international trade. Further, competition in the world market remains constant. This has made prices even lower. Last, if the quality of the imported goods is better but the price is not higher compared with the domestic cost, there is still a cost advantage.

2. Various Goods or Services

International trade means that countries can provide a wider variety of products for their consumers and thus help to improve the living standard of the people. Countries trade because there is a cost advantage and because competition in the world market has made prices even lower.

3. Wider Markets

International trade can greatly expand the market. The expansion enables manufacturers to take advantage of economies of scale in both research and production. Besides, since markets around the world are often in different development stages, newly expanded markets can help extend the life of products.

4. Economic Growth

International trade provides a stimulus to economic growth. It provides wealth to the economy. It develops beneficial links between countries; encourages tourism education and creates jobs, which is of great importance for the economic growth of a country as well as the advancement of the whole world.

The primitive "goods-for-goods" trade still remain today in some countries that do not have enough foreign currency reserves to settle payment with. This form of trade is called barter. Another trade form is "exchange of goods for money", where people settle payment, chiefly with US dollar, British pound, Swiss franc, the euro, Hong Kong dollar, and Japanese yen.

Words and Terms

acceleration [əkselə'reɪʃn]	n. 加速
exchange [ɪks'tʃeɪndʒ]	v. 交换，互换
classified ['klæsɪfaɪd]	adj. 分类的，归类的
transaction [træn'zækʃn]	n. 交易
characteristic [ˌkærəktə'rɪstɪk]	n. 特征
currency ['kʌrənsɪ]	n. 货币
luggage ['lʌgɪdʒ]	n. 行李
restriction [rɪ'strɪkʃən]	n. 限制，管制
minimize ['mɪnɪmaɪz]	v. 减少
barter [bɑːtə(r)]	n. 以货易货；易货贸易

Chapter Three   International Trade

import trade	进口贸易
export trade	出口贸易
transit trade	过境贸易
visible goods trade	有形商品贸易
invisible goods trade	无形商品贸易

Notes

1. Trade began to exist almost the same time as human being did. Without trade, there would have been no society.

贸易几乎与人类同时出现。没有贸易，就不会有社会。

2. International trade, also known as world trade, foreign trade or oversea trade, is the exchange of goods and service between nations. 国际贸易也被称为世界贸易、国外贸易或是海外贸易，是国家之间进行商品和服务交易的活动。

世界贸易组织(World Trade Organization，简称 WTO)，中文简称世贸组织。1994 年 4 月 15 日，在摩洛哥的马拉喀什市举行的关贸总协定乌拉圭回合部长会议决定成立更具全球性的世界贸易组织，以取代成立于 1947 年的关贸总协定。世界贸易组织是当代最重要的国际经济组织之一，拥有 164 个成员，成员贸易总额达到全球的 98%，有"经济联合国"之称。

3. In today's complex economic world, neither individuals nor nations are self-sufficient.

在当今复杂的经济领域中，没有任何个人或是国家能够做到自给自足。

4. The difference in these factors enables some countries to grow certain plants and leaves other countries with the only choice to import the produces they consume.

这些因素的不同导致一些国家种植某些作物，其他国家只能选择进口它们所生产的农产品。

5. For example, Country A and Country B may have the same capability in producing card and computers, but the cost for the production of them will decrease if the goods are produced on a large scale. 例如，A 国家和 B 国家在生产卡片和计算机方面可能具有相同的能力，但是如果大规模生产的话，它们的生产成本就会降低。

6. The primitive "goods-for-goods" trade still remain today in countries that do not have enough foreign currency reserves to settle payment with.

现今，原始的"以物换物"贸易在一些国家中依然存在。以物换物是有社会契约或明确协议条件下的交换价值模式。与物品经济自由价值模式相反。用自己已有的物品或服务与别人交换，以换取别人的物品或服务，是一种现有贸易模式出现之前已有的交易方式。在人类使用货币之前，人类已经懂得以物易物。以物换物不同于买卖，并没有使用任何金钱做交易的工具，所以以物易物不一定是一场等价交换。和市场经济一样，以物易物属于等级制度的文化体系，有明显的"经济"体系特性。

 Notes

I. Answer the following questions according to the text.

1. How long is the history of trade?
2. What is international trade?
3. How many types of international trade are mentioned in the text? What are they?
4. What's the definition of "transit trade"?
5. Does "goods-for-goods" trade still exist in the world?

II. Identify the key words or main ideas of the following parts.

Part 1	The _____ of international trade
Part 2	The _____ of international trade
Part 3	_____ for international trade
Part 4	_____ of international trade

III. Match the words or phrases in Column A to the words or phrases in Column B.

A	B
1. _____ import trade	A. 限制，管制
2. _____ invisible goods trade	B. 有形商品贸易
3. _____ transit trade	C. 过境贸易
4. _____ currency	D. 好处，益处，盈利
5. _____ exchange	E. 出口贸易
6. _____ self-sufficient	F. 货币
7. _____ export trade	G. 进口贸易
8. _____ restrictions	H. 自给自足的
9. _____ visible goods trade	I. 交换，互换
10. _____ benefit	J. 无形商品贸易

IV. Choose the best translation.

1. In international trade, likewise, we not only import and export goods, we also import and export services. (   )

　　A. 同样地，在国际贸易当中，我们不仅进行商品的进出口贸易，同时也进行服务的进出口贸易。

　　B. 同样地，在国际贸易当中，我们仅进行商品的进出口贸易，并没有进行对服务的进出口贸易。

　　C. 同样地，在国际贸易当中，我们不仅进行商品的出口贸易，同时也进行服务的进口贸易。

D. 同样地，在国际贸易当中，我们不仅进行商品的进口贸易，同时也进行服务的出口贸易。

2. Trade, the exchange of goods and services, is the most basic social activity. (　　)
   A. 贸易，即商品及劳务交换，是最重要的社会活动之一。
   B. 贸易，即商品及劳务交换，是最重要的社会活动。
   C. 贸易，即商品及服务交换，是最重要的社会活动之一。
   D. 贸易，即产品及服务交换，是最重要的社会活动。

3. Very often the things we buy are a "real" thing that we can touch or see and can make use of, such as cars, wines, shoes etc. (　　)
   A. 我们经常购买的东西是"虚幻"的东西，也就是我们不能触摸到或看到，但能够使用的东西，比如汽车、酒、鞋等。
   B. 我们购买的东西常常是"虚幻"的东西，也就是我们不能触摸到或看到，但能够使用的东西，比如汽车、酒、鞋等。
   C. 我们经常购买的东西是"实实在在"的东西，也就是我们能触摸到或看到并能够使用的东西，比如汽车、酒、鞋等。
   D. 我们购买的东西常常是"实实在在"的东西，也就是我们能触摸到或看到并能够使用的东西，比如汽车、酒、鞋等。

4. In today's complex economic world, neither individuals nor nations are self-sufficient. (　　)
   A. 在当今复杂的经济领域里，没有任何个人或国家是自给自足的。
   B. 在当今变化无常的经济领域里，没有任何个人或国家是自给自足的。
   C. 在当今变化无常的政治领域里，没有任何个人或国家是自给自足的。
   D. 在当今复杂的政治领域里，没有任何个人或国家是自给自足的。

5. The primitive "goods-for-goods" trade still remain today in some countries. (　　)
   A. 至今，原始的"以物换物"贸易在所有国家中依然存在。
   B. 现今，原始的"以物换物"贸易在一些国家中依然存在。
   C. 现今，原始的"以物换物"贸易在所有国家中依然存在。
   D. 至今，原始的"以物换物"贸易在一些国家中依然存在。

Reading Skills (3)
Recognizing the Signal Words

What Is Recognizing the Signal Words?

"Signal words" give hints about what is about to happen in what you're reading. understanding them is a key to comprehension. In the case of research question, students should begin by deciding what type of question they're trying to answer.

In the case of a reading assignment, students should decide early on how the passage is organized.

In both cases, students can look for some of the signal words listed below to help them to make decisions.

The following is a list of signal words.

1. Chronological Sequence

after	afterward	as soon as	before
during	finally	first	later
then	inexact	not long after	meanwhile
immediately	initially	now	on(date)
preceding	third	soon	when
following	second	today	until

2. Process/ Cause

accordingly	as a result of	because	because of
in order to	how to	first	fianlly
for this reason	is caused by	so that	if…then
next	initially	lead/led to	may be due to
thus	when…then	steps involved	therefore
consequently	effects of	today	until

3. Comparison/ Contrast

although	as well as	as opposed to	both
but	compared with	different from	either…or
even though	how ever	instead of	in common
on the other hand	otherwise	similar to	similarly
still	yet		

4. Description

above	across	in front of	along
below	behind	in back of	beside
appear to do	down	on top of	onto
outside	near	such as	to the right/left
as in	over	under	

Chapter Three　International Trade

Further Development

Passage I

Trade in the Balance
—Can Globalization Make Everyone Better off ?

　　The past two decades have left working-class voters in many countries leery of globalization. Donald Trump, the billionaire television star who promises to slap a 45% tariff on Chinese goods if elected president of America, has partly based his candidacy on this angst. Economists tend to scoff at such brash protectionism; they argue, rightly, that trade does far more good than harm. Yet new research reveals that for many, the short-term costs and benefits are more finely balanced than textbooks assume.

　　David Autor of MIT, David Dorn of the University of Zurich and Gordon Hanson of the University of California, San Diego, provide convincing evidence that workers in the rich world suffered much more from the rise of China than economists thought was possible. In their most recent paper, published in January, they write that sudden exposure to foreign competition can depress wages and employment for at least a decade.

　　Trade is beneficial in all sorts of ways. It provides consumers with goods they could not otherwise enjoy: without it only Scots would sip lovely Islay single malts. It boosts variety: Americans can shop for Volvos and Subarus in addition to Fords. Yet its biggest boon, economists since Adam Smith have argued, is that it makes countries richer. Trade creates larger markets, which allows for greater specialization, lower costs and higher incomes.

　　Economists have long accepted that this overall boost to prosperity might not be evenly spread. A paper published by Wolfgang Stolper and Paul Samuelson in 1941 pointed out that trade between an economy in which labor was relatively scarce (like America) and one in which labor was relatively abundant (like China) could cause wages to fall in the place that was short of workers. Yet many were skeptical that such losses would crop up much in practice. Workers in industries affected by trade, they assumed, would find new jobs in other fields.

　　Most research concluded that trade's effects on workers were benign. But China's subsequent incorporation into the global economy was of a different magnitude. From 1991 to 2013 its share of global exports of manufactured goods rocketed from 2.3% to 18.8%. For some categories of goods in America, Chinese import penetration—the share of domestic consumption met through Chinese imports—was near total.

　　The gain to China from this opening up has been enormous. Average real income rose from 4% of the American level in 1990 to 25% today. Hundreds of millions of Chinese have moved out of poverty thanks to trade. Many think, firms profit from a larger global market and reduced supply costs, and should also gain—eventually—from the reallocation of labor away from shrinking manufacturing to more productive industries.

But those benefits are only visible after decades. In the short run, the same study found, America's gains from trade with China are minuscule. The heavy costs to those dependent on industries exposed to Chinese imports offset most of the benefits to consumers and to firms in less vulnerable industries. Economists' assumption that workers would easily adjust to the upheaval of trade seems to have been misplaced. Manufacturing activity tends to be geographically concentrated. So the disruption caused by Chinese imports was similarly concentrated, in hubs such as America's Midwest. The competitive blow to manufacturers rippled through regional economies, write Messrs Autor, Dorn and Hanson, battering suppliers and local service industries. Such places lacked growing industries to absorb displaced workers, and the unemployed proved reluctant (or unable) to move to more prosperous regions. Labor-market adjustment to Chinese trade was thus slower and less complete than expected.

As a result, according to a 2013 paper, competition from Chinese imports explains 44% of the decline in employment in manufacturing in America between 1990 and 2007. For any given industry, an increase in Chinese imports of US$1,000 per worker per year led to a total reduction in annual income of about US$500 per worker in the places where that industry was concentrated. The offsetting rise in government benefits was only US$58 per worker. In a paper from 2014, co-written with Daron Acemoglu and Brendan Price, of MIT, and focusing on America's "employment sag" in the 2000s, the authors calculate that Chinese import competition reduced employment across the American economy as a whole by 2.4 million jobs relative to the level it otherwise would have enjoyed.

The costs of Chinese trade seem to have been exacerbated by China's large current-account surpluses: China's imports from other countries did not grow by nearly as much as its exports to other countries. China's trade with America was especially unbalanced. Between 1992 and 2008, trade with China accounted for 20%~40% of America's massive current-account deficit; China imported many fewer goods from America than vice verse.

Trade generates enormous global gains in welfare. Generous trade-adjustment assistance, job retraining and other public spending that helps to build political support for trade are therefore sound investments. To make any of these policies work, however, economists and politicians must stop thinking of them as political goodies designed to buy off interest groups opposed to trade. They are essential to fulfilling trade's promise to make everyone better off.

Words and Terms

globalization[ˌgləubəlaiˈzeiʃən]	n.	全球化
billionaire[bɪljəˈneə]	n.	亿万富翁
candidacy[ˈkændɪdəsɪ]	n.	候选人资格
evidence[ˈevɪdəns]	n.	证词；证据
specialization[ˌspeʃəlaɪˈzeɪʃən]	n.	专业化

assumption[əˈsʌmpʃn]	n.	假定，假设
adjustment[əˈdʒʌstmənt]	n.	调解，调整
exacerbate[ɪgˈzæsəbeɪt]	v.	使恶化；使加重
enormous [ɪˈnɔːməs]	adj.	巨大的
prosperous[ˈprɒspərəs]	adj.	繁荣的；兴旺的
welfare[ˈwelfeə]	n.	福利；幸福；繁荣
political[pəˈlɪtɪkl]	adj.	政治的；政党的

Notes

1. Economists tend to scoff at such brash protectionism; they argue, rightly, that trade does far more good than harm. 经济学家们大都对这种冒进的贸易保护措施嗤之以鼻，他们认为全球化贸易无疑是利大于弊的。

2. Trade creates larger markets, which allows for greater specialization, lower costs and higher incomes. 贸易使得市场更广阔，专业分工更细化，成本更低，而收入更高。

3. A paper published by Wolfgang Stolper and Paul Samuelson in 1941 pointed out that trade between an economy in which labor was relatively scarce (like America) and one in which labor was relatively abundant (like China) could cause wages to fall in the place that was short of workers. 沃尔夫冈·斯托尔帕和保罗·萨缪尔森在1941年发表的一篇论文中指出，在两个经济体之间的贸易中，如果一国劳动力相对稀缺(如美国)而另一国劳动力相对丰富(如中国)，可能导致劳动力相对稀缺的国家的工资水平下降。

4. Many think, firms profit from a larger global market and reduced supply costs, and should also gain—eventually—from the reallocation of labor away from shrinking manufacturing to more productive industries. 很多人认为，全球市场更大，供应成本降低，劳动实现了再分配，企业不再局限于萎缩的制造业而把目光转向了生产率更多的其他行业，因此受益良多。

5. In a paper from 2014, co-written with Daron Acemoglu and Brendan Price, of MIT, and focusing on America's "employment sag" in the 2000s. 2014年，一篇由麻省理工的达龙·阿西莫格鲁和丹·普莱斯共同撰写的文章，研究了21世纪美国的"就业凹陷"。

6. Between 1992 and 2008, trade with China accounted for 20%～40% of America's massive current-account deficit; China imported many fewer goods from America than vice verse. 在1992年到2008年期间，美国经常账户赤字中20%～40%都源于与中国的贸易，中国从美国进口的商品锐减不少，反之亦然。

Exercises

I. Read the following statements and decide whether they are True(T) or False (F).

1. The past two decades haven't left working-class voters in many countries leery of globalization.   (   )

2. Economists tend to scoff at such brash protectionism; they argue, rightly, that trade does far more harm than good. (   )

3. Trade creates larger markets, which allows for greater specialization, lower costs and higher incomes. (   )

4. The gain to China from this opening up has been enormous, but Hundreds of millions of Chinese haven't moved out of poverty thanks to trade. (   )

5. Labor-market adjustment to Chinese trade was thus slower and less complete than expected.
(   )

II. Choose the correct answer according to Passage I.

1. What does the trade can bring to the market? It creates larger markets, which allows for _____. (   )

   A. lower costs

   B. higher incomes

   C. greater specialization

   D. all of the above

2. According to a 2013 paper, competition from Chinese imports explains _____ of the decline in employment in manufacturing in America between 1990 and 2007. (   )

   A. 44%

   B. 20%

   C. 25%

   D. 4.4%

3. Which article is focusing on America's "employment sag" in the 2000s? (   )

   A. The article was co-written by Donald Trump and Brendan Price.

   B. The article was co-written by Daron Acemoglu and Brendan Price.

   C. The article was co-written by Daron Acemoglu and Wolfgang Stolper.

   D. The article was co-written by Donald Trump and Daron Acemoglu.

4. Who promises to slap a 45% tariff on Chinese goods if elected president of America? (   )

   A. Donald Trump

   B. Brendan Price

   C. Daron Acemoglu

   D. Wolfgang Stolper

5. Which of the following statement is true? (   )

   A. From 1991 to 2013 its share of global exports of manufactured goods rocketed from 2.3% to 18.8%.

   B. From 1991 to 2013 its share of global exports of manufactured goods rocketed from 3.3% to 8.8%.

   C. From 1991 to 2013 its share of global exports of manufactured goods rocketed from 3.3% to 28.8%.

   D. From 1991 to 2013 its share of global exports of manufactured goods rocketed from 2.3% to 19.8%.

Chapter Three International Trade

III. Fill in the missing information.

Trade is _____ in all sorts of ways. It provides _____ with goods they could not otherwise enjoy. Yet its biggest boon, economists since Adam Smith have argued, is that it makes countries _____ . Trade creates larger markets, which allows for greater _____, lower costs and higher_____ .

Passage II

Protectionism Doesn't Pay

The global financial crisis is no doubt a catalyst for trade protectionism. As the world economy deteriorates, some countries try to boost growth prospects by erecting trade barriers. China calls on these governments not to replay history and revert to protectionism and economic isolationism.

Previous global economic crises were usually accompanied by frequent trade disputes. The United States' erection of large-scale tariffs in 1930, for example, triggered a retaliatory global trade war. During the two oil shocks in the 1970s and 1980s, trade frictions emerged when major economies attempted to increase exports by depreciating their currencies. And in the wake of the 1997 Asian financial crisis, there was a notable uptick in anti-dumping actions, countervailing duties and other protectionist measures.

The financial crisis is now spilling over into the real economy, hitting sectors like manufacturing and services. In almost all countries, factories are closing and unemployment is rising, creating political pressure and social problems. More and more governments are strengthening intervention in their economies under the excuse of "economic security" and protecting vulnerable domestic industries to curb imports from other countries, especially those in emerging markets.

Trade protectionism differs from legally acceptable measures to protect trade. It is an abuse of remedies provided by multilateral trade rules. This kind of protectionism is morphing into more complex and disguised forms, ranging from conventional tariff and non-tariff barriers to technical barriers to trade, industry standards and industry protectionism.

With the economic crisis worsening, caution must be taken even in employing trade protection measures consistent with World Trade Organization rules. At the Group of 20 Financial Summit in November 2008, world leaders called for countries to resist trade protectionism and committed themselves to refraining from erecting new barriers to trade and investment, a message strongly echoed by the Asia-Pacific Economic Cooperation summit at the end of last year, and the World Economic Forum held in Davos last month.

History tells us that trade protection measures hurt not only other countries, but eventually the country that erected that trade barrier in the first place.

To counter the Great Depression, the U.S. adopted the Smoot-Hawley Act in 1930, which raised import duties of over 20,000 foreign products significantly and provoked protectionist retaliation from other countries. Faced with that crisis, other countries pursued beggar-thy-neighbor policies that slashed global trade volumes from US$36 billion in 1929 to US$12 billion in 1932. Among the victims, not the least was the U.S. itself, where exports shrank from US$5.2 billion in 1929 to US$1.2 billion in 1932. Even in the U.S., the Smoot-Hawley Act was widely believed to be a catalyst that aggravated the effects of Great Depression.

Global trade is now in dire straits. Thanks to shrinking external demand caused by the economic crisis, major trading countries have seen their export growth tumble or have suffered huge contractions. Germany's exports dropped 10.6% in November 2008, compared to the same period the prior year — the highest one-month drop since 1990. China also experienced negative export growth in November, and a 17.5% decline last month, when compared to the prior year. Protectionist policies would make things even worse and the consequences would be hard to predict.

In the heat of the crisis, it's critical that all countries refrain from pointing fingers at each other or pursuing their own interests at the expense of others. The financial crisis reflects a chronic illness resulting from global economic structural imbalance and financial risk accumulation, and there is no quick fix to this malady. The fundamental interest of every country is to step up consultation and cooperation and keep international trade smoothly flowing. Healthy international trade can help revive the world economy. During the Great Depression, the U.S. recovered from its economic woes because the Franklin D. Roosevelt administration implemented the New Deal and shunned protectionism.

Today's unprecedented financial crisis has inflicted a severe impact on China and other countries as well. China's economic growth has slowed, exports have plunged and unemployment pressure has mounted. Yet even so, China still firmly believes that trade protectionism isn't a solution to the world's problems. In 2008, amid a contraction in global trade, China imported US$1.133 trillion worth of goods from countries around the world — an 18.5% increase over the prior year. These imports are boosting the economic development of China's trading partners. Since the crisis broke out, the Chinese government has decisively put forward a series of measures aiming at stimulating domestic demand. Given the size and openness of our country, the growth in China's domestic markets can be translated into greater market potential and investment opportunities for other countries. This year, China will continue to increase imports and send buying missions abroad for large-scale purchase of equipment, products and technology.

China has always championed our mutually beneficial opening-up policy and advocated international economic cooperation. We maintain that the Doha Round of global trade negotiations should be taken forward in a way that meets the interests of members and complies with the multilateral trading system already established. China is ready to stand together with all nations in the world to face up to the challenges of today, tackle the financial crisis through cooperation and guide the world economy into a new period of prosperity.

Chapter Three International Trade

 Exercises

I. Choose the correct answer according to Passage II.

1. According to the text, how to research and review the exec's "business agenda". (   )

   A. use your contacts in the firm and your own business acumen

   B. get information about him by his family.

   C. get information about him by his customers.

   D. get information about him by computer or books.

2. Why are execs often unaware meeting on their agenda. (   )

   A. Because they are too busy to remember.

   B. Because they don't want to remember it.

   C. Because the meeting is too difficult to remember.

   D. Because the meeting isn't need to remember.

3. When is the good time to show that you've done your homework and understand the company? (   )

   A. Within the last few minutes during the conversations.

   B. After finishing the talking.

   C. Within the first few minutes during the conversations.

   D. Before finishing the talking.

4. What do Execs care about features and functions; they want to know how you're going to change the bottom line? (   )

   A. They care about features

   B. They care about functions

   C. They care about features and functions

   D. They care about the ways you're going to change the bottom line.

5. According to the text, what the author's suggestion for conversations with Exec? (   )

   A. Try to talk as much as you can.

   B. Just listen to Exec.

   C. Talk more than you listen.

   D. Listen more than you talk.

II. Choose the best translation.

1. 在这场前所未有的世界金融危机中，中国与其他国家一样都受到严重冲击。(   )

   A. Today's precedence financial crisis has inflicted a severe impact on China and other countries as well.

   B. Today's unprecedented political crisis has inflicted a severe impact on China and other countries as well.

C. Today's unprecedented financial crisis has inflicted a severe impact on Japan and other countries as well.

D. Today's precedence financial crisis has inflicted a severe impact on Korea and other countries as well.

2. 当前，金融危机已蔓延到制造业、服务业等实体经济领域。（   ）

A. The financial crisis is now spilling over into the real economy, hitting sectors like manufacturing and services.

B. The political crisis is now spilling over into the unreal economy, hitting sectors like manufacturing and services.

C. The currency crisis is now spilling over into the real economy, hitting sectors like manufacturing and services.

D. The banking crisis is now spilling over into the real economy, hitting sectors like manufacturing and services.

3. 历史告诉我们。任何针对他国的贸易保护措施，不仅会损害对方，最终也会伤及自身。（   ）

A. History tells us that import trade protection measures hurt not only other countries, but eventually the country.

B. History tells us that tangible trade protection measures hurt not only other countries, but eventually the country.

C. History tells us that export trade protection measures hurt not only other countries, but eventually the country.

D. History tells us that trade protection measures hurt not only other countries, but eventually the country.

4. 今年，中国将继续扩大进口，积极组织企业采购团，赴海外大规模采购，进口设备、商品和技术。（   ）

A. This year, China will continue to increase imports and send buying missions abroad for large-scale purchase of equipment, products and technology.

B. This year, China will continue to increase exports and send buying missions abroad for large-scale purchase of equipment, products and technology.

C. This year, China won't continue to increase imports and send buying missions abroad for large-scale purchase of equipment, products and technology.

D. This year, China will continue to increase imports and send buying missions abroad for small-scale purchase of equipment, products and technology.

5. 中国始终奉行互利共赢的开放战略，倡导国际经济合作。（   ）

A. China has always championed our mutually beneficial opening-up policy and advocated national economic cooperation.

B. China has always championed our mutually beneficial opening-up policy and advocated international economic cooperation.

C. China has always championed our mutually beneficial closing-up policy and advocated international economic cooperation.

D. China has always championed our mutually beneficial opening-up policy and advocated national economic cooperation.

Special Terms

international trade	国际贸易
oversea trade	海外贸易
import trade	进口贸易
export trade	出口贸易
transit trade	过境贸易
domestic market	国内市场
international market	国际市场
visible goods trade	有形商品贸易
invisible goods trade	无形商品贸易
financial crisis	金融危机
trade disputes	贸易争端
trade protectionism	贸易保护主义
emerging market	新兴市场
trade barriers	贸易壁垒

Chapter Four

Financial Management

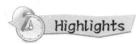

Text
Introduction to Financial Management
Reading Skills (4)
Guessing the Meanings from the Context
Further Development
Passage I
2016: A Big Year for Shanghai's Financial Sector
Passage II
Top Ten Financial Aid Tips for Parents

  This is the 4th chapter of the book. In the first section, you will learn a text, and you will have some information about the importance of international financial management. In the second section, you will have a deeper understanding about financial management. In this section, you will learn two passages about financial sectors and financial aid tips and they will help you have a further development on mastering reading skills of guessing the meanings from the context.

Starter

"Boundless risk must pay for boundless gain." — William Marris
Do you agree with this saying?

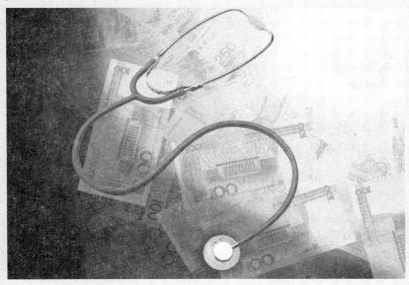

Text

Introduction to Financial Management

The Importance of International Financial Management

International financial management deals with the financial decisions taken in the area of international business. The growth in international business is, first of all, evident in the form of highly inflated size of international trade. In the immediate post-war years, the General Agreement on the Trade and Tariffs was set up in order to boost trade. It axed the trade barriers significantly over the years, as a result of which international trade grew manifold. Naturally, the financial involvement of the exporters and importers and the quantum of the cross country transactions surged significantly.

Normally, with the growth of international trade, the products of the exporter become mature in the importing countries. When the product becomes mature in the importing countries, the exporter starts manufacturing the product there so as to evade tariff and to supply it at the least cost.

Thus it would not be wrong to say that the emergence of the multinational companies was the by-product of the expansion in world trade. With growing operation of multinational companies, a number of complexities arose in the area of their financial decisions. Apart from the considerations of where, when and how much to invest, the decision concerning the management of working capital among their different subsidiaries and the parent units become more complex especially because the basic polices varied from one multinational companies to the other. Those multinational companies that were more interested in maximizing the value of global wealth adopted a centralized approach while those not interfering much with their subsidiaries believed in a decentralized approach.

The nature of the movement of funds become so complex that proper management become a necessity and the study of international finance management become highly relevant. In fact, international finance management suggests the most suitable technique to be applied at a particular moment and in a particular case in order to hedge the risk.

Three Major Decision Functions of the Financial Manager

Financial management is the efficient and effective planning and controlling of financial resources so as to maximize profitability and ensuring liquidity for an individual (called personal finance), government (called public finance) and for profit and non-profit organization/firm (called corporate or managerial finance). Generally, it involves balancing risks and profitability.

The decision function of financial management can be divided into the following three major areas:

A. Investment Decision

It is the most important decision. It begins with the firm determining the total amount of assets needed to be held by the firm. There are two types of investment decision:

a. Capital Investment Decision

It involves large sums of money. The impact is critical. Examples: acquire a new machine or to set up a new plant.

b. Working Capital Investment Decision

It is a more routine or schedule form of decision. Examples are determination of the amount of inventories, cash and account receivables to hold within a certain period.

B. Financing Decision

It is the second major decision. After deciding on what assets to buy or what securities to invest in, the financial manager would have to decide on how to finance these assets.

C. Assets Management Decision

It is the third and the last decision. Once the assets have been acquired and appropriate financing provided, these assets must be managed efficiently. By managing currents assets effectively and efficiently, the company can increase its returns and minimize its risk of illiquidity.

Role of Finance Managers

In the area of finance and financial management, finance manager is important authority. Not only to raise the finance of company, finance managers do also other lots of works for company. We can explain his role in following words.

A. Role of Finance Manager for Raising Funds of the Company

A Finance manager checks different sources of company. He did not get fund from all sources. First, he check his need in short term and in long term and after this he select best source of fund. He has also power to change the capital structure of the company for giving more benefit of the company.

B. Role of Finance Manager for Taking Maximum Benefits from Leverage

The finance manager uses both operating and financial leverage and tries to use it for taking maximum benefit from leverage.

C. Role of Finance Manager for International Financial Decision

The finance manager finds opportunities in international financial decision. In these opportunities, he does the contracts of credit default swap, interest rate swap and currency swap.

D. Role of Finance Manager in Investment Decisions

The finance manager checks the net present value of each investment project before actual investment in it. Net present value of project means what net profit at discount rate the company will gets if the company invests him money in that project. High NPV project will be accepted. So, due to high responsibility, role of the finance manager in this regard is very important.

E. Role of Finance Manager in Risk Management

Happening of risks means facing different losses. The finance manager is very serious on risk and its management. He plays an important role to find new ways to control risk of company. Like other parts of management, he estimates all his risks and organizes the employees who are responsible to control risk. He also calculates risk adjusted NPV. He meets all risk controlling organizations like insurance companies, rating agencies at pervasive level. He is able to convert company's misfortunes into fortunes. By good estimations of averse situations, he tries his best to safeguard the money of the company.

Words and Terms

inflated [ɪnˈfleɪtɪd]	adj.	膨胀的
post-war [ˈpəʊstˈwɔː]	adj.	战后的
boost [buːst]	v.	提高
barrier [ˈbærɪə]	n.	障碍
axe [æks]	v.	消除
manifold [ˈmænɪfəʊld]	adj.	多种多样的
quantum [ˈkwɒntəm]	n.	总量，总额
tariff [ˈtærɪf]	n.	关税
by-product [ˈbaɪprɒdʌkt]	n.	副产品
subsidiary [səbˈsɪdɪərɪ]	n.	子公司
hedge [hedʒ]	v.	回避

liquidity [lɪˈkwɪdətɪ]	n.	流动资金	
capital [ˈkæpɪtl]	n.	资本	
security [sɪˈkjʊərətɪ]	n.	证券	
leverage [ˈliːvərɪdʒ]	n.	杠杆作用	
pervasive [pəˈveɪsɪv]	adj.	普遍的	
averse [əˈvɜːs]	adj.	不好的	

Notes

1. Naturally, the financial involvement of the exporters and importers and the quantum of the cross country transactions surged significantly. 自然而然地，进出口贸易中涉及的财务工作和跨国交易总量越来越多。

2. Apart from the considerations of where, when and how much to invest, the decision concerning the management of working capital among their different subsidiaries and the parent units become more complex especially because the basic polices varied from one multinational companies to the other. 除了要考虑投资的地点、时间和金额，各子公司和总公司运营资金管理的决定越来越复杂，因为基本政策从一家跨国公司到另一家跨国公司是不同的。

3. In these opportunities, he does the contracts of credit default swap, interest rate swap and currency swap. 在这些机会中，他做信用违约互换、利率互换和货币互换合同。

4. Net present value of project means what net profit at discount rate the company will gets if company invests him money in that project. 投资项目的净现值是指公司如果投资该项目应获得的折现率的净利润。

Exercises

I. Answer the following questions according to the text.

1. Why can we say that international financial management is important?
2. What are the three decision functions of the financial manager?
3. How many roles can a finance manager play according to the text?
4. Why can we say that the emergence of the multinational companies was the by-product of the expansion in world trade?
5. What does a finance manager do in international financial decision?

II. Identify the key words or main ideas of the following parts.

Part 1	_____ of international financial management
Part 2	_____ of the financial manager
Part 3	Role of finance manager for _____
	Role of finance manager for _____

Chapter Four Financial Management

	Role of finance manager for_____
	Role of finance manager for_____
	Role of finance manager for_____

III. Match the words or phrases in Column A to the words or phrases in Column B.

        A   B

1. _____ trade and tariff   A. 飙升
2. _____ surge   B. 贸易和壁垒
3. _____ evade   C. 副产品
4. _____ by-product   D. 避开
5. _____ multinational companies   E. 子公司
6. _____ subsidiary   F. 个人理财
7. _____ personal finance   G. 跨国公司
8. _____ security   H. 净现值
9. _____ net present value   I. 证券
10. _____ risk   J. 风险

IV. Choose the best translation.

1. Naturally, the financial involvement of the exporters and importers and the quantum of the cross country transactions surged significantly. (　　)
   A. 自然而然地，进出口贸易中涉及的财务工作和跨国交易总量越来越多。
   B. 自然地说，金融涉及出口进口贸易和跨国业务总量急剧上升。
   C. 自然地，进出口贸易中涉及的金融工作和跨国业务总量急剧上升
   D. 自然地，财务涉及出口进口的贸易人总量越来越多。

2. Thus it would not be wrong to say that the emergence of the multinational companies was the by-product of the expansion in world trade. (　　)
   A. 然而这并不是错的，跨国公司的出现是世界贸易扩张的结果。
   B. 因此，跨国公司的出现是国际贸易扩大的副产品，这种说法并没有错。
   C. 因此，跨国公司的出现是国际贸易扩大的副产品是没有错的。
   D. 然而跨国公司的出现并不是错的，它是国际贸易扩大的产物。

3. Examples are determination of the amount of inventories, cash and account receivables to hold within a certain period. (　　)
   A. 例子是存货金额、现金和一定时间内的应收金额的确定。
   B. 榜样是确定存货金额、现金和一定时间内的应收金额。
   C. 例子是存货金额、现金和一定时间内的应收金额的决心。
   D. 比如存货金额、现金和一定时间内的应收金额的决策。

4. He has also power to change the capital structure of the company for giving more benefit of the company. (　　)

A. 他有权力改变公司的资金结构，给公司带来更多的利益。
B. 他有力量改变公司的资金结构，给公司带来更多的利益。
C. 他有权利改变公司的总部结构，为了给公司更多的利益。
D. 他有权利改变公司的资产结构，给公司带来更多的利益。

5. Once the assets have been acquired and appropriate financing provided, these assets must be managed efficiently. (   )
A. 一旦资产被得到，合适的财务被提供，这些资产必须被有效管理。
B. 一旦得到资产并作出正确的财务决策，这些资产必须被有效地管理。
C. 曾经得到资产，作出合适的财务，这些资产必须被有效地管理。
D. 曾经得到资产并作出正确的财务决策，这些资产必须被有效地管理。

Reading Skills (4)
Guessing the Meanings from the Context

Guessing from the context refers to the ability to infer the meaning of an expression using contextual clues. These clues may be purely linguistic or situational:

• Linguistic context: the linguistic environment in which a word is used within a text。

• Situational context: extra linguistic elements that contribute to the construction of meaning this may involve background knowledge of the subject.

What this amounts to is that learners should be able to infer the meaning of an unknown word using:

• the meaning of vocabulary items that surrounds it;

• the way the word is formed;

• background knowledge of the subject and the situation.

Techniques for Guessing

Texts are often full of redundancy and consequently students can use the relation between different items within a text to get the meaning. Our prior knowledge of the world may also contribute to understand what an expression means.

Synonyms and definitions

Kingfishers are a group of small to medium-sized brightly colored birds

When he made insolent remarks towards his teacher they sent him to the principal for being disrespectful.

Antonym and contrast

He loved her so much for being so kind to him. By contrast, he abhorred her mother.

Cause and effect

He was disrespectful towards other members. That's why he was sent off and penalized.

Parts of speech

Whether the word is a noun, a verb, an adjective or an adverb, functioning as a subject, a predicate or a complement.

Examples

Trojan is an example of a computer virus.

Word forms (the morphological properties of the word)

Getting information from affixes (prefixes and suffixes) to understand a word. Examples: dis- (meaning not), -less (meaning without)…

General knowledge

The French constitution establishes laïcité as a system of government where there is a strict separation of church and state.

These techniques help students get the meaning of words or at least narrow the possibilities. If needed using the dictionary should be the last resort to fine tune the understanding of a vocabulary item.

Further Development

Passage I

2016: A Big Year for Shanghai's Financial Sector

Shanghai, the Chinese metropolis that is building itself into an international financial center, has been working on a range of measures in the finance sector over the past year. Those measures include deepening financial reforms, improving the sector's infrastructure, furthering innovation of the financial system and increasing the city's global influence in the finance industry.

The China Financial Information Center and the Shanghai branch of the China Economic Information Service reviewed the city's efforts in the financial sector in 2016 and released the following top 10 events on Jan 9.

1. Financial reform in Shanghai's free trade zone deepened

About 40 innovative financial reform measures were introduced in Shanghai's free trade zone in October 2015. More detailed rules were released successively in 2016 to further explain and guide the implementation of various measures.

2. The investment-loan linkage mechanism piloted in Shanghai

In April, the Zhangjiang National Innovation Demonstration Zone and three commercial banks — the Bank of Shanghai Bank, Huarui Bank and SPD Silicon Valley Bank — were selected as pilots for trials of an investment-loan linkage mechanism. The mechanism aims to give small and medium-sized technology companies easier access to financial services which would help their development.

3. Shanghai Insurance Exchange launched

China's first insurance asset trading platform, the Shanghai Insurance Exchange, was inaugurated on June 12, 2016 to boost transparency and efficiency in the world's third-largest insurance market. Its other purpose is to attract more international insurance and reinsurance giants to Shanghai. A national insurance investment fund was also established in the Shanghai free trade zone after the launch of the insurance exchange.

4. Shanghai Commercial Paper Exchange Corp. and China Trust Registration Co. open

December 2016 witnessed the opening of the Shanghai Commercial Paper Exchange Corp. and the China Trust Registration Co. The exchange, a nationwide platform for centralized commercial paper trading, broadens the existing financial infrastructure that serves increasing market demand and will improve regulation of the market. The China Trust Registration Co. , which opened on Dec 26, focuses on centralized registration, issuing and trading of trust products as well as supervision of the trust industry.

5.National Internet Finance Association of China launches in Shanghai

The National Internet Financial Association of China, which was founded in Shanghai on March 25 last year, is playing a crucial role in the healthy development of China's burgeoning Internet finance sector. The association focuses on formulating and introducing industry rules and self-disciplinary mechanisms to better regulate the internet finance sector and to promote its further development.

6. CCP12 registers in Shanghai

The Global Association of Central Counterparties (CCP12) registered in the China (Shanghai) Pilot Free Trade Zone as a non-profit organization on June 8, 2016. The association was formed in 2001 and has been working to further the industry's discussions on the adoption of the best clearing and risk management practices. It also supports strategic progress on regulatory harmonization and the achievement of global standards. Its arrival in Shanghai reflects China's progress in financial market development and risk prevention and has won international recognition.

7. Shanghai Gold Exchange launches yuan-denominated gold benchmark price

The Shanghai Gold Exchange (SGE), the world's largest physical gold exchange, launched a yuan-denominated benchmark price on April 19, 2016 in Shanghai, a measure that will benefit both China's domestic gold market and the global precious metals market. SGE said that the launch of the Shanghai Gold Benchmark Price will be useful in adequately reflecting gold supply and demand in China and in representing price trends in the nation's gold market. It is also considered a necessary addition to the international gold market and should make the pricing of physical gold more open to the play of market forces.

8. Yuan-denominated green bonds issued by BRICS New Development Bank and Shanghai Pudong Development Bank

In January, Shanghai Pudong Development Bank issued a green bond of 20 billion yuan (US$2.9 billion), which was China's first domestic green bond.

In July, BRICS New Development Bank issued its first renminbi-denominated green financial bond of 3 billion yuan, the first of its kind issued by a China-headquartered international financial institution. The issuing of the bond shows the international financial institution's confidence in the internationalization of the renminbi (RMB) as well as its contribution to the growth and development of the global green economy.

9. Shanghai Finance Bureau issues local government bonds

Shanghai Finance Bureau issued a local government bond of 30 billion yuan in November through a government bond issuance system recently developed by the Shanghai Stock Exchange. The move was considered conducive to expanding the issuance channels of the local government bond market, to optimizing the structure of investors and to improving the fluidity of the bonds.

In December, the bureau issued a local government bond of 3 billion yuan, targeting Chinese and foreign investors who have opened free trade accounts in the Shanghai free trade zone. This was the first bond issued in a Chinese free trade zone and is helping to broaden backflow channels for offshore RMB and to push forward the internationalization of the Chinese currency.

10. China Development Bank opens Shanghai office and Lujiazui Financial City reforms its management mechanism

The branch office of the China Development Bank in Shanghai opened on June 23. The branch will support development of the infrastructure of the bond market in Shanghai's free trade zone. It will also take part in local financial market transactions and promote the internationalization of the RMB.

Words and Terms

metropolis [mɪˈtrɒpəlɪs]	n.	大都市
infrastructure [ˈɪnfrəstrʌktʃə]	n.	基础设施
release [rɪˈliːs]	v.	发布；释放
successively [səkˈsesfəlɪ]	adv.	先后地
implementation [ˌɪmplɪmenˈteɪʃn]	n.	贯彻，实施
linkage [ˈlɪŋkɪdʒ]	n.	联动，联系，关联
inaugurate [ɪˈnɔːgjʊreɪt]	v.	开创；创始
burgeoning [ˈbɜːdʒənɪŋ]	adj.	迅速成长的

benchmark ['bentʃmɑːk]	n.	基准
conducive [kən'djuːsɪv]	adj.	有利于……的
backflow ['bækfləʊ]	n.	回流
offshore ['ɒfʃɔː]	adj.	境外的，离岸的
financial sector		金融部门
international financial center		国际金融中心
financial reforms		金融改革
financial system		金融体系
China Financial Information Center		中国金融信息中心
Shanghai's free trade zone		上海自由贸易区
Shanghai Insurance Exchange		上海保险交易所
Shanghai Commercial Paper Exchange Corp.		上海票据交易所
China Trust Registration Co.		中国信用注册公司
National Internet Finance Association		中国互联网金融协会
CCP12		全球中央对手方协会
China (Shanghai) Pilot Free Trade Zone		中国(上海)自由贸易试点区
Shanghai Finance Bureau		上海财政局
China Development Bank		国家开发银行
investment loan		投资放贷
yuan-denominated		以人民币计价的

Notes

1. Those measures include deepening financial reforms, improving the sector's infrastructure, furthering innovation of the financial system and increasing the city's global influence in the finance industry. 这些措施包括深化金融改革，提高行业的基础设施建设，深化金融体制创新，提高城市在金融行业的国际影响力。

2. More detailed rules were released successively in 2016 to further explain and guide the implementation of various measures. 2016年先后发布了更详细的规则，进一步解释和指导各项措施的落实。

3. In April, the Zhangjiang National Innovation Demonstration Zone and three commercial banks — the Bank of Shanghai Bank, Huarui Bank and SPD Silicon Valley Bank——were selected as pilots for trials of an investment-loan linkage mechanism. 4月，张江国家自主创新示范区和三家商业银行——上海银行、华瑞银行和浦发硅谷银行——被选为投资贷款联动机制试行的试点银行。上海张江高新技术产业开发区——是1991年国务院批准成立的中国首批国家级高新区，是2011年国务院批准建设的第三个国家自主创新示范区。

4. The exchange, a nationwide platform for centralized commercial paper trading, broadens the existing financial infrastructure that serves increasing market demand and will improve regulation

of the market. 此交流为集中式商业票据交易提供了一个全国性的平台，并拓宽现有的金融基础设施，该设施服务于日益增长的市场需求，促进市场调控。

5. The association focuses on formulating and introducing industry rules and self-disciplinary mechanisms to better regulate the internet finance sector and to promote its further development. 协会研究制定和引入行业规则和自律机制，更好地规范互联网金融领域并促进其进一步发展。

6. In July, BRICS New Development Bank issued its first renminbi-denominated green financial bond of 3 billion yuan, the first of its kind issued by a China-headquartered international financial institution. 7月，金砖国家新开发银行首次发行以人民币计价的绿色金融债券30亿元，这是债券是首次由总部在中国的国际金融机构发行。

Exercises

I. Read the following statements and decide whether they are True (T) or False (F).

1. About 40 innovative financial reform measures were introduced in Shanghai's free trade zone in October 2015.　　　　　　　　　　　　　　　　　　　　　　　　　( )

2. The mechanism aims to give big and medium-sized technology companies easier access to financial services which would help their development.　　　　　　　　　( )

3. China's first insurance asset trading platform, the Shanghai Insurance Exchange, was inaugurated on June 12, 2015 to boost transparency and efficiency in the world's third-largest insurance market.　　　　　　　　　　　　　　　　　　　　　　　　　　　( )

4. The China Trust Registration Co, which opened on Dec 26, focuses on centralized registration, issuing and trading of trust products as well as supervision of the trust industry. ( )

5. The Global Association of Central Counterparties (CCP12) registered in the China (Shanghai) Pilot Free Trade Zone as a profit organization on June 8, 2016.　　　( )

II. Choose the correct answer according to Passage I.

1. In April, the Zhangjiang National Innovation Demonstration Zone and _____ commercial banks were selected as pilots for trials of an investment-loan linkage mechanism. ( )

A. one
B. Two
C. three
D. four

2. _____ focuses on formulating and introducing industry rules and self-disciplinary mechanisms to better regulate the internet finance sector and to promote its further development. ( )

A. Shanghai Gold Exchage
B. The National Internet Finance Association
C. CCP12
D. Shanghai Commercial Paper Exchange

3. The Global Association of Central Counterparties (CCP12) registered in the China (Shanghai) Pilot Free Trade Zone as a _____ organization on June 8, 2016. (   )

A. non-profit

B. profit

C. official

D. non-official

4. BRICS New Development Bank issued its first renminbi-denominated green financial bond of 3 billion yuan, the first of its kind issued by a _____ international financial institution. (   )

A. Brazil-headquartered

B. China-headquartered

C. India-headquartered

D. Russia-headquartered

5. The branch office of the China Development Bank in Shanghai opened on June 23. The branch will support development of the infrastructure of the _____ in Shanghai's free trade zone. (   )

A. security market

B. bond market

C. insurance market

D. gold market

III. Fill in the missing information.

Shanghai, the Chinese _____ that is building itself into an international _____, has been working on a range of measures in the finance sector over the past year. Those measures include deepening _____, improving the sector's infrastructure, furthering innovation of the _____ and increasing the city's global influence in the _____.

The China Financial Information Center and the Shanghai branch of the China Economic Information Service reviewed the city's efforts in the financial sector in 2016 and released the following top 10 events on Jan 9.

Passage II

Top Ten Financial Aid Tips for Parents

Looking for financial aid to help foot the tuition bill? Follow these 10 tips to help you secure the funding. You need and remember — don't wait until your child's senior year to start thinking about student aid. The sooner you start, the more money you may be able to find.

1. Get an early idea of your EFC

Estimate your Expected Family Contribution (EFC) during your child's junior year. By getting an idea of what you might pay, you can find colleges within your price range and identify what you might need in scholarships and loans to manage your tuition costs. The more financial aid information you can gather, the better.

2. Reduce your child's savings

An entire 20 percent of your child's assets are considered available for college, as opposed to just 5.6 percent of yours. Encourage your child to save, but keep college funds in a custodial account.

3. Learn a little about marketing

This is one of the most important aspects of competing for merit-based awards. Highlight your child's accomplishments and an award committee will be that much more likely to consider giving a scholarship to your son or daughter.

4. Make financial aid a part of your campus visits

Ask to speak with someone in the student financial aid office — it's the best way to get your family on the radar for campus-based awards. Afterwards, take some notes! These contacts could come in handy later.

5. Do a bit of detective work

Determine if your child's application for aid affects the probability of admittance. If so, find out how.

6. Make a decision on early decision

If your child is thinking of applying Early Decision or Early Action, determine how it will affect your chances for student aid. Early Decision acceptance may prevent you from comparing awards, because your child will have to commit to the school before you see the aid offers from other applications. (This is not a factor if your child is accepted under an Early Action or Single-Choice Early Action application, as these are non-binding offers.)

7. Determine the effect of outside awards

If your child receives an outside scholarship, find out how it will affect your student financial aid award. Some schools will lessen grant aid, and others will pare down on loans. The school's policy will affect the amount you'll have to borrow.

8. Pay attention to deadlines

The sooner your child files his or her college applications, the better your chances of receiving aid. To assist with financial aid for college forms, file your taxes as early in the year as possible. Keep in mind that if you are applying to schools that require the PROFILE financial aid application, it may have an earlier deadline than the FAFSA.

9. Complete the FAFSA

Fill out this form, even if you think you won't qualify — very affluent families sometimes qualify for aid at certain high-tuition schools. This single application is your gateway to all federal loan, grant, and work-study awards that total in the billions of dollars.

10. Make your college aware of special circumstances

If you have lost your job since completing the FAFSA or PROFILE, inform schools about your situation. Most have standard policies that allow for the use of projected income, which could increase financial assistance.

Exercises

I. Choose the correct answer according to Passage II.

1. _____ you start, _____ money you may be able to find. (　　)
A. The earlier, the less
B. The sooner, the more
C. The sooner, the less
D. The later, the more

2. Determine if your child's application for aid _____ the probability of admittance. (　　)
A. affects
B. changes
C. provides
D. tells

3. To _____ with financial aid for college forms, file your taxes as early in the year as possible. (　　)
A. fill
B. help
C. assist
D. deal

4. This single application is your _____ to all federal loan, grant, and work-study awards that total in the billions of dollars. (　　)
A. way
B. choice
C. answer
D. gateway

5. If you have lost your job since completing the FAFSA or PROFILE, _____ schools about your situation. (　　)
A. tell
B. stop
C. prevent
D. inform

II. Choose the best translation.

1. 这些联系方式可能用得着。(　　)
A. These connection may be can used.
B. These contacts could come in handy later.
C. These contacts may be can used.
D. We may use these contacts.

2. 一些学校会减少资助，其他将削减贷款。(　　)
A. Some schools will reduce financial aid, other people will reduce the loan.
B. Some schools will cut financial aid, and others may reduce the loan.
C. Financial aid will be decreased by school and loans will be reduced.

D. Some schools will lessen grant aid, and others will pare down on loans.

3. 如果你的孩子想申请提前录取，确定这将如何影响申请学生经济援助的机会。（   ）

A. If your child is thinking of applying Early Decision or Early Action, determine how it will affect your chances for student aid.

B. If your child wants to apply Early Decision or Early Action, check how it will affect your chances for student aid.

C. If your child wants to apply Early Decision or Early Action, make sure how it will affect your chances for student aid.

D. If your child wants to apply Early Decision or Early Action, ensure how it will affect your chances for student aid.

Special Terms

security	证券
subsidiary	子公司
tariff	关税
by-product	副产品
liquidity	流动资金
capital	资本
yuan-denominated	以人民币计价的
investment loan	投资放贷
financial sector	金融部门
international financial center	国际金融中心
financial reforms	金融改革
financial system	金融体系
Shanghai Finance Bureau	上海财政局
Shanghai's free trade zone	上海自由贸易区
Shanghai Insurance Exchange	上海保险交易所
Shanghai Commercial Paper Exchange Corp.	上海票据交易所
China Financial Information Center	中国金融信息中心
China Trust Registration Co.	中国信用注册公司
National Internet Finance Association	中国互联网金融协会
CCP12	全球中央对手方协会
China Development Bank	中国国家开发银行
China (Shanghai) Pilot Free Trade Zone	中国(上海)自由贸易试点区

Chapter Five

Business Management

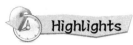

Text
Manager and Management—The Eternal Topic of the Workplace
Reading Skills (5)
Drawing Conclusions
Further Development:
Passage I
Workplaces' Skills
Passage II
Job Interview—7 Rules for Meetings with Top Execs

This is the 5th chapter of the book. In the first section, you will learn a text, and you will have some information about Manager and Management. In the second section, you will have a deeper understanding about workplace's skills. In this section, you will learn two passages about workplace's skills and job interview and they will help you have a further development on mastering reading skills of drawing conclusions.

Starter

Why are managers the most expensive resource in most organizations?

Text

Managers and Management
— The Eternal Topic of the Workplace

Management and managers are the specific need of all organization, from the smallest to the largest one. They are the specific organ of every institution. They are what holds it together and makes it work. None of our organization could function without managers. But what is manager? What kind of person belongs to manager? And what's the duty of a manager?

Members in Organization

Managers work in an organization, but not everyone who works in an organization is a manager. In an organization, we can divide organizational members into two categories: managers and operative employees. Operative employees are people who work directly on a job or task and have no responsibility for overseeing the work of others, such as farmers in the farm, workers in the factory, cleaners in the street belong to operative employees. In contrast, a manager is the person who can direct the activities of other people in an organization. In a word, the distinction between managers and operative employees — is that managers have employees who report directly to them.

Levels of Managers

Managers are the basic resource of the organizational enterprise. In a fully automated factory,

Chapter Five Business Management

there may be almost no rank-and-file employees. But there will be managers. Managers are the most expensive resource in most organizations — and the one that depreciates the fastest and needs the most constant replenishment. It takes years to build a management team, but it can be depleted in a short period of misrule.

There are three levels of managers. It is classified as the first-line managers, middle managers, or top managers. Identifying exactly who managers are in an organization is often not a difficult task, although you should be aware that management positions come with a variety of titles. First-line managers are usually called supervisors. They may also be called team leaders, coaches, or unit coordinators. They are responsible for directing the day-to-day activities of operatives. In college, for example, dean would be a first-line manager overseeing the activities of the departmental faculty and the operatives. Middle managers represent levels of management between the first-line manager and top manager. These individuals manage other managers — and possibly some operative employees — and typically responsible for translating the goal set by top manager into specific details that lower-level managers can perform. In organizations, middle managers may have such titles as project leader, district manager and so on.

At or near the top of an organization are top managers. These individuals are responsible for making decisions about the direction of the organization and establishing policies that affect all organization members. Top managers typically have titles such as president, vice president, chief financial officer(CFO), chief operating officer(COO), chief executive officer(CEO), chairperson of the board.

What Is Management

The term management refers to the process of getting things done, effectively and efficiently, through and with other people. Several components in this definition need discussion. Components that represent planning, organizing, leading and controlling are in an organization.

Functions of Management

In the early part of the twentieth century, the French industrialist Henri Fayol wrote that all managers perform five management activities referred to as the "Functions of Management". They include plan, organize, command, coordinate and control. But now, it have been condensed to the basic four aspects: planning, organizing, leading and controlling.

Planning defines what the organization wants to be in the future and how to get there. Planning means defining goals for future organization performance and deciding on the tasks and use of resources needed to attain them. A lack of planning — or poor planning — can hurt organization's performance. However, for example, clothing retailer Merry-Go-Round, a once ubiquitous presence in malls across America, slid into bankruptcy and ultimately disappeared as a result of poor planning. Top managers' lack of vision in perceiving market direction and demographic trends, weak planning efforts regarding acquisitions and growth, and the failure to prepare for management succession helped to kill a 1,500 store, US$1 billion national wide chain.

Organizing typically follows planning and reflects how the organization tries to accomplish the plan. Organizing involves the assignments of tasks, the grouping of tasks into departments, and the allocation of resources to departments. For example, Honeywell managers reorganized new product development into "tiger team" consisting of marketing, engineering and design employees. The new structural design reduced the time to produce a new thermostat from 5 years to 12 months. Many companies today are following Honeywell's lead by reorganizing into teams that have the responsibility for self-management.

Leading is the use of influence to motivate employees to achieve organizational goals. Leading means creating a shared culture and values, communicating goals to employees throughout the organization, and infusing employees with the desire to perform at a high level. Leading involves motivating entire department and divisions as well as those individuals working immediately with the manager. In an era of uncertainty, international competition, and a growing diversity of workforce, the ability to shape culture, communicate goals, and motivate employees is critical to business success.

Controlling means monitoring employees' activities, determining whether the organization is on target toward its goals and making corrections as necessary. Managers must ensure that the organizations are moving toward its goals. New trends toward empowerment and trust of employees have led many companies to place less emphasis on top-down control and more emphasis on training employees to monitor and correct themselves.

 Words and Terms

workplace ['wɜːkpleɪs]	n.	职场，工作场所
institution [ɪnstɪ'tjuːʃn]	n.	组织，机构
function ['fʌŋkʃn]	n.	功能，职能，运作
category ['kætɪgɪ]	n.	种类
distinction [dɪ'stɪŋkʃn]	n.	区别
replenishment [rɪ'plenɪʃmənt]	n.	补给，补充
supervisor ['suːpəvaɪzə]	n.	主管
responsible [rɪ'spɒnsɪbl]	adj.	负有责任的
bankruptcy ['bæŋkrʌptsɪ]	n.	破产

operative employees	作业人员
first-line manager	基层管理人员
middle manager	中层管理人员
top manager	高层管理人员
chief financial officer(CFO)	财务总监；首席财务官
chief operating officer(COO)	首席运营官
chief executive officer (CEO)	首席执行官

 *Notes*

1. Managers are the most expensive resource in most organizations — and the one that depreciates the fastest and needs the most constant replenishment. 管理人员是大多数企业的宝贵资源，也是消耗最快、最需要经常补充的资源。在这个句子中，the one 指代前半句所提到的 resource。

2. Middle managers represent levels of management between the first-line manager (the supervisor) and top manager. 中层管理人员是指介于基层管理人员和高层管理人员之间的管理人员。

3. Top managers' lack of vision in perceiving market direction and demographic trends, weak planning efforts regarding acquisitions and growth, and the failure to prepare for management succession helped to kill a 1,500 store, US$1 billion national wide chain. 企业的高层管理人员缺乏对市场趋势和人口发展趋势的洞察力，对如何获取利润和促进增长所做的计划不周详，另外，他们为管理继任所做的准备也失败了，这几个因素最终导致了这家拥有 1500 间店铺、市值 10 亿美元的全国性连锁企业的失败。

management succession：管理继任。管理继任计划(Management Succession Planing)是确定和培养潜在的继承人以便在将来接管要职的过程和行动。主要内容是发现并追踪具有高潜质的人才。高潜质的人才是指那些企业相信他们具有胜任高层管理职位潜力的人。这些高层职位包括战略经营部门的管理者、职能领域的指导者(比如营销总监)或是首席执行官。与一般重置计划不同的是，继任计划更具有战略性、事先性、长期性和发展导向。它保证了企业合格经理人的持续供给，从而继续领导和推动业务增长。

4. For example, Honeywell managers reorganized new product development into "tiger team" consisting of marketing, engineering and design employees. 例如，霍尼韦尔国际公司的管理人员重新组织了新产品开发活动，选拔擅长于市场营销、工程学和设计的员工组成"老虎队"来进行新产品的开发。

Honeywell：霍尼韦尔国际公司(以下简称"霍尼韦尔")成立于 1999 年，由原世界两大著名公司——美国联信公司及霍尼韦尔公司合并而成，是一家年收入超过 200 亿美元，在多元化技术和制造业方面占世界领导地位的跨国公司，连续 50 年位列"《财富》500 强"排行榜。在全球，其业务涉及航空产品及服务；住宅及楼宇控制和工业控制技术；自动化产品；特种化学、纤维、塑料、电子和先进材料及交通和动力系统及产品等领域。霍尼韦尔在全球 95 个国家拥有 10.8 万名员工，公司总部设在美国新泽西州莫里斯镇。

5. In an era of uncertainty, international competition, and a growing diversity of workforce, the ability to shape culture, communicate goals, and motivate employees is critical to business success. 在这个充满不确定性、国际竞争日益激烈、劳动力日益多元化的时代，塑造文化、传达目标、激励员工的能力对于企业的成功来说是至关重要。

这句话中，主语是 the ability，不定式 to shape culture, communicate goals, and motivate employees 作后置定语修饰 ability，In an era of uncertainty, international competition, and a growing diversity of workforce 作状语。

6. New trends toward empowerment and trust of employees have led many companies to place less emphasis on top-down control and more emphasis on training employees to monitor and correct themselves. 倾向于授权和信任员工的新趋势使得许多企业减少自上而下的控制力度，重视培训员工以期他们能够进行自我监督和自我纠正。

在这句话中，主语是 New trends toward empowerment and trust of employees，many companies 作宾语，不定式 to place less emphasis on top-down control and more emphasis on training employees to monitor and correct themselves 作宾语补足语。

Exercises

I. Answer the following questions according to the text.

1. What's the best definition of "manager"?
2. What's the difference between operative employees and managers?
3. What are the levels of managers?
4. What is the management?
5. What are the functions of management?

II. Identify the key words or main ideas of the following parts.

Part 1	The _____ to management and managers
Part 2	The _____ in organization
Part 3	_____ of managers
Part 4	_____ of management
Part 5	_____ of management

III. Match the words or phrases in Column A to the words or phrases in Column B.

A	B
1. _____ bankruptcy	A. 管理
2. _____ supervisor	B. 功能，职能，运作
3. _____ institution	C. 组织，机构
4. _____ distinction	D. 基层管理人员
5. _____ first-line manager	E. 管理人员
6. _____ chief executive officer	F. 作业人员
7. _____ manager	G. 破产
8. _____ management	H. 主管，监管人
9. _____ operative employees	I. 首席执行官
10. _____ function	J. 区别

IV. Choose the best translation.

1. Managers work in an organization, but not everyone who works in an organization is a manager. (   )
   A. 管理人员在企业中工作，但不是每个在企业中工作的都是管理人员。
   B. 管理人员在企业中工作，而且每个在企业中工作的都是管理人员。
   C. 管理人员在企业中运作，在企业中工作的肯定都是管理人员。
   D. 管理人员在企业中运作，但在企业中工作的都是作业人员。

2. Managers are the most expensive resource in most organizations — and the one that depreciates the fastest and needs the most constant replenishment. (   )
   A. 管理人员是大多数企业中最廉价的资源，也是消耗最快，最需要经常补充的资源。
   B. 管理人员是大多数企业中最昂贵的资源，也是消耗最快，最需要经常补充的资源。
   C. 管理人员是大多数企业中最廉价的资源，也是消耗最慢，不需要经常补充的资源。
   D. 管理人员是大多数企业中最昂贵的资源，也是消耗最快，不需要经常补充的资源。

3. For example, clothing retailer Merry-Go-Round, a once ubiquitous presence in malls across America, slid into bankruptcy and ultimately disappeared as a result of poor planning. (   )
   A. 例如，服饰批发商旋转木马曾经遍布美国的各大商场，但由于计划不周，业绩下滑导致破产，最后消失在商界。
   B. 例如，服饰批发商旋转木马曾经遍布法国的各大商场，但由于计划不周，业绩下滑导致破产，最后消失在商界。
   C. 例如，服饰零售商旋转木马曾经遍布美国的各大超级市场，但由于计划不周，业绩下滑导致破产，最后消失在商界。
   D. 例如，服饰零售商旋转木马曾经遍布美国的各大商场，但由于计划不周，业绩下滑导致破产，最后消失在商界。

4. Many companies today are following Honeywell's lead by reorganizing into teams that have the responsibility for self-management. (   )
   A. 现今很多公司都效仿霍尼韦尔国际公司，重新组织能够更好地进行自我管理的团队。
   B. 现今很多公司都效仿霍尼韦尔国际公司，重新监控能够更好地进行自我反思的团队。
   C. 现今很多公司都跟随霍尼韦尔国际公司，重新组织能够更好地进行自我管理的团队。
   D. 现今很多公司都效仿霍尼韦尔国际公司，重新组织能够更好地进行自我反省的团队。

5. Controlling means monitoring employees' activities, determining whether the organization is on target toward its goals and making corrections as necessary. (   )
   A. 领导指的是监督员工的活动，确定企业是否正在朝着目标前进，在必要时进行改正。
   B. 控制指的是监督员工的活动，确定企业是否正在朝着目标前进，在必要时进行纠正。
   C. 指挥指的是监督员工的活动，确定企业是否正在朝着目标前进，在必要时进行纠正。
   D. 控制指的是干涉员工的活动，确定企业是否正在朝着终点前进，在必要时进行修改。

Reading Skills (5)
Drawing Conclusions

What Is Drawing Conclusions?

Careful and thoughtful readers always think about what they are reading, trying to interpret — explain and understand the ideas presented in a reading passage. In doing so they are able to draw conclusions based on what the author tells them. Therefore, drawing a conclusion means arriving at one decision justified by the stated evidence. Now read the following paragraph and try to answer the questions.

Much discussion has, in recent years, surrounded various ways and special courses designed to help people to increase their reading speed. So much depends on definition. Even among experts there is no complete their agreement as to exactly what we mean when we speak of "reading" a page of print. For some, it is attention to, and interpretation of most of the words on the page. Others seem to mean simply " dealing with large groups of words by speeding through them and picking out highlights". Most reading experts stress the importance of increasing the level of comprehension — the rate at which words and ideas they stand for can be truly understood. They believe that there has been overemphasis on the "numbers game" of increasing the number of words a person can "run through" per minute.

Further Development

Passage I

Workplaces' Skills

Twelve Tips for Becoming a Successful Manager

As a manager, you have the opportunity to lead, supervise, mentor and motivate others — and your ability to do so effectively making a huge difference to your company's overall success. Here are some tips for becoming a successful manager:

1. Don't try to be someone you are not

The temptation is to emulate the previous. This is bad news as you are not the previous manager, you are you. Think about successful managers you have enjoyed working for and identify what it was they did that gave you that feeling. Also, think about managers you have not enjoyed working for and identify what it was they did that gave you that feeling. These two activities will give you a framework from which to start your career towards becoming a successful manager.

2. Start as you mean to go on

Set clear standards and then model them — always. People respond positively to certainty as they generally don't like surprises. Everyone needs to know what is expected of them and clear standards will help them understand that this is the way we are going to do things around here. So why not ask your team to put together their ideas on what the standards should be and then agree them with you? That way they have the ownership so you don't need to motivate them to live by the standards.

3. Share your department's objectives with your staff

People respond to being given responsibility. You always get one or two people who moan and groan about you abdicating your responsibilities to them. Get rid of these people, or re-train them, as they will be trying to infect the team against you. Being decisive like this is a key step towards becoming a successful manager as you will impress your team and show them that you care about your responsibilities and about them as people.

4. Hold regular team reviews to ensure everyone is clear about what is expected of them

You can do this both as a team and more regularly as individuals. Once a month on an individual basis is a good way to work. Talk to each person about what he is working towards and the resources he has to do it with. Give them feedback about how they are performing (good and developmental feedback) and show what you can do to help them in the following month.

5. Initiate new rituals for the team

Rituals are important as they confirm to the team members that they each belong to something. Such rituals might include regular social events, team building days and team meetings.

6. Give feedback openly

Nothing engenders trust more in a successful manager than being honest. OK, so you also need to be sensitive about how you do it. But remember, feedback is not just telling someone they have got it wrong — it is also about telling them when they have got it right. When you give feedback, be specific. Don't say, "You dealt with that customer well." Do say, "I particularly liked the way you calmed down that angry customer. You showed empathy for her needs and yet still managed to help her understand that she was the one who had caused the problem."

7. Acknowledge the expertise of your staff

You are now a manager which means that your job is to manage other people doing the work. If you find yourself doing the work, then you are not being a successful manager but an overpaid worker. If you look to their expertise in doing the job they will respect your expertise in managing them.

8. Encourage creativity in your team

Look to your team for the solutions to problems rather than try and solve them for yourself. People like problem solving and will be motivated by you involving them. Creativity is in all of us. It just needs encouraging out. They will probably come up with better solutions than you could have anyway.

9. Don't be too weak to admit your mistakes

You will make mistakes — that is, if you are human. Be open about them and ask your team for help in avoiding making the same mistake again. If you make yourself approachable they will be relaxed about giving you feedback which may help prevent mistakes in the future.

10. Managing and leading are not the same thing

Some successful managers are not good leaders. The art is in knowing when to delegate. You will be developing your staff if you delegate leadership experiences. You will still retain overall control because you will always retain accountability, so learn to trust your staff — they don't have a choice with you.

11. Carry on developing yourself

Becoming a successful manager is not an end point but the start of a new direction in your career. Managing is a skill which needs to be learned and practiced and then learned some more. You will never reach the point where you will not need training and developing, so get yourself on some good courses, read management books (some of them are fun to read believe it or not) and sign up for some e-learning.

12. You can still be friends with your staff

Just because you are now a successful manager, it doesn't mean you have to change your staff. They need to understand that you are being held accountable for their work and so there will be times when you have to be directive but there will be more times when you have to rely on them to help you. Successful managers do not build barriers against people.

Words and Terms

supervise [ˈsuːpəvaɪz]	v.	监督，管理，指导
motivate [ˈməʊtɪveɪt]	v.	激发，诱导，刺激
temptation [tempˈteɪʃn]	n.	诱惑，引诱；诱惑物
previous [ˈpriːvɪəs]	adj.	先前的；以前的
identify [aɪˈdentɪfaɪ]	v.	识别，认出
career [kəˈrɪə(r)]	n.	生涯；职业
expertise [ˌekspɜːˈtiːz]	n.	专门知识或技能
approachable [əˈprəʊtʃəbl]	adj.	可亲近的；可接近的
creativity [ˌkriːeɪˈtɪvɪtɪ]	n.	创造性，创造力
feedback [ˈfiːdbæk]	n.	反馈；回应
direction [dɪˈrekʃn]	n.	方向；趋势
accountable [əˈkaʊntəbl]	adj.	负有责任的

Notes

1. As a manager, you have the opportunity to lead, supervise, mentor and motivate others — and your ability to do so effectively makes a huge difference to your company's overall success. 作

为一名经理，你有领导、监督、指导和激励他人的机会。而有能力这样做的你，将会对企业取得整体性的成功有着巨大的影响。make a difference to 对……有影响

2. Everyone needs to know what is expected of them and clear standards will help them understand that this is the way we are going to do things around here. 每个人都需要知道他们的期望和明确的标准是什么，这样才会让他们明白，自己将要做的事情是什么。

3. Rituals are important as they confirm to the team members that they each belong to something. 团队仪式很重要，它会让团队成员有归属感。

4. You showed empathy for her needs and yet still managed to help her understand that she was the one who had caused the problem. 你可以向她表明你能站在她的立场去理解她，但同时也应让她明白一个事实——她是导致事情发生的因素之一。

5. Managing is a skill which needs to be learned and practiced and then learned some more. 管理是那种需要不断学习和实践，然后慢慢提升的一门技能。

这是一个定语从句，先行词是 skill，which 是连接代词。

6. They need to understand that you are being held accountable for their work and so there will be times when you have to be directive but there will be more times when you have to rely on them to help you. 要让他们(员工)理解你对他们的工作负有责任。因此，有时候你不得不发号施令，但更多的时候，你必须依靠他们的帮助。

 Exercises

I. Read the following statements and decide whether they are True(T) or False(F).

1. According to the text, there are 12 tips for becoming a successful manager. (   )
2. As a successful manager, you should try to be someone you are not, especially imitate your previous manager. (   )
3. Managers do not share their department's objectives with their staff, but keep it on their own. (   )
4. Becoming a successful manager is not an end point for one's career. (   )
5. Being a successful manager means you have right to lead, supervise, mentor and motivate your staff, even can change your staff. (   )

II. Choose the correct answer according to Passage I.

1. As a manager, you have the opportunity to _____ others. (   )
A. lead, supervise
B. mentor , motivate
C. lead, supervise and mentor
D. lead, supervise, mentor and motivate

2. For feedback, which of the following statement is true? (   )
A. Feedback shouldn't be specific.

B. Feedback should only tell something wrong.

C. Feedback should only tell something right.

D. Feedback is not only telling something wrong, but also telling them something right.

3. When the customers got angry, what should the staff do? (   )

A. Calmed down angry customers.

B. Showed empathy for customers' needs.

C. Try to help the customers understand the whole situation.

D. All of the above.

4. As a successful manager, what does he need to do? (   )

A. Share department's objectives with staff.

B. Stop carrying on developing himself.

C. Couldn't make friends with his staff.

D. Try to imitate previous manager as he could.

5. Which of the following statement is true? (   )

A. Managing and leading are not the same thing.

B. Managers do not share their department's objectives with staff.

C. Don't be too weak to admit mistakes during the work.

D. Don't carry on developing yourself when you are a successful manager.

III. Fill in the missing information.

Nothing _____ trust more in a successful manager than being_____. OK, so you also need to be _____ how you do it. But remember, _____ is not just telling someone they have got it wrong — it is also about telling them when they have got it right. When you give feedback, be _____.

Passage II

Job Interview

— 7 Rules for Meetings with Top Execs

Congratulations! You've finally landed a one-on-one meeting with a top exec, a powerful player inside your customer's firm. It's a great opportunity, but you've got to be certain to take advantage of it. Make sure you follow these simple steps.

1. Do your research

Before the meeting, research and review the exec's "business agenda" — what he or she needs to accomplish organizationally. Then use your contacts in the firm and your own business acumen to understand the exec's "personal agenda" — likely career goals, the job that he or she is angling for, and so forth.

2. Don't assume the exec knows who you are

Busy execs are often unaware (or can't remember) why a particular meeting is on their agenda. Introduce yourself and explain why you're there, tying the subject matter to both the business agenda and, more subtly, the personal agenda of the executive in question. For example: "I'm John Doe from Acme and I'm here to discuss how to increase profitability through improvements in quality control."

3. Establish credibility immediately

Within the first few minutes, demonstrate that you've done your homework and understand the company, its challenges and its place in its industry. Focus on business issues that the executive faces — never the specific bells and whistles on your product. Execs don't care about features and functions; they want to know how you're going to change the bottom line.

4. Ask intelligent questions

Frame everything according to the drivers that affect the business and the metrics that this exec uses to evaluate activities. For example, if you're talking to a CFO, you might ask questions about the ROI expectations that the firm uses to make purchasing decisions. If you're talking to a chief technology officer, you might ask questions about the how the rest of the company measures IT performance.

5. Listen more than you talk

Once you've asked a question, hear what the exec has to say. A productive conversation with a customer is one in which the customer does most of the talking. Your job is to guide the conversation so that you discover what you need to know in order to be of service to that customer. You need to fully understand a company's problem before proposing a solution.

6. Add value to the conversation

Resist the temptation to present your solution right then and there. Anything resembling a sales pitch will make it seem as if your haven't been listening or (worse) don't care about what the exec just told you. Instead, bring additional value to the conversation by introducing a different business perspective and your experience dealing with similar problems.

7. Close on a next step

Involve the exec directly in planning any subsequent actions concerning your offering. In most cases, this will involve an opportunity for you to present some kind of customized solution to the problems you've been discussing. However, take the exec's lead on how to go about this. Ideally, you want the executive to make some kind of public commitment to the project, even if it's just to schedule a group meeting to discuss the idea further.

Exercises

I. Choose the correct answer according to Passage II.

1. According to the text, how to research and review the exec's "business agenda"? (   )

A. Use your contacts in the firm and your own business acumen.

B. Get information about him by his family.

C. Get information about him by his customers.

D. Get information about him by computer or books.

2. Why are execs often unaware meeting on their agenda? (   )

A. Because they are too busy to remember.

B. Because they don't want to remember it.

C. Because the meeting is too difficult to remember.

D. Because the meeting isn't need to remember.

3. When is the good time to show that you've done your homework and understand the company? (   )

A. Within the last few minutes during the conversations.

B. After finishing the talking.

C. Within the first few minutes during the conversations.

D. Before finishing the talking.

4. What do execs care about features and functions; they want to know how you're going to change the bottom line? (   )

A. They care about features

B. They care about functions

C. They care about features and functions

D. They care about the ways you're going to change the bottom line.

5. According to the text, what the author's suggestion for conversations with execs? (   )

A. Try to talk as much as you can.

B. Just listen to the exec.

C. Talk more than you listen.

D. Listen more than you talk.

II. Choose the best translation.

1. 恭喜你！你终于有机会与一位高管面谈了。(   )

A. Lucky you! You've finally landed a one-on-one meeting with a top exec.

B. Congratulations! You've finally landed a one-on-one meeting with a top exec.

C. Lucky you! You've finally landed a one-on-one meeting with a low exec.

D. Congratulations! You've finally landed a one-on-one meeting with a low exec.

2. 高管们太忙了，他们常常不知道为什么自己的日程里有某个会议。（　　）
A. Busy execs are often unaware why a particular meeting is on their agenda.
B. Busy execs are often aware why a particular meeting is on their agenda.
C. Top execs are often unaware why a particular meeting is on their agenda.
D. Top execs are often aware why a particular meeting is on their agenda.

3. 会谈开始了，最初的几分钟是你证明自己在会谈前已经认真做功课的好机会。（　　）
A. Within the last few minutes, demonstrate that you've done your homework and understand the company.
B. After finishing the conversations with top execs, demonstrate that you've done your homework and understand the company.
C. Before the conversations with top execs, demonstrate that you've done your homework and understand the company.
D. Within the first few minutes, demonstrate that you've done your homework and understand the company.

4. 控制住自己，别急着一下子就把自己的解决方案说出来。（　　）
A. Resist the temptation to present your solution right then and there.
B. Release the temptation to present your position right then and there.
C. Resist the temptation to present your position right then and there.
D. Release the temptation to present your solution right then and there.

5. 在提出一个解决方案之前，你需要先充分了解公司现有的问题。（　　）
A. You don't need to fully understand a company's problem before proposing a solution.
B. You need to fully understand a company's problem before proposing a solution.
C. You don't need to fully understand a company's problem after proposing a solution.
D. You need to fully understand a company's problem after proposing a solution.

Special Terms

operative employee	作业人员
first-line manager	基层管理人员
middle managers	中层管理人员
top managers	高层管理人员
chief financial officer(CFO)	财务总监；首席财务官
chief operating officer(COO)	首席运营官
chief executive officer (CEO)	首席执行官
chairperson of the board	董事会主席
supervisor	主管，监管人
vice president	副总裁
district manager	区域经理

Chapter Six

Investment and Financing

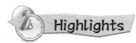
Highlights

Text

Five Really Dumb Money Moves You've Got to Avoid

Reading Skills (6)

Skimming

Further Development

Passage I

Companies' Investment Plans

Passage II

Student Finance: Top 10 Student Money Saving Tips

Preview

This is the 6th chapter of the book. In the first section, you will learn a text, and you will have some information about the five really dumb money moves you've got to avoid. In the second section, you will have a deeper understanding about Investment and Financing. In this section, you will learn two passages about companies' investment plans and student finance and they will help you have a further development on mastering reading skills of skimming.

Chapter Six Investment and Financing

Starter

"Famous men get their pictures on money; rich men get their hands on money." How do you understand this sentence?

Text
Five Really Dumb Money Moves You've Got to Avoid

You know the smartest things to do with your money. But what are the worst moves? What should you avoid?

Weirdly enough, they are things that a surprising number of people are still doing — even though they probably know, in their heart of hearts, how foolish they really are.

Any list is going to be incomplete. But here are five to avoid.

1. Reaching for yield

What this country needs is a good 5% certificate of deposit. Instead the collapse in interest rates, and the Federal Reserve's policy of keeping them down for as long as possible, is driving people crazy — especially people who need to generate income from their investments.

In these circumstances, people start to do really foolish things in the desperate hunt for higher interest rates. That includes taking on crazy amounts of risk, or investing in complex products they don't understand, in the hope of higher yields. The Fed is producing a bull market in scams, Ponzi schemes and associated rackets.

The Securities and Exchange Commission recently warned about an epidemic of bogus high-yield "corporate promissory notes" being marketed to investors by scam artists.

The Wall Street Journal's Jason Zweig highlighted the woes of those sold complex "reverse convertibles," a legal but complicated product with embedded risks. Eric Lewis, chief investment officer of Bedrock Capital Management in Los Altos, Calif., suggests that if you can't explain an investment to a friend, including what might go wrong, you should think twice.

A high-yield bond fund such as the iShares High Yield Corporate Bond exchange-traded fund (HYG), which lends money to risky companies, sports a yield of about 5%. That's the maximum yield you can earn without taking on much more risk.

2. Going into the poor house to send Junior to a country-club college

Over the past 40 years, the cost of tuition and fees at a private university has tripled — after accounting for inflation. The cost of a public university has quadrupled.

The cost of getting a bachelor's degree has become a scandal in this country. Students spend US$160,000 on a four-year degree and the results are too often questionable.

Financial planners strongly advise parents against plundering their own retirement savings, which they are likely to need, to pay for this.

Admittedly, a degree has become a protection racket — you can't get a job without one, but there are fewer jobs for those with them. But the smart move for the budget-constrained is to get a bachelor's degree at a public university. The tuition and fees average less than US$9,000 a year instead of US$30,000 at a private college.

3. Owning stock in your employer

This is one of the silliest and riskiest moves any investor can make. If the company hits trouble, you get whacked twice. You can lose your job and your savings — all in one fell swoop. Ask anyone who worked for Enron or Lehman Brothers.

The law, amazingly, actually encourages this crazy move. While employers' 401(k) plans are subject to punitive regulations, lest they allow you to take on too much "risk", employers are allowed to offer their own stock among the investment options. Many do.

The Employee Benefit Research Institute says that the percentage of 401(k) assets held in employers' stock has been halved since 2000, but the numbers are still alarming. Furthermore, it's the youngest workers — those best able to take a gamble — who are shunning their employers' company stock.

At companies where the 401(k) plan offers the option, workers aged 40 or over typically hold about 20% of their entire 401(k) account in the company's stock, according to EBRI data. Crazy.

4. Taking social security too early

If you can afford to delay taking your Social Security retirement benefit, do.

Someone earning US$50,000 a year who starts claiming Social Security as soon as he or she is able, age 62, will typically collect a monthly check of about US$1,000, according to the Social Security Administration. If they wait until they are 70, that amount would double.

Taking Social Security too early, or without thinking through the consequences, is one of the biggest financial blunders people can make — roughly on a par with buying tech stocks in 2000 or a

Las Vegas condo in 2006. The lure of getting money early can blind people to the big cost down the road. (Many retirees may not have much of a choice. Hard labor at low pay over a lifetime takes its toll on a person. Also, many companies all but force older workers into early retirements.)

In any case, it doesn't take more than just a few years before the total money accrued with the higher, later benefits surpasses the total earned starting at the earlier retirement age.

But that understates the bigger issue. Social Security is insurance. For many retirees, the big risk isn't that they will run out of money before they turn 70, but after 85. According to the Centers for Disease Control, more than half of women currently age 65 will live to 85 or longer, and three out of eight men.

David Blanchett, head of retirement research for financial research firm Morningstar, says it makes sense for women, married couples and those with good health to wait longer for a bigger paycheck.

5. Buying long-term bonds

A surprising number of people still subscribe to the flawed and circular argument that bonds, including long-term government bonds, are "safe." In reality, bonds — especially long-term government bonds — are the rare example of a bubble that has been explicitly declared.

The Fed is openly printing money and using it to buy up such bonds, driving up the price and driving down the interest rates, in order to help the economy. There is no dispute about this. It's public policy.

A 30-year Treasury bond currently sports an interest rate of just 3.1%. That's barely half a percentage point above long-term inflation forecasts. Based on history, the yield should be at least 4.5%, or two percentage points above inflation. Thirty-year Treasury inflation-protected securities, known as TIPS, sport a "real" or inflation-adjusted yield of 0.6% a year. Again, it should be 2%.

The only reason to buy such bonds in any quantity is to gamble on a 1930s-style depression and worldwide deflation. Such bonds are a gamble, not a safe haven.

(From:http://www.24en.com)

 Words and Terms

certificate [sə'tɪfɪˌkeɪt]	n.		证书，文凭
scam [skæm]	n.		骗局，欺诈
bogus ['bəʊgəs]	n.		假冒的，伪造的
promissory ['prɒmɪsərɪ]	adj.		约定的，允诺的
convertible [kən'vɜːtɪbl]	adj.		可转变的
tuition [tjuː'ɪʃn]	n.		学费
inflation [ɪn'fleɪʃn]	n.		膨胀
quadruple ['kwɒdrʊpl]	n.		四倍，翻两番
admittedly [əd'mɪtɪdlɪ]	adv.		承认地，无可否认地
whacked [wækt]	adj.		疲惫不堪的

punitive ['pju:nɪtɪv]	adj.	惩罚的
blunder ['blʌndə]	n.	疏忽
paycheck ['peɪtʃek]	n.	薪水

take a gamble	冒险
heart of hearts	内心深处
long-term bonds	长期债券
high-yield bond fund	高收益债券基金
treasury bond	财政部发售的公债，美国的长期国库券
Securities and Exchange Commission	证券交易委员会

1. reaching for yield 追求高收益率

2. What this country needs is a good 5% certificate of deposit. Instead the collapse in interest rates, and the Federal Reserve's policy of keeping them down for as long as possible, is driving people crazy — especially people who need to generate income from their investments. 美国这个国家需要的是收益率能够达到5%的定期存单。然而，这里有的只是利率的一降再降，以及联邦储备委员会(Federal Reserve)尽量将利率维持在低位的政策，这样的现状逼得人们愈加疯狂——对于那些需要从投资中获取收益的人而言尤其如此。

美国联邦储备委员会(The Board of Governors of the Federal Reserve System)，简称美联储委员会(Federal Reserve Board)，是美国联邦储备系统(The Federal Reserve System)的核心管理机构，它是一个美国联邦政府机构，其办公地点位于美国华盛顿特区(Washington D.C.)。"美联储"一般是对整体储备系统的简称，而非对其委员会的简称。

3. The Fed is producing a bull market in scams, Ponzi schemes and associated rackets. 美联储正在打造着一个各类阴谋、庞氏骗局和欺诈手段层出不穷的牛市。

4. The Securities and Exchange Commission recently warned about an epidemic of bogus high-yield "corporate promissory notes" being marketed to investors by scam artists. 美国证券交易委员会最近提醒投资者警惕，目前市场中有一种由骗子发行的虚假高收益"企业本票"在大量传播。

5. The Wall Street Journal's Jason Zweig highlighted the woes of those sold complex 'reverse convertibles, ' a legal but complicated product with embedded risks. 《华尔街日报》的杰森·茨威格指出了那些卖出"反向可转债"这一复杂产品的投资者所面临的困境，"反向可转债"是一种合法的金融产品，不过此类产品结构复杂，其本身存在着潜在的风险。

6. While employers' 401 plans are subject to punitive regulations, lest they allow you to take on too much "risk", employers are allowed to offer their own stock among the investment options. 虽然企业的401(k)计划受到监管部门监管，若企业让员工承担过高"风险"，则会受到惩罚，但是监管规定允许企业向员工提供企业自己的股票作为投资选择之一。

401K 计划的名称取自美国 1978 年《国内收入法》中的(section 401K)条款。其是美国一种特殊的退休储蓄计划，其深受欢迎的原因是可以享受税收优惠。作为"雇员福利"项目之一的养老金计划一直是美国人生活中不可或缺的组成部分。401(k)计划起源于 20 世纪 80 年代初美国税法修改及相关免税条款的出台。其名称来自《国内税收法案》第 401(k)节，它允许员工将一部分税前工资存入一个储蓄计划，积累至退休后使用。在此基础上，一种新的养老金计划——"401(k)"开始出现，并大受欢迎。到 2000 年底，其资产规模已达 17000 亿美元，参与人数超过 4200 万。

7. At companies where the 401(k) plan offers the option, workers aged 40 or over typically hold about 20% of their entire 401(k) account in the company's stock, according to EBRI data. 根据员工福利研究所的数据，在那些在 401(k)计划中提供了持有本公司股票这一投资选择的公司中，年龄在 40 岁或者以上的员工通常会将自己的 401(k)账户中大约 20%的资产用于投资本公司股票。

8. A surprising number of people still subscribe to the flawed and circular argument that bonds, including long-term government bonds, are "safe." In reality, bonds — especially long-term government bonds — are the rare example of a bubble that has been explicitly declared. 令人吃惊的是，仍有很多人接受这样的观点：包括长期政府债券在内的债券是"安全的"。实际上，债券——特别是长期政府债券——是少有的一种已经被明确宣告的泡沫。

9. A 30-year Treasury bond currently sports an interest rate of just 3.1%. That's barely half a percentage point above long-term inflation forecasts. Based on history, the yield should be at least 4.5%, or two percentage points above inflation. 30 年期美国国债目前的收益率仅为 3.1%。这比长期通货膨胀预期仅高出半个百分点。如果以过往的标准来衡量，30 年期国债的收益率应该至少达到 4.5%，比通货膨胀率高出两个百分点。

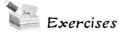

Exercises

I. Answer the following questions according to the text.

1. What does this country need and what is the policy of the Federal Reserve?
2. What kinds of foolish things do people start to do?
3. How about the cost of tuition and fees at a private university and a public university over the past 40 years?
4. How much do students spend on a four-year degree?
5. What do financial planners strongly advise parents?

II. Identify the key words or main ideas of the following parts.

Part 1	Reaching for _____	
Part 2	Going into _____ to send junior to _____	
Part 3	Owning _____ in your employer	
Part 4	Taking _____ too early	
Part 5	Buying _____	

III. Match the words or phrases in Column A to the words or phrases in Column B.

A

1. _____ certificate
2. _____ scam
3. _____ bogus
4. _____ promissory
5. _____ convertible
6. _____ tuition
7. _____ inflation
8. _____ whacked
9. _____ punitive
10. _____ take a gamble

B

A. 约定的，允诺的
B. 学费
C. 可转变的
D. 证书，文凭
E. 惩罚的
F. 疲惫不堪的，重击
G. 伪币，假的，伪造
H. 冒险
I. 膨胀
J. 骗局，欺诈

IV. Choose the best translation.

1. In these circumstances, people start to do really foolish things in the desperate hunt for higher interest rates. ( )

A. 在此环境下，人们不顾一切地寻找更高的收益率，并为此开始犯下着实愚蠢的错误。
B. 这样子说来，人们正在高兴地寻求更高的收益率，并犯下了非常低级的错误。
C. 在此情况下，人们不顾一切地寻找更高的收益率，并为此开始做一些傻事。
D. 在此天气下，人们开始愚蠢地，绝望地犯下错误去寻找更高的收益。

2. Over the past 40 years, the cost of tuition and fees at a private university has tripled — after accounting for inflation. ( )

A. 在过去的 40 年，学费的花费在一所私立大学已经翻了 3 倍。
B. 过去 40 年来，美国私立大学的学费以及各种开销增长了两倍——扣除了通货膨胀因素之后。
C. 超过过去的 40 年，美国公立大学的学费以及各种开销是过去的三倍，因为通货膨胀的原因。
D. 过去 40 年来，美国私立大学的学费因为通货膨胀的原因，增长了两倍。

3. Financial planners strongly advise parents against plundering their own retirement savings, which they are likely to need, to pay for this. ( )

A. 金融策划师们强烈建议父母们不要掠夺自己的退休金，他们很有可能把这些钱用来支付学费。
B. 理财专家们强烈建议学生家长们将自己的养老积蓄用来为孩子付学费，这笔钱他们自己可能还用得着。
C. 理财专家们强烈建议学生家长们将自己很可能还用得着的养老金用来为孩子付学费。
D. 理财专家们强烈建议学生家长们不要将自己的养老积蓄用来为孩子付学费，这笔钱他们自己可能还用得着。

4. Someone earning US$50,000 a year who starts claiming Social Security as soon as he or she is able, age 62, will typically collect a monthly check of about US$1,000, according to the Social Security Administration. (   )
   A. 根据美国社会安全局的数据，年薪五万美元的员工若在自己年满 62 岁这一支取社保金的规定年龄后即开始使用社保，则通常每月可以得到大约 1 000 美元。
   B. 根据美国社会安全局的数据，月薪五万美元的员工从自己 62 岁开始提取养老金，那他每个月可以拿到 1000 美金。
   C. 年薪五万美元的员工若在自己年满 62 岁这一支取社保金的规定年龄后即开始使用社保，则通常每月可以得到大约 1 000 美元，根据美国社会安全局的数据。
   D. 年薪五万美元的员工一到 62 岁就立刻提取养老金，则通常每月可以得到大约 1 000 美元。

5. The Fed is openly printing money and using it to buy up such bonds, driving up the price and driving down the interest rates, in order to help the economy. (   )
   A. 美联储公开地印刷钞票，并用这些钱买国债，从而降低这些国债的价格，提高利率，以便能够帮助促进美国经济。
   B. 美联储在毫不掩饰地大肆印着钞票，并用这些印出来的钞票买国债，从而抬高这类债券的价格，压低利率，以便能够帮助提振美国经济。
   C. 美联储在毫不掩饰地大肆印着钞票，并用这些印出来的钞票买股票，从而抬高这类债券的价格，压低利率，以便能够帮助提振美国经济。
   D. 美联储私下地印刷钞票，并用这些钱买国债，从而抬高这些国债的价格，降低利率，以便能够帮助促进美国经济。

Reading Skills (6)

Skimming

What Is Skimming

Skimming is very fast reading. When you skim, you read to get the main idea and a few, but not all of the details. People often skim when they have lots of material to read in a limited amount of time. To skim is to read quickly in order to get the general idea of a passage. Skimming is done at a speed three to four times faster than normal reading. For example, a student's normal reading speed is 150 wpm, (words per minute) he is supposed to achieve a skimming rate of 300 wpm or better.

Unlike scanning which involves searching for details or isolated facts, skimming requires you to note only information and clues which provide an idea of the central theme or topic of a piece of prose. Skimming is quickly looking over a selection to get the general idea rather than reading every word. Here is a step-by-step procedure to follow in skimming for main ideas of an article:

1. Read the title, the headings and subheadings.

2. Notice the author's name and the source of the text.

3. Read the introduction, notice the pictures, charts or graphs included.

4. Read the first paragraph completely to see what the general topic is about.

5. Keep the general theme in mind, and look for key sentences or words and phrases related to the theme. The first sentence or last sentence is usually your best bet, but it's a good idea to let your eyes glide rapidly over the in-between lines for names, dates, or key words.

6. Skip sections within the paragraph that seem to contain nothing more than examples or illustrations.

7. Look for general ideas related to the theme of the selection.

8. If the final paragraph appears to be a summary, read it completely.

Further Development

Passage I

Companies' Investment Plans

Computers, research and software will be the big-ticket items in 2016. There have been three great waves of corporate investment in the past two decades. First came the dotcom splurge of 1997—2001, when cash was poured into building mobile-phone networks and the Internet's backbone. Then there was the emerging-market frenzy of 2003—2010. Western firms threw about US$2 trillion into factories and other facilities in places like China and India. In 2005—2013 there was a craze for commodities, partly driven by great Chinese demand. Global energy and metals firms spent US$6 trillion digging in the Australian outback and drilling for oil in North Dakota and deep beneath Brazil's coastal waters.

The dotcom boom turned to bust, emerging markets are now in poor shape and commodity prices have slumped in the past year (costing some firms' bosses their jobs). So where are companies looking to invest now? A new study by Hugo Scott-Gall, of Goldman Sachs, a bank, crunches the numbers for capital investment at more than 2,500 firms worldwide, forecasting how things will look in 2017 compared with 2014. It finds a startling divergence across industries.

Energy, mining and chemicals firms are expected to slash their capital-investment budgets by 20—50%. Property firms are cutting back too, in part reflecting the end of China's building boom. This has a knock-on effect on those capital-goods firms that supply equipment to these industries. For example, Caterpillar, which makes diggers used by mining and construction firms, expects its capital investment in 2016 to be half the level of 2012.

In contrast, internet, software and other tech firms are on a high, with their budgets expected to expand by a quarter or more. Though some tech firms have gone asset-light, renting their processing power and data storage in the online "cloud", others—including cloud-providers themselves—are splurging on hardware. In 2016 the combined capital spending of Google and Apple will be US$24 billion, almost equal to Exxon's US$28 billion budget.

Measured in dollars, the overall picture is of a 15% fall in corporate capital spending by 2017. Allowing for the greenback's big rise since 2014, the fall will be just 5% or so in local-currency terms. And the figures exclude research-and-development (R&D) spending. That is rising quickly. America's national accounts, for example, show an economy-wide decline in investment in physical plant being offset by a rise in R&D and software spending.

However you slice the numbers, growth in capital investment is unusually concentrated. Of the industries that Goldman studied, 22 are forecast to have shrinking budgets in dollar terms and 12 are expected to grow. The top 20 spenders on R&D—firms such as Samsung, Roche, Novartis and Microsoft—account for 25% of worldwide R&D spending by listed firms, according to Bloomberg, an information provider. The corporate world seems mostly destined to stagnation, with only a few hotspots of investment and growth.

So investors might hope that an elite of investment-intensive, technology-based firms will conquer new markets and increase profits faster than all others. That is certainly what Silicon Valley's boosters think will happen. They cheer each time tech firms unveil some new area of expansion—smart watches, driverless cars, virtual-reality goggles, delivery drones.

Yet history suggests that whenever there is a near-unanimous view on what to invest in, disaster follows as firms in those industries lose their spending discipline. The shares of Western firms exposed to energy and emerging markets have lagged the S&P 500 index by over 50% in the past two years. In 2016 it should become clearer whether the present funnelling of investment into tech-based industries reflects a step change in the way the economy works, or is just a symptom of a stagnant climate in which pockets of opportunity are hyped beyond their true potential.

(From: The Economist)

Words and Terms

dotcom[ˈdɒtkɔm]	n.	网站
splurge[splɜːdʒ]	n.	挥霍
frenzy [ˈfrenzɪ]	n.	狂潮
commodity[kəˈmɒdɪtɪ]	n.	商品
slump[slʌmp]	vt.	暴跌
divergence [daɪˈvɜːdʒəns]	n.	分歧
slash [slæʃ]	vt.	大幅度削减
stagnation [stæɡˈneɪʃən]	n.	停滞
lag [læɡ]	v.	延迟
potential [pəˈtenʃl]	n.	潜能
big-ticket items		投资热点

1. First came the dotcom splurge of 1997—2001, when cash was poured into building mobile-phone networks and the Internet's backbone. (此句为倒装句)第一次是互联网投资热是在1997—2001年期间，大量资金注入手机网络和互联网主干的建设。

2. In 2005—2013, there was a craze for commodities, partly driven by great Chinese demand. 2005年至2013年又成了大宗商品的疯狂年代，大宗商品走俏的部分原因是中国对此类商品需求大。

3. The dotcom boom turned to bust, emerging markets are now in poor shape and commodity prices have slumped in the past year. 如今，互联网泡沫破裂、新兴市场后继乏力、大宗商品价格也在过去一年中大幅跳水。

4. Property firms are cutting back too, in part reflecting the end of China's building boom. 房地产公司也会采取同样的措施，这也从一定程度上反映了中国房地产热的终结。

5. This has a knock-on effect on those capital-goods firms that supply equipment to these industries. For example, Caterpillar, which makes diggers used by mining and construction firms, expects its capital investment in 2016 to be half the level of 2012. 削减投资的举措会连带影响为这些产业提供设备的企业。以卡特彼勒公司为例，它专为矿业及建筑公司生产挖掘机，预计其2016年度的资本投资额会削减至2012年的一半。

卡特彼勒是财富500强公司之一，总部所在地美国，主要经营工业农业设备。80年以来，卡特彼勒公司一直致力于全球的基础设施建设，并与全球代理商紧密合作，在各大洲积极推进持续变革。2005年，卡特彼勒销售和收入达到363.4亿美元，是建筑机械、矿用设备、柴油和天然气发动机以及工业用燃气轮机领域的技术领导者和全球领先制造商。

6. Though some tech firms have gone asset-light, renting their processing power and data storage in the online "cloud", others—including cloud-providers themselves—are splurging on hardware. 尽管一些科技企业走轻资产化路线，将公司的数据处理及存储都交给网络"云"，但其他科技企业，包括云服务提供商本身却在大量购进硬件设施。

7. In 2016 the combined capital spending of Google and Apple will be US\$24 billion, almost equal to Exxon's US\$28 billion budget. 2016年，谷歌和苹果公司的投资额总和将达到240亿美元，几乎等同于埃克森公司280亿美元的投资预算。

Exxon: 艾克森石油公司

8. Allowing for the greenback's big rise since 2014, the fall will be just 5% or so in local-currency terms. And the figures exclude research-and-development (R&D) spending. 考虑到美元自2014年起已大幅增值，因此对地方货币来说，降幅应该只有5%左右。这个数字还不包括研发支出。

greenback: 美元

Chapter Six Investment and Financing

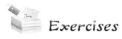 *Exercises*

I. Read the following statements and decide whether they are True(T) or False(F).

1. There have been three great waves of corporate investment in the past twenty years. (   )
2. In 2005—2013 there was a craze for emerging-market, partly driven by insatiable Chinese demand. (   )
3. The dotcom boom turned to bust, emerging markets are now in poor shape and commodity prices have increased in the past year. (   )
4. Energy, mining and chemicals firms are expected to cut their capital-investment budgets by 20—50%. (   )
5. The top 20 spenders on R&D — firms such as Samsung, Roche, Novartis and Microsoft — account for 35% of worldwide R&D spending by listed firms, according to Bloomberg, an information provider. (   )

II. Choose the correct answer according to Passage I.

1. The three great waves of corporate investment in the past two decades are as follows except_____. (   )
   A. the dotcom splurge of 1997—2001
   B. the emerging-market frenzy of 2003—2010
   C. a craze for commodities
   D. the increase of the stock market

2. According to paragraph 2, which one is NOT true about the situation in the past year? (   )
   A. The dotcom boom turned to bust.
   B. The dotcom boom began to prosper.
   C. Emerging markets are now in good shape.
   D. Commodity prices have slumped in the past year.

3. Energy, mining and chemicals firms are expected to slash their capital-investment budgets by _____. (   )
   A. 20—50%
   B. 10—20%
   C. 15—30%
   D. 30—55%

4. In 2016 the combined capital spending of _____ will be US$24 billion, almost equal to Exxon's US$28 billion budget. (   )
   A. Samsung and Roche
   B. Google and Apple
   C. Microsoft and Google
   D. Samsung and Apple

97

5. Which of the following statement is NOT true? (   )

A. The overall picture is of a 15% fall in corporate capital spending by 2017.

B. America's national accounts how an economy-wide increase in investment in physical plant being offset by a rise in R&D and software spending.

C. The corporate world seems mostly destined to stagnation, with only a few hotspots of investment and growth.

D. The shares of Western firms exposed to energy and emerging markets have lagged the S&P 500 index by over 50% in the past two years.

III. Fill in the missing information.

There have been three great waves of corporate investment in the past two decades. First came _____ of 1997—2001, when cash was poured into building _____ and _____. Then there was the _____ of 2003—2010. Western firms threw about US$2 trillion into factories and other facilities in places like China and India. In 2005—2013 there was _____, partly driven by great Chinese demand. Global energy and metals firms spent US$6 trillion digging in the Australian outback and drilling for oil in North Dakota and deep beneath Brazil's coastal waters.

Passage II

Student Finance: Top 10 Student Money Saving Tips

Whether it's your first or your third year, the temptation to spend is everywhere — not least at the union bar. Problem is, you'll need cash left at the end of term if you fancy joining the university ski trip. Here are ten great money saving tips for old and new students alike.

Budget during the first weeks of term

With the living expenses fresh in your account, you're so far; in the black; that you're positively itching to spend. Beware — you have entered the danger zone. Someone organises a fancy dress party: you fork out on an expensive costume. You need a new hobby: you acquire a ukulele. It's hard to budget when you're keen to have fun, but it is worth holding off on extravagant spending early on. If you want to go out and celebrate at the end of term, check out some student budget apps to make sure you have something left to spend.

Plan meals in advance

Walking back from a lecture, you're likely to want to pick up lunch and a coffee with friends. Pay attention to jaunts like these — if they become too much of a habit, they will significantly impact your finances. Preparing food at home is a great way to save money over the week, and there's no need to cut back on the ingredients you love if you budget correctly.

Enjoy student discounts

Congratulations — you are now eligible for a ridiculous number of discounts. This doesn't mean you should be increasing your spending just to enjoy them, but it does mean savings when you do go shopping. Be sure to check the list of offers before registering for a card, as it's only worth buying if you are likely to use it.

Travel smarter

Travelling home for a weekend or visiting friends at other universities can be a costly affair, but that doesn't have to put you off. There is the railcard that can get you up to a fifth off rail fares. Alternatively — your friends will only turn 21 once — so get to their birthday celebrations with a ride-sharing service. If you have a car, you can offer seats to paying passengers, raking back a third of your petrol costs for each person you take on board.

Sell, sell, sell

Your textbooks are surprisingly valuable, so when you're sure that a book's future is to sit and gather dust, head to Amazon to trade it in for a gift card. The same applies to your clothes. Rid yourself of fashion faux-pas at eBay, or head to flea markets if you think they're worth a buck or two.

Head online for money saving tips

Once you've arrived at university, chances are you'll spend more time online than can really be healthy — generally at 1a.m. As you're already connected, make the most of your browsing time by heading to some websites for offers, discounts and budgeting tips.

Buy non-branded

We understand that there's something less than glamorous about supermarket value ranges. Don't let that stop you — the quality is often indistinguishable from that of branded produce. Avoiding the household names can mean a hefty saving on filling the fridge, so you'd be wise to look beyond the labels. Next time an all-nighter leaves you with a headache; remember that the same principle also applies to medicines. Branded pain killers can be significantly more expensive than supermarket versions, which often sell for less than 1 pound.

Avoid the kebab shop

You're on your way home from another night in the KTV and trying to converse over a deafening beat. It's time for something greasy, and you can already smell the kebab shop on the crisp morning air. Stop! Adding fast food to each and every night out is going to take its toll, not only on your waistline, but also on your finances. Indulge in some cheesy chips from time to time, but if you're serious about saving money, try returning home to a bowl of cereal or some toasted pitta.

Get paid to do stuff

Shouldn't that say "get a job"? Well, sort of — but we're aware that not every university gives you time to put your all into studying while working in a bar along the way. If you think you can balance it, by all means apply for a job. If you can't, try taking part in paid online surveys or market research focus groups. After all, everyone secretly loves a good survey! Ipsos rewards users for completing surveys online, offering vouchers from the likes of Amazon and John Lewis. If you have a little more time, a focus group like Saros will pay 30 to 100 for two hours' work — a welcome boost to your budget.

"Pre-drinks"

We're not advocating drinking, but you're a student now, so we suspect you're doing it anyway. Take our advice on this, though — you'll save money if you drink before going out. Your local supermarket is almost always going to beat student bars on price, so buy accordingly, and start your evening at home with friends. Bonus: you'll actually be able to hear what they're saying.

(From:http://www.hjenglish.com)

Exercises

I. Choose the correct answer according to Passage II.

1. It's hard to budget when you're keen to have fun, but it is worth_____. ( )

   A. to go out to have fun with friends on weekends

   B. going to the cinema together

   C. holding off on extravagant spending early on

   D. refusing your friends when you're busy

2. _____ is a great way to save money over the week. ( )

   A. Preparing food at home

   B. Buying some fast food

   C. Going to the canteen

   D. Eating the leftovers

3. Be sure to _____ before registering for a card, as it's only worth buying if you are likely to use it. ( )

   A. investigate thoroughly

   B. go to the shop

   C. check the list of offers

   D. check the price of all things

4. There is the railcard that can get you up to _____ off rail fares. ( )

   A. a fifth

   B. a third

   C. a sixth

   D. a fourth

5. What is the author's suggestion when you're sure that a book's future is to sit and gather dust? (   )

A. Throw them away in the rubbish bin.

B. Put them away in the bookshelf.

C. Leave them to your sister.

D. Head to Amazon to trade it in for a gift card.

II. Choose the best translation.

1. 学期末想要出去庆祝，先在相关学生预算应用上查查自己的账户，确保你还负担得起外出花费。(   )

   A. If you wants to go out and celebrate in the end of term, check out some student budget apps to make sure you have something left to spend.

   B. If you want to go out and celebrate at the end of term, check out some student budget apps to make sure you have something left to spend.

   C. Going out and celebrate at the end of term, check out some student budget apps to make sure you have something left to spend.

   D. Checking out some student budget apps to making sure you have something left to spend, if you want to celebrate.

2. 下课走在路上，你免不了会想和朋友一起买午餐，喝咖啡。(   )

   A. When you are walking on the road after class, you will definitely want to buy lunch and coffee with friends.

   B. Class walk on the road, you will inevitably want to buy lunch with friends, drink coffee.

   C. After Class walk on the road, you will inevitably want to buy lunch with friends, drink coffee.

   D. Walking back from a lecture, you're likely to want to pick up lunch and a coffee with friends.

3. 无论是要回家还是去找其他的大学朋友玩，都会是一件花钱的事情，但这些不应该阻挡你出行。(   )

   A. Travelling home for a weekend or visiting friends at other universities can be a costly affair, but that doesn't have to put you off.

   B. Whether to go home or go to other college to find friends will be a matter of money, but these should not stop you.

   C. Whether to go home or go to other college to find friends will cost a lot of money, but these should not prevent you doing it.

   D. Travel home for a weekend or visit friends at other universities can be a costly affair, but that doesn't have to put you off.

4. 知名品牌的止痛药会比超市卖的普通品牌贵很多，超市的品牌一般只卖不到一英镑。(   )

   A. Famous brand of relief will be more expensive than the ordinary supermarket sells brand many, supermarket brand to sell only commonly less than a pound.

B. Branded pain killers can be significantly cheaper than supermarket versions, which often sell for less than 1 pound.

C. Branded pain killers can be significantly more expensive than supermarket versions, which often sell for less than 1 pound.

D. Famous brand of relief will be more expensive than the ordinary supermarket sells brand many, supermarket brand to sell only commonly more than a pound.

5. 我们都知道，不是每所大学都有让你一边上学，一边在酒吧打工的时间。(　　)

A. We all knows that not every university has time for you to go to school while working at the bar.

B. We all know that every university has time for you to go to school while working at the bar.

C. We're aware that not every university giving you time to put your all into studying while work in a bar along the way.

D. We're aware that not every university gives you time to put your all into studying while working in a bar along the way.

Special Terms

Federal Reserve Board	美联储委员会
greenback	美元
long-term bonds	长期债券
high-yield bond fund	高收益债券基金
treasury bond	财政部发售的公债，美国的长期国库券
commodity prices	大宗商品价格
Securities and Exchange Commission	美国证券交易委员会
Wall Street Journal	《华尔街日报》

Chapter Seven

Banking

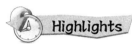

Text
Banking in China
Reading Skills (7)
Guessing the Meanings from the Context
Further Development
Passage I
Mobile Banking—A Platform for Engagement
Passage II
China Traditional Banks Strike Back Against Threat from Internet Finance

This is the 7th unit of the book. In the first section, you will learn a text, and you will have some information about the banking in China. In the second section, you will have a deeper understanding about banking. In this section, you will learn two passages about mobile banking and traditional banks strike back against threat from internet finance and they will help you have a further development on mastering reading skills of guessing the meanings from context.

Starter

The Chinese RMB to join SDR basket as IMF reserve currency together with the U.S. dollar, the euro, the yen and the British pound. What will this promotion really mean for the RMB?

Text

Banking in China

China's banking system has undergone significant changes in the last two decades, banks are now functioning more like western banks than before. Nevertheless, China's banking industry has remained in the government's hands even though banks have gained more autonomy.

Seen from the present situation, China's banking system has a clear gradation and possesses its own character. It can divided into four layers. The first layer is the leading bank — People's Bank of China; the second layer is five state-owned banks — Agriculture Bank of China, Bank of China, Industrial and Commercial Bank of China, China Construction Bank and China Bank of Communications; the third layer is other small and medium banks, including local bank, private bank, foreign bank, rural credit cooperative banks and postal savings bank. All the banks of these three layers are controlled by the adjustment of People's Bank of China.

Supervisory Body

The People's Bank of China (PBC) is China's central bank, which formulates and implements monetary policy according to the law independently. The PBC maintains the banking sector's payment, clearing and settlement systems of the country, and manages official foreign exchange and gold reserves. It oversees the State Administration of Foreign Exchange (SAFE) for setting foreign-exchange policies. The main role of PBC is to regulate currency policy, macro-control the economy of our country through adjusting interest rate and reserve fund rate, and reduce overall risk and promote stability of the financial system.

Domestic Key Players

China's four major banks consist of the Bank of China (BOC), the Agricultural Bank of China (ABC), and the Industrial and Commercial Bank of China (ICBC) and the China Construction Bank (CCB). In 1983, these four specialized banks were established (or re-established) to take over part of the banking business from PBC, allowing PBC to focus on regulation and monetary policy.

1. Bank of China

The Bank of China (BOC) specializes in foreign-exchange transactions and trade finance. It is not only one of China's major bank, but also plays a principal role in international trade. The business scope of BOC covers a lot of fields such as financial bank, investment bank and insurance. It provides comprehensive and fine financial service for individual, company clients all over the world and holds financial institutions like BOC Hong Kong, BOC International and BOC Insurance etc. In 2002, BOC Hong Kong (Holdings) was successfully listed on the Hong Kong Stock Exchange, which was a significant move in the reform of China's banking industry.

2. The Agricultural Bank of China (ABC)

The Agricultural Bank of China (ABC) specializes in providing loans to China's agriculture, offers wholesale and retail banking services to farmers, township and village enterprises and other businesses in rural areas.

3. The Industrial and Commercial Bank of China (ICBC)

The Industrial and Commercial Bank of China is a Chinese multinational banking company, the largest commercial bank in terms of assets and the largest bank in the world by total assets and by market capitalization. It has always been global 500 and ranks number 1 in the Banker's Top 1000 World Banks ranking. ICBC differentiates itself from the other state owned commercial banks by being second in foreign exchange business and 1st in RMB clearing business. It used to be the major supplier of funds to China's urban areas and manufacturing sector. As of August 19, 2016, ICBC had a market capitalization of over US$235 billion.

4. The China Construction Bank (CCB)

The China Construction Bank (CCB) is the fourth biggest bank in China which provides a comprehensive range of commercial banking products and services, such as infrastructure loans, residential mortgage and bank cards. Besides, it owns a foundation of extensive clients and has business relationship with many group companies and the leading enterprise in China's economic strategic industries whose marketing network covers the main areas of China. In 2015 CCB was the 2nd largest bank in the world by market capitalization. It has approximately 14,917 domestic branches and 68 overseas institutions covering 14 countries and regions. And in Hong Kong, Singapore, Tokyo, New York, Frankfurt, Seoul, Sydney, Johannesburg, Melbourne, Auckland and Ho Chi Minh, CCB all has its own overseas branches. What's more, it has representative office in Moscow and Taipei and a wholly owned subsidiary in London.

Besides the four major banks mentioned above, Bank of Communications becomes the fifth biggest commercial bank of China. Nowadays it has been one of pillar enterprises in China's banking system with a long history.

Policy Banks

The Bank of China, the Agricultural Bank of China, the China Construction Bank and the Industrial and Commercial Bank of China remained as specialized banks until 1994 when three policy banks were established to take over the government-directed spending and lending functions of the four state-owned commercial banks. They are the Agricultural Development Bank of China (ADBC), China Development Bank (CDB), and the Export-Import Bank of China.

CBRC and Unionpay

In China's banking system, there exists two big organizations — CBRC and Unionpay. CBRC (China Banking Regulatory Commission) is a government agency, established to regulate financial organizations such as bank and asset management companies, safeguard the legitimate and sound working of banks. It shares some functions with the central bank, shares out the work and cooperate with the central government and takes charge of China's banking sector together.

Established in March 2002, UnionPay is a national bankcard association established under the approval of the State Council and the People's Bank of China and launched by more than 80 internal financial institutions. At present, the Shanghai-headquartered UnionPay has  about 400 domestic and overseas associate members. It is the only interbank network in China that links all the ATMs of all banks throughout the country and also an EFTPOS network. It proceeds nationwide currency through bank card to promote the fast development of bank card. Now UnionPay carries a big weight in China's banking system, and plays an essential role in the industry development. In response to the economic and social development in China and to fulfill the industrial mission and social responsibilities, UnionPay has joined hands with domestic commercial banks to create an independent bankcard brand — UnionPay card. In August 2003, UnionPay officially launched the UnionPay card. The standard cards with a mark of UnionPay are in common use on a nationwide scale, which makes people's daily life and cash flow a big convenience. As of today, UnionPay card can be smoothly used at 160 countries and regions worldwide, making it the third-largest payment network by value of transactions processed, behind Visa and MasterCard. UnionPay cards are not only well accepted by the domestic cardholders, but also highly appreciated by cardholders in more and more countries and regions.

Chapter Seven Banking

 Words and Terms

undergone [ˌʌndəˈɡɔːn]	v.	经历；承受
industry [ˈɪndəstrɪ]	n.	行业；工业；产业
autonomy [ɔːˈtɒnəmɪ]	n.	自主权；自治权
gradation [ɡrəˈdeɪʃn]	n.	等级；分级；层次性
credit [ˈkredɪt]	n.& v.	信用；学分；赞颂
supervisory [ˈsjuːpəˌvaɪzərɪ]	v.	监督的；管理的
formulate [ˈfɔːmjʊleɪt]	v.	制定；规划
settlement [ˈsetlmənt]	n.	结算；协议
currency [ˈkʌrənsɪ]	n.	货币
regulation [ˌreɡjʊˈleɪʃn]	n.	管理；规定；规则
reform [rɪˈfɔːm]	n.	改革
township [ˈtaʊnʃɪp]	n.	乡镇
multinational [ˌmʌltɪˈnæʃnəl]	adj.	跨国的
infrastructure [ˈɪnfrəstrʌktʃə]	n.	基础设施；基础建设
mortgage [ˈmɔːɡɪdʒ]	n.	抵押
subsidiary [səbˈsɪdɪərɪ]	n.& adj.	子公司；附属的
legitimate [lɪˈdʒɪtɪmət]	adj.	合法的；合理的

monetary policy	货币政策
gold reserve	黄金储备
interest rate	利率
reserve fund rate	准备金率
market capitalization	市值
rural credit cooperative bank	农村信用社
postal savings bank	邮政储蓄银行
CBRC (China Banking Regulatory Commission)	中国银监会
State Administration of Foreign Exchange	国家外汇管理局

 Notes

1. The PBC maintains the banking sector's payment, clearing and settlement systems of the country, and manages official foreign exchange and gold reserves. 中国人民银行维护国家银行业金融机构的支付、清算及结算系统，并管理官方外汇和黄金储备。

2. The main role of PBC is to regulate currency policy, macro-control the economy of our country through adjusting interest rate and reserve fund rate, and reduce overall risk and promote stability of the financial system. 中国人民银行的主要任务是调控货币政策、通过调整利率与准

备金率来宏观调控我国经济，减少整体风险及促进金融体系稳定。

3. It owns a foundation of extensive clients and has business relationship with many group companies and the leading enterprise in China's economic strategic industries whose marketing network covers the main areas of China. 它还拥有广泛的客户基础，与多个大型企业集团及中国经济战略性行业的主导企业有银行业务联系，营销网络覆盖全国的主要地区。

4. CBRC is a government agency, established to regulate financial organizations such as bank and asset management companies, safeguard the legitimate and sound working of banks. 中国银行业监督管理委员会是一个政府机构，监督管理金融机构，比如银行和金融资产管理公司，维护银行业的合法、稳健运行。

5. The standard cards with a mark of UnionPay are in common use on a nationwide scale, which makes people's daily life and cash flow a big convenience. 带有银联标志的标准卡已在全国范围内普遍使用，给人们的日常生活和现金流动带来了很大的方便。

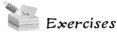

Exercises

I. Answer the following questions according to the text.

1. What is the main role of PBC?
2. What are the five stated-owned commercial banks in China?
3. How many policy banks are there in China? What are they?
4. What does CBRC stand for? And what is the definition of it?
5. What is UnionPay? What convenience does UnionPay card bring to people?

II. Identify the key words of main ideas of the following parts.

Part 1	The _____ to China's banking system
Part 2	_____ of China's banking system
Part 3	_____ in China's banking industry
Part 4	Three _____ in China
Part 5	Two big organizations in China's banking system—_____

III. Match the words of phrases in Column A to the words or phrases in Column B.

A	B
1. _____ settlement	A. 基础设施
2. _____ subsidiary	B. 制订
3. _____ infrastructure	C. 子公司
4. _____ monetary policy	D. 准备金率
5. _____ formulate	E. 结算
6. _____ postal savings bank	F. 改革

7. _____ regulation   G. 邮政储蓄银行
8. _____ market capitalization   H. 货币政策
9. _____ reserve fund rate   I. 规定
10. _____ reform   J. 市值

IV. Choose the best translation.

1. The People's Bank of China is China's central bank, which formulates and implements monetary policy according to the law independently. (　　)
    A. 中国人民银行是中国的中心银行，依法独立制定与完成国家货币政策。
    B. 中国人民银行是中国的中央银行，依法独立制定与执行国家货币政策。
    C. 中国人民银行是中国的中央银行，依法独立制定国家货币政策。
    D. 中国人民银行是中国的中心银行，依法独立执行国家货币政策。

2. Bank of China provides comprehensive and fine financial service for individual, company clients all over the world and holds financial institutions like BOC Hong Kong, BOC International and BOC Insurance etc. (　　)
    A. 中国银行在全球范围内为个人和公司客户提供全面、优良的金融服务，旗下有中银香港、中银国际、中银保险等控股金融机构。
    B. 中国银行为个人和公司客户提供全面、好的金融服务，旗下有中银香港、中银国际、中银保险等控股金融机构。
    C. 中国银行在全国范围内为个人和公司客户提供全面、优质的金融服务，旗下有中银香港、中银国际、中银保险等控股金融机构。
    D. 中国银行在全国范围内为个人提供全面、好的金融服务，旗下有中银香港、中银保险等控股金融机构。

3. ICBC has always been global 500 and ranks number 1 in the banker's Top 1000 World Banks ranking. (　　)
    A. 中国工商银行一直位于全球 500 强，在全球 1000 家银行中排名中位居第一。
    B. 中国工商银行一直位于全国 500 强，在《银行家》的全国 1000 家银行中位居全国第一。
    C. 中国工商银行一直位于世界五百强企业之列，在《银行家》杂志的全球 1000 家大银行排名中位居全球首位。
    D. 中国工商银行一直位于世界五百强企业之列，在全球 1000 家大银行排名中位居首位。

4. UnionPay cards are not only well accepted by the domestic cardholders, but also highly appreciated by cardholders in more and more countries and region. (　　)
    A. 银联卡不仅被消费者广泛接受，而且受到越来越多的国家和地区的消费者的高度喜爱。
    B. 银联卡不仅被持卡者广泛接受，而且受到越来越多的国家的持卡人的高度赞赏。
    C. 银联卡不仅被持卡者广泛接受，而且受到越来越多的国家和地区的人的高度赞赏。
    D. 银联卡不仅被国内持卡者广泛接受，而且受到越来越多的国家和地区的持卡人的高度赞赏。

5. It owns a foundation of extensive clients and has business relationship with many group companies and the leading enterprise in China's economic strategic industries whose marketing network covers the main areas of China. (   )
   A. 它还拥有很广的客户基础，与多个大型企业集团及龙头企业有业务联系，营销网络覆盖全国的主要地区。
   B. 它还拥有广泛的客户基础，与多个大型企业集团及中国经济战略性行业的主导企业有银行业务联系，营销网络覆盖全国的主要地区。
   C. 它还拥有广泛的客户基础，与多个大型企业集团及中国经济战略性的企业有银行联系，营销网络覆盖全国的多个地区。
   D. 它还拥有很广的客户基础，与多个大型企业集团及企业有银行业务联系，营销网络覆盖全国的主要地区。

Reading Skills (7)
Guessing the Meanings from the Context

Everyone knows that new words and expressions are always easily found when reading an article. Some of them can be ignored because they are not so necessary for you to grasp the main idea of an article or answer the questions. However, there are also a lot of new words which are key words to the article. Not knowing the meanings of these words will greatly affect the understanding of the article. So the ability of guessing the meanings of the new words is very important in reading comprehension. For this reason, you must try to improve your ability of conjecturing the meanings from the context.

The meanings of the words can be guessed from the given information in the contexts, for example: Mr. Joes got on the motorbike, I sat behind him on the pillion, and we roared off into the night. Suppose you don't know the meaning of the word "pillion", you can guess it in the following way. Since the above sentence tells that "Mark got on the motorbike" and "I sat behind him". The meaning of the word "pillion" probably means: saddle for a passenger behind the driver of a motorbike.

Further Development

Passage I

Mobile Banking — A Platform for Engagement

Mobile banking, as an important application of mobile commerce, is an important extension of

Chapter Seven Banking

banking business. It is a service provided by a bank or other financial institutions that allows its customers to conduct financial transactions remotely using a mobile device such as a mobile phone or tablet. It is usually available on a 24-hour basis. Mobile users can check accounts, make transfer, pay bills of spending, and manage company accounts or process instructions through mobile banking.

In December 2015, the value of transactions made from mobile phones in India was the highest. India's mobile banking users made Rs 49,000 crore worth of transactions, up more than four times from December 2014. Indian bankers say that a substantial number of customers have taken to mobile banking without going the Internet banking route.

In a country where the Internet is accessed mainly on mobile, mobile banking is gaining traction among consumers, and not just those from the younger generations. Importantly, just as the mobile is not just a phone anymore, mobile banking is not just another channel of banking; rather, it is a platform for engaging the digital customer.

India's progressive banks are riding this opportunity to deploy mobility in three important aspects of customer engagement, namely, the efficiency of transaction, the quality of experience, and the intensity of engagement. Firstly, by enabling transactions on mobile, banks are helping customers bank better, faster and easier. A simple example is funds transfer, which can be accomplished within a few taps on a mobile banking app.

Secondly, mobile banking is ideally suited to deliver rich, intuitive experience. The native capabilities of the smartphone make it possible to provide location-based offers, financial advice on the go, biometric-based banking, and so on. For instance, mobile banking can make tedious authentication by password and additional factors redundant by facilitating biometric identification and verification. We at Infosys Finacle call it the "death of passwords" — an idea that is deeply appreciated by all our clients.

Thirdly, customers are engaging with their banks more intensively on mobile than on channels like the branch or Internet. A research study from the United Kingdom says that British current account customers made 427 million branch visits and 895 million mobile app logins in 2015. This disparity is expected to grow sharply and in 2020, branch visits will number about 268 million only whereas mobile app usage instances will touch 2.3 billion. The data for Indian banks is likely to be a lot more in favor of mobile-led engagement due to the country's demographic advantage and lack of reach of branches for various segments of consumers. Clearly there is a huge opportunity for banks to convert the frequency of visits into deep customer engagement.

The key question before Indian banks is whether they are doing enough to leverage this opportunity for engagement. Most banks are still oriented to delivering services to customers only after they approach them. They need to change their approach to make banking unobtrusive but ubiquitous, so that it is simply there when customers need it. An example of this comes from Poland's Alior Bank, winner at the BAI — Infosys Finacle Global Banking Innovation Award, which devised a lending product that was approved in minutes — even real-time in certain cases — ensuring ecommerce customers in need of a loan got one on the spot. In fact engagement is the only way to establish differentiation in a business that is so commoditized. One way to build it is by improving quality of experience; another by inspiring customers' trust and confidence by showing them that their bank has their financial well-being at heart. The mobile supports this beautifully by allowing banks to integrate and share insights with customers in real-time — at the moment of the transaction, so that they can make smarter and more responsible financial decisions.

(Published by Puneet Chhahira, Global Head of Marketing, Infosys Finacle)

Words and Terms

platform ['plætfɔ:m]	n.	平台
transaction [træn'zækʃn]	n.	交易；事务
tablet ['tæblət]	n.	平板电脑
account [ə'kaʊnt]	n.	账户；账目
traction ['trækʃn]	n.	牵引力
digital ['dɪdʒɪtl]	adj.	数字的；数据的
deploy [dɪ'plɔɪ]	v.	有效地利用；施展；部署
mobility [məʊ'bɪləti]	n.	移动性；流动性
intuitive [ɪn'tju:ɪtɪv]	adj.	直观的；直觉的
authentication [ɔ:ˌθentɪ'keɪʃən]	n.	认证；鉴定
password ['pɑ:sw3:d]	n.	密码；口令
biometric [ˌbaɪəʊ'metrɪk]	adj.	生物识别的
verification [ˌverɪfɪ'keɪʃn]	n.	核实；验证
demographic [ˌdemə'græfɪk]	adj.	人口的；人口统计学的
leverage ['li:vərɪdʒ]	v. & n.	影响；杠杆作用
unobtrusive [ˌʌnəb'tru:sɪv]	adj.	不张扬的；不唐突的
ubiquitous [ju:'bɪkwɪtəs]	adj.	无处不在的；随处可见的
mobile banking		移动银行；手机银行
Global Banking Innovation Award		全球银行业创新奖

Notes

1. It is a service provided by a bank or other financial institution that allows its customers to conduct financial transactions remotely using a mobile device such as a mobile phone or tablet. 它是由银行或者其他金融机构提供的允许其客户使用移动设备，比如手机或者平板电脑进行金融交易的一种服务。

2. Importantly, just as the mobile is not just a phone anymore, mobile banking is not just another channel of banking; rather, it is a platform for engaging the digital customer. 重要的是，正如手机不再只是手机，移动银行不仅仅是银行的另一个服务渠道，它是服务于数字化客户的一个平台。

3. India's progressive banks are riding this opportunity to deploy mobility in three important

aspects of customer engagement, namely, the efficiency of transaction, the quality of experience, and the intensity of engagement. 印度有先进移动技术的银行利用移动银行业务的便利性从三个重要方面吸引客户，即银行交易效率、用户体验质量及交易强度。

4. A simple example is funds transfer, which can be accomplished within a few taps on a mobile banking app. 一个简单的例子是转账，只要在手机银行 APP 上轻点几下就能完成。

5. The mobile supports this beautifully by allowing banks to integrate and share insights with customers in real-time — at the moment of the transaction, so that they can make smarter and more responsible financial decisions. 移动银行业务完美地实现了这一点，银行可以在实时交易时，与客户共享远见，达成一致，从而做出更明智、更可靠的金融决策。

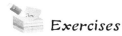

Exercises

I. Read the following statements and decide whether they are True (T) or False (F).

1. Mobile banking is a platform for engaging the digital customer. （ ）
2. There is no opportunity for banks to convert the frequency of visits into deep customer engagement. （ ）
3. Mobile banking a service provided by a bank or other financial institutions that allows its customers to conduct financial transactions remotely using a mobile device.
4. In October 2016, the value of transactions made from mobile phones in(　　) India was the highest. （ ）
5. British current account customers made 427 million mobile app logins in 2015. （ ）

II. Choose the correct answer according to Passage I.

1. Mobile users can check accounts, manage company accounts, _____, and pay bills of spending, or process instructions through mobile banking. （ ）
   A. make friends　　　　　　　　B. do business
   C. make transfer　　　　　　　　D. chat with partners

2. A substantial number of customers in India have taken to _____. （ ）
   A. mobile banking　　　　　　　B. branch
   C. Internet banking　　　　　　　D. phone banking

3. According to the passage, customers in India are engaging with their banks more intensively on _____. （ ）
   A. branch　　　　　　　　　　　B. mobile
   C. Internet　　　　　　　　　　　D. phone

4. India's progressive banks are riding the opportunity to deploy mobility in three important aspects of customer engagement, namely, the intensity of engagement, the efficiency of transaction and _____. （ ）
   A. the intensity of engagement

B. the quality of experience

C. the satisfaction of customers

D. the advantage of price

5. Which bank devised a lending product that was approved in minutes? (   )

A. Bank of China

B. Swiss Bank

C. Poland's Alior Bank

D. Citibank

III. Fill in the missing information.

Mobile banking is a service provided by a bank or other_____that allows its customers to conduct financial transactions remotely using a mobile device. Mobile users can check accounts, make transfer,_____and manage company accounts or process instructions through_____. In December 2015, the value of transactions made from mobile phones in India was_____. India's progressive banks are riding the opportunity to deploy mobility in three important aspects of customer engagement, namely_____, the quality of experience, and the intensity of engagement.

Passage II

China Traditional Banks Strike Back Against Threat from Internet Finance

China's brick-and-mortar banks are launching a counter-attack against the assault on their business from Alibaba and other Internet heavyweights, in a bid to staunch the outflow of bank deposits into high-yielding online investment products.

In less than eight months, Alibaba Group Holding Ltd.'s money market fund, Yu'e Bao, has attracted 400 billion yuan (US$66.0 billion) in assets under management, more than the customer deposits held by the five smallest listed Chinese banks.

Similar online products from Baidu Inc. and Tencent Holdings Ltd. also contributed to a fall of one trillion yuan in traditional bank deposits in January.

Now traditional lenders, initially caught flat-footed, are striking back.

Industrial and Commercial Bank of China, Bank of China, Bank of Communications and Ping An Bank have all launched new products in recent weeks that match the attractive features of Yu'e Bao.

Banks are also lobbying regulators to introduce curbs on the growth of on-line funds offered by non-banks.

Ultimately, however, competition for deposits will drive up banks' funding costs and crimp profit margins this year.

As China gradually moves to liberalize deposit interest rates, banks will be forced to compete among themselves to attract customers, which means offering higher yields. The development of new deposit-like money market products designed to compete with online rivals will further accelerate the trend toward higher funding costs.

Cash on demand

Chinese savers in recent years have flocked to so-called wealth management products (WMPs)that banks market as a higher-yielding alternative to traditional savings deposits, which remain subject to a cap of 3.3 percent for one-year savings.

Alibaba super-charged the switch away from traditional deposits last June when it launched Yu'e Bao in partnership with Tianhong Asset Management Co. Ltd., in which it owns a 51 percent stake. The product is currently yielding 6.2 percent.

Beyond, the attractive yield, several innovations allowed Yu'e Bao and other online money-market funds to draw funds away from bank deposits and offline WMPs. Unlike most bank WMPs, the Yu'e Bao fund allows investors to redeem shares for cash at any time, rather than locking up their funds for months at a time. Yu'e Bao also requires no minimum threshold to buy in.

The product's seamless integration with Alibaba's widely used third-party payments platform Alipay, also makes buying into the product simple and convenient.

Now banks are getting in on the act with their own cash-on-demand money market products.

ICBC, the world's largest bank by assets, launched a money-market WMP called "Tiantian Yi", which translates as "Everyday Benefit." So far only account holders based in the eastern province of Zhejiang are allowed to purchase, but the pilot is likely to ramp up quickly.

ICBC hopes to gain an edge over Alibaba by allowing customers to transfer up to 30 million yuan into its product, known as "Everyday Increase." ICBC has also fought back by limiting its depositors monthly transfers to Alipay to 50,000 yuan per month.

Bocom, China's fifth largest lender, has launched "Quick Benefit Channel," while Ping An Bank has a product called "Ping An Profit."

Bank of Beijing Co. Ltd., a mid-sized lender, on Wednesday announced a partnership with smartphone maker Xiaomi Tech on mobile payments and sales of WMPs and insurance products.

Banks are also tweaking WMPs to make them more competitive. "We're trying to increase the convenience of our WMPs, like letting people buy them during non-working hours. We're also asking the bank regulator to let us lower the 50,000 yuan minimum investment for some products," said a wealth product manager at a mid-sized bank in Shanghai.

Calls for regulation

UBS estimates that if 10 percent of total bank deposits flow into online products, it could reduce banks' net interest margin by 0.1 percentage points, while lost fee income would amount to 4 percent of estimated 2014 net profit.

The China Securities Regulatory Commission said last week that it is working with other agencies to develop rules for Internet finance. Industry observers say that banks are lobbying for curbs on the proliferation of online products from third-party payment services.

"Regulators are trying to walk a fine line. They don't want to kill innovation that benefits consumers, but they also don't want deposit-taking activity that's completely unregulated," said Yan.

Analysts say that even if banks are able to draw funds into their own money-market products the trend of rising funding costs will continue, as the banks' products would have to match the yields offered by online rivals.

Indeed, funds invested in Yu'e Bao and similar products eventually end up with banks anyway. Tianhong uses Yu'e Bao funds to invest mainly in interbank deposits and repurchase agreements. So whether banks borrow from Tianhong or raise funds from their own products, the cost is still higher than on ordinary deposits.

(From: http://m.kekenet.com/read/201403/278218.shtml)

Exercises

I. Choose the correct answer according to Passage II.

1. Unlike most bank WMPs, the Yu'e Bao fund allows investors to _____ for cash at any time. (   )

   A. lock up funds

   B. redeem shares

   C. withdraw shares

   D. deposit money

2. _____ launched a money-market WMP called "Tiantian Yi". (   )

   A. Industrial and Commercial Bank of China

   B. Bank of China

   C. Ping An Bank

   D. Bank of Communications

3. All of the following banks have all launched new products in recent weeks that match the attractive features of Yu'e Bao, except _____. (   )

   A. Bank of Communications

   B. Ping An Bank

   C. Industrial and Commercial Bank of China

   D. China Construction Bank

4. Which of the following product requires no minimum threshold to buy in? (   )

   A. Tiantian Yi

   B. Yu'e Bao

   C. Ping An Profit

   D. Quick Benefit Channel

5. Tianhong uses Yu'e Bao funds to invest mainly in _____ and repurchase agreements. (   )

   A. funds investment   B. money-market products

C. interbank deposits   D. treasury bills

II. Choose the best translation.

1. 随着中国存款利率不断地自由化，中国传统银行将会被迫进行内部竞争，提供更高回报率的产品来吸引客户。（   ）

    A. As China gradually moves to liberalize deposit interest rates, banks will be forced to compete among themselves to attract customers, which means offering higher yields.
    B. As China gradually moves to liberalize interest rates, banks will be forced to compete among themselves to attract customers, which means offering higher yields.
    C. As China gradually moves to liberalize reserve fund rates, banks will be forced to compete among themselves to attract customers, which means offering lower yields.
    D. As China gradually moves to liberalize deposit interest rates, banks will compete among themselves to attract customers, which means offering lower yields.

2. 余额宝与支付宝的完美结合，也使得购入该产品更为简单方便。（   ）

    A. Yu'e Bao's integration with Wechat pay, also makes buying into the product simple and convenient.
    B. Yu'e Bao's integration with Alipay, also makes buying into the product simple and convenient.
    C. Yu'e Bao's seamless integration with Alipay, also makes buying into the product simple and convenient.
    D. Yu'e Bao's seamless integration with Wechat pay, also makes buying into the product convenient.

3. 工商银行希望赢得与阿里巴巴的竞争，借"天天益"吸收存款达 3000 万元。（   ）

    A. ICBC hopes to gain an edge over Alibaba by allowing customers to transfer up to 30 billion yuan into its product, known as "Everyday Increase."
    B. ICBC hopes to gain an edge over Alibaba by allowing customers to transfer up to 30 million yuan into its product, known as "Everyday Increase."
    C. ICBC hopes to get an edge over Alibaba by allowing customers to transfer 30 million yuan into its product, known as "Everyday Increase."
    D. ICBC hopes to get an edge over Alibaba by allowing customers to transfer 30 billion yuan into its product, known as "Everyday Increase."

4. 不管银行是向天弘借贷，还是从自己的产品中融资，成本仍旧比普通存款高。（   ）

    A. Whether banks borrow money or raise funds from their investment products, the cost is still higher than on deposits.
    B. Whether banks borrow money or raise funds from other products, the cost is still high than on ordinary deposits.
    C. Whether banks borrow from Tianhong or raise funds from their own products, the cost is still higher than on ordinary deposits.
    D. Whether banks borrow from Tianhong or raise funds from products, the cost is still higher than on deposits.

5. 与大多数银行理财产品不同的是，余额宝允许投资者随时赎回资金，而不是一次就锁定他们的资金好几个月。

A. Like most bank WMPs, the Yu'e Bao fund allows investors to lock up their funds at any time, rather than redeeming shares for cash for months at a time.

B. Like most bank WMPs, the Yu'e Bao fund allows investors to redeem shares for cash at any time, rather than locking up their funds for months at a time.

C. Unlike most bank WMPs, the Yu'e Bao fund allows investors to redeem shares for cash at any time, rather than locking up their funds for months at a time.

D. Unlike most bank WMPs, the Yu'e Bao fund allows investors to lock up their funds at any time, rather than redeeming shares for cash for months at a time.

Special Terms

Industrial and Commercial Bank of China	中国工商银行
China Construction Bank	中国建设银行
Agricultural Bank of China	中国农业银行
Postal Savings Bank of China	中国邮政储蓄银行
monetary policy	货币政策
mobile banking	移动银行；手机银行
interest rate	利率
gold reserve	黄金储备
reserve fund rate	准备金率
market capitalization	市值
CBRC (China Banking Regulatory Commission)	中国银监会
State Administration of Foreign Exchange	国家外汇管理局

Chapter Eight

Insurance

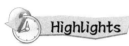

Text
Social Insurance
Reading Skills (8)
Using Word Part Clues for Word Meanings
Further Development
Passage I
Life Insurance
Passage II
Auto Insurance Market

This is the 8th chapter of the book. In the first section, you will learn a text, and you will have some information about social insurance in China. In the second section, you will have a deeper understanding about insurance. In this section, you will learn two passages about life insurance and auto insurance market and they will help you have a further development on mastering reading skills of using word part clues for word meanings.

Starter

An insurance broker said: "The longer you wait, the more expensive it gets." Do you think so?

Text

Social Insurance

China is experiencing rapid population aging. The one-child policy and significant improvement in the living standard accelerate the aging process and make China's aging problem more serious than any other countries in the world. According to a World Bank report, China's aging population will reach the peak by 2030 (The World Bank, 1994). There will be 0.3 billion people over 60, which will account for 22 percent of the total population. Old age dependency ratio is expected to rise from currently six workers for every retired person to only two workers for a retired person by 2030. China faces the greatest challenge to support the huge aging population. Therefore, establishing the system of social insurance is essential, which enables citizens to share the achievements of development and promoting social harmony and stability.

Social insurance is a sign of social progress and it is something people care about nowadays, so China is now trying hard to build a system to ensure that everyone can enjoy a happy life after retirement by way of imposing law on it. The state raises social insurance through various channels and provides support for social insurance through preferential tax free. Moreover, the people's governments at and above the county level have put social insurance into their national economic and social development planning and provided necessary fund support for social insurance.

The social security system in China consists of five different types of insurance, plus one mandatory housing fund, introduced in the chart below. How companies register and deregister their employees often varies depending upon the city and the employee's location or residency.

China Social Insurance and Housing Fund						
Particulars	Pension	Medical	Unemployment	Maternity	Injury	Housing Fund
Company contributions	12%-22%	5%-12%	0.2-2%	0.5%-1%	0.5-2%	5%-20%
Individual contributions	8%	0.5%-2%	0-1%	N/A	N/A	5%-20%

Let's take a brief look at the functions of each of these insurances.

Pension

As in many countries, China has put in place a system to ensure its citizens, which will be able to maintain some incomes after their retirement. It operates by receiving contributions on a monthly basis from both the employee and the employer. The portion contributed by the employee goes into a personal fund (the contribution directly accrues to the individual) and after retirement the individual can draw on the funds in this pool directly. In contrast, the contributions made by the employer go into a social pool. Funds in this pool are distributed to all citizens that have made contributions into the system during their working life. In terms of the amount of contributions that need to be made each month by both employee and employer, pension is generally the largest component of social insurance.

Medical Insurance

By contributing to the medical insurance fund Chinese citizens can defray some of the costs of medical expenses in the event of illness or injury. Both employees and employers are required to make contributions to this fund.

Unlike in some countries where medical treatment is provided for free, in most cities in China the patient is required to bear a certain percentage of the total hospital fee. In addition, each month individuals receive a small amount of money onto their medical insurance card. The funds can be used to purchase medicine or other goods at pharmacies, or to pay small medical expenses at hospitals.

Unemployment Insurance

Employers in all major cities are expected to make a contribution towards unemployment insurance and most cities also require a contribution from the employee. In the event an individual becomes unemployed they will be able to make a claim to receive unemployment benefits on the precondition that contributions have been made for a period of at least one year.

However the amount that can be received will be a fixed amount determined locally, and will be unrelated to the salary received by the individual previously or the amount of accumulated contribution. The benefits can be received for a maximum of 24 months.

Maternity Insurance

Maternity insurance is paid by employers rather than employees. In the event that an employee becomes pregnant, she will be entitled to receive a lump sum to defray some of the costs of the childbirth. During the period of maternity leave from the company the maternity fund will cover payment of salary.

Occupational Injury Insurance

Contributions to this fund are made only by the employer and the amount of the contribution depends upon the nature of the work being carried out by the employees. The more dangerous the work is deemed to be, the higher the percentage contribution (usually the range is from 0.4% to 2% of the gross salary). The precise amount of the percentage premium will be made by the local social insurance bureau according to the category of industry the company is deemed to be affiliated to.

In the event that an employee is injured at work, the employer will collect evidence concerning the injury and the associated costs and apply for reimbursement from the occupational insurance fund. Note that the employer will still need to pay the salary to the employee during the recuperation period.

Housing Fund

The housing fund is fundamentally different from the above insurances in two ways. First of all the contributions made by both employee and employer accrue directly to the employee. Secondly, administration of this fund is handled by the housing fund center separately from social insurance.

Funds accrued in this account can be used to make the initial down-payment as well as to repay mortgages taken out when purchasing a house. Individuals that have sufficient funds accrued in a housing fund account can also apply for a lower mortgage rate compared to a normal commercial loan.

Administration of housing fund differs greatly around the country. In Shenzhen no contribution is required from the employee at all, while the employer is required to pay a fixed rate of 13 percent. In contrast, in Dalian the employer can be required to pay up to 25 percent (although there are some special reduced rates that can be applied) while the employee contributions can be a maximum of 15 percent. The housing fund can be quite a significant additional cost for employers.

Together, social insurance and housing fund are commonly referred to as "mandatory benefits." Employers are usually required to handle the administration of mandatory benefits on behalf of their employees, which means first of all affiliating the employees to the company "accounts" and then calculating and making the contributions (both the employer's and the employee's portion) on a monthly basis.

 Words and Terms

accelerate [əkˈseləreɪt]	v.	(使)加快，(使)增速
harmony [ˈhɑːmənɪ]	n.	协调，融洽
stability [stəˈbɪlətɪ]	n.	稳定
preferential [ˌprefəˈrenʃl]	adj.	优先的，特惠的

Chapter Eight Insurance

channel ['tʃænl]	n.	渠道，途径
pension ['penʃn]	n.	养老金
accrue [ə'kru:]	v.	(使)逐渐增加；积累
defray [dɪ'freɪ]	v.	支付
pharmacy ['fɑ:məsɪ]	n.	药房
pregnant ['pregnənt]	adj.	怀孕的
premium ['pri:mɪəm]	n.	保险费，附加费
reimbursement [ˌri:ɪm'bɜ:smənt]	n.	报销偿还
recuperation [rɪku:pə'reɪʃn]	n.	恢复
affiliate [ə'fɪlɪeɪt]	v.	使隶属于

one-child policy	独生子女政策
account for	(在数量、比例上)占
dependency ratio	抚养比例
maternity insurance	生育险
occupational injury insurance	工伤险
mandatory benefits	强制性福利
in the event	如果
housing fund	住房公积金

 Notes

1. According to a World Bank report, China's aging population will reach the pea by 2030. 根据世界银行组织的一份报告，中国老龄人口到2030年将达到顶峰。
World Bank: 世界银行是世界银行集团的简称，是由国际复兴开发银行、国际开发协会、国际金融公司、多边投资担保机构和国际投资争端解决中心五个成员机构组成。其主要任务是资助国家克服穷困，各机构在减轻贫困和提高生活水平的使命中发挥独特的作用。世界银行与国际货币基金组织(IMF)、世界贸易组织(WTO)成为国际经济体制中最重要的三大支柱。

2. The people's governments at and above the county level has put social insurance into their national economic and social development planning and provided necessary fund support for social insurance. 县级及县级以上人民政府把社会保险列入经济和社会发展计划中，并对其给予必要的基金支持。

3. The portion contributed by the employee goes into a personal fund (the contribution directly accrues to the individual) and after retirement the individual can draw on the funds in this pool directly. 职工所缴比例进入个人基金(缴款直接归于个人)，退休后个人可直接从中提取基金。

4. In the event an individual becomes unemployed they will be able to make a claim to receive unemployment benefits on the precondition that contributions have been made for a period of at least one year. 如果个人失业，他们可以申请补偿以领取失业金，前提是失业险缴费至少要一年以上。

5. The precise amount of the percentage premium will be made by the local social insurance bureau according to the category of industry the company is deemed to be affiliated to. 保险费所缴比例的具体总额由当地社保局根据该公司被认定隶属于的行业类别决定。

Exercises

I. Answer the following questions according to the text.

1. Why does China's aging problem become more serious?
2. What does the social security system in China consist of?
3. What is the function of medical insurance card?
4. Under what conditions can an individual make a claim to receive unemployment benefits?
5. What are the differences between housing fund and other insurances?

II. Identify the key words or main ideas of the following parts.

Part 1	The _____ of establishing social insurance system
Part 2	The _____ of establishing social insurance system
Part 3	The _____ of social insurance
Part 4	_____ of five social insurances
Part 5	_____ between housing fund and five social insurances

III. Match the words or phrases in Column A to the words or phrases in Column B.

A		B
1. _____	accelerate	A. 失业
2. _____	mandatory	B. 支付
3. _____	pension	C. 生育
4. _____	benefits	D. 强制的
5. _____	unemployment	E. 养老金
6. _____	insurance	F. 缴款
7. _____	mortgage	G. 保险
8. _____	maternity	H. 抵押
9. _____	contributions	I. 救济金
10. _____	defray	J. 增加

IV. Choose the best translation.

1. Old age dependency ratio is expected to rise from currently six workers for every retired person to only two workers for a retire person by 2030. (   )

A. 老年抚养比率预期从现在的六个工人养一个退休人员上升到 2030 年两个工人养一个退休人员。

B. 老年抚养比率预期从现在的六个工人养一个退休人员到 2030 年变成只有两个工人抚养一个退休人员。

C. 老人抚养比率期待从目前六个工人扶持一个退休人员到 2030 年变成只有两个工人扶持一个退休人员。

D. 老人抚养比率期待从目前的六个工人扶持一个退休人员上升到 2030 年两个工人扶持一个退休人员。

2. The state raises social insurance through various channels and provides support for social insurance through preferential tax free. (   )

　　A. 政府通过多种渠道增加社会保险资金，通过税收优先政策向社会保险事业提供支持。
　　B. 政府多渠道增加社会保险，通过免税政策支持社会保险事业。
　　C. 国家多渠道筹集社会保险，通过免税政策支持社会保险事业。
　　D. 国家多渠道筹集社会保险资金，通过税收优惠政策支持社会保险事业。

3. How companies register and deregister their employees often varies depending upon the city and the employee's location or residency. (   )

　　A. 用人单位如何为他们职工登记和注销社会保险通常取决于该城市及其员工所在地。
　　B. 用人单位如何为他们职工登记和注销社会保险经常取决于员工所在城市和居住地。
　　C. 企业如何为他们职工登记和注销社会保险通常决定了职工所在城市和居住地。
　　D. 企业如何为他们职工登记与注销社会保险经常依赖于该城市和员工所住地。

4. In most cities in China the patient is required to bear a certain percentage of the total hospital fee. (   )

　　A. 在中国大多数城市，病人需要负担全部医院费用中的一部分。
　　B. 在中国大多数城市，病人需要承担一定比例的医疗费用。
　　C. 在中国大多数城市，要求病人承担全部医药费中的一定比例。
　　D. 在中国，大多数城市的病人要求负担一定比例的医疗费用。

5. During the period of maternity leave from the company the maternity fund will cover payment of salary. (   )

　　A. 在生产离开公司阶段，生育基金包含工资。
　　B. 在生产离开公司阶段，生育基金包括支付工资。
　　C. 在生育离岗期间，生育基金包含薪水的支付。
　　D. 在生育离岗期间，生育基金将包括支付工资。

Reading Skills (8)
Using Word Part Clues for Word Meanings

　　In the previous chapter, you've learned how to guess the meaning of unkown words by using context clues. There is another way of guessing the meaning of unknown words: it is the root or main part of a noun, a verb, etc., and is also a word from which other words are made. The basic part of any word is the root or the stem. The root often expresses the basic meaning of a word, The part added before it is called prefix, and the part added after it is called suffix.

1. Prefixes

A prefix is a word or syllable put at the beginning of a word to change its meaning or add to its meaning. By recognizing prefixes, you will be able to learn many new words. For example, the word "prefix" is made up of the prefix "pre" and the base word (or root word) fix; the word "irregular" is made up of the prefix "ir" and "regular". Here are some of the prefixes.

Prefix	Meaning	Example
re	again or back	rewrite
pre	before	preschool
un	not	unbelievable
ex	former	ex-minister
dis	not	disadvantage
anti	against, opposite	antiwar
mis	bad(ly) or wrong(ly)	misunderstand
super	greater	supermarket
under	not enough, not sufficiently	underdeveloped
counter	opposite	counterattack

2. Suffixes

A suffix is a syllable or syllables added to the end of a word. Suffixes can also offer clues to meanings of new words as they usually just change the parts of speech of the base words. For example, the word "teacher" is made up of the suffix "er" and the root word "teach"; the word "employee" is made up of the suffix "ee" and the root word "employ". Here are some of the suffixes.

Suffix	Meaning	Example
ee	one who receives	trainee
less	without	useless
ize	make or cause to become	modernize
ity	having the quality of	similarity
ish	having the quality of	childish
ive	having the quality of, inclined to	active
ful	full of	helpful
ess	female	actress
hood	condition, state	manhood
ion, ation	action of, process of	action

Further Development

Passage I

Life Insurance

The first image that comes to most people's minds upon hearing this phrase life insurance is some variation of an old couple playing with their grand kids. We are often misled by the thought that life insurance is for old people and that we could invest in it about thirty-odd years later. In fact, people in their twenties don't even think about life insurance as something that they need to invest in at their current stage in life. We may say that an investment in life insurance while in your twenties is much more beneficial than one when you are in your fifties.

Life insurance is not something that any individual with insurable interests can decide to do away with. After all, as morbid as it may sound, the fact remains that it is the certainty of death that makes the life insurance industry thrive. It is also what makes every individual realize the importance of life insurance, especially those people who have some dependents such as a spouse and children. So it is definitely not something anyone can avoid investing in. However, it is true that investing in life insurance from an earlier age is always more beneficial than investing in it as a senior citizen, either at the same cost or even at a lower cost. Following are some of the most prominent and valid benefits of buying a life insurance policy when you are in your tender twenties:

Health is Wealth

One of the biggest reasons for this is the fact that one is much healthier in their twenties than they would be in their fifties and insurance companies charge a relatively lower premium to a healthier younger individual. As one grows older and accumulates more and more health ailments and problems, insurance companies are more and more reluctant to allow lower premiums. Hence, this is a direct impact on one's cost of life insurance. In any case, there is an absolute undeniable guarantee that your insurance premium, once locked at a particular amount (comparatively lower when you are young) is going to stay the same and not increase.

Loyalty Benefits

Another reason that life insurance works out cheaper in the long run is the fact that most insurance providers stay competitive by providing a lot of loyalty benefits to their customers. Either premiums get reduced or the coverage of the policy modifies conditional to the loyalty of the customer with that particular insurer. Hence, if insured at twenty, by the time one is fifty, he would have a much more beneficial cover than someone who invests in a new policy at fifty.

Saving Can Save You

Another advantage of opting for a life insurance policy at an early age when one has just begun earning is the fact that setting aside a monthly or periodical amount to pay off as one's life insurance premium helps to ensure that we are constantly saving a certain amount every month or at regular intervals, depending on the insurance policy requirements. In simpler words, paying a premium at regular periods helps to get one in the habit of saving at a very early age, even from a comparatively nominal salary in one's early years of their career. If you can save some amount from even such a nominal amount, you'll definitely be able to save up for the bigger things in life.

It is definitely safe to say that life insurance is an absolute necessity in one's life, however healthy one's lifestyle maybe. Death is, of course, certain and while there is nothing that can be done to bring somebody back to life, leaving a protective cover for the deceased's loved ones is some form of comfort and solace. However, what is more important that simply having a life insurance policy is investing in this policy when you are just starting out, that is, sometime in your twenties as soon as you have some stability in life. The earlier you start investing, the bigger is your pool of funds, after all.

Words and Terms

insurable [ɪnˈʃuərəbl]	adj.	可保险的
morbid [ˈmɔːbɪd]	adj.	病态的，不健康的
thrive [θraɪv]	v.	兴盛，成长
prominent [ˈprɒmɪnənt]	adj.	显著的，突出的
accumulate [əˈkjuːmjʊleɪt]	v.	积累
undeniable [ʌndɪˈnaɪəbl]	adj.	不可否认的，不可争辩的
guarantee [gærənˈtiː]	n.	保证，担保
loyalty [ˈlɔɪəlti]	n.	忠实
modify [ˈmɒdɪfaɪ]	v.	改变
insure [ɪnˈʃuə]	v.	为…保险，投保
opt [ɒpt]	v.	选择
nominal [ˈnɒmɪnl]	adj.	微不足道的，票面上的
decease [dɪˈsiːs]	n.	死亡
solace [ˈsɒlɪs]	n.	安慰
do away with		消灭，去除
in any case		不管怎样
work out		解决，作出
in the long run		从长远来看
set aside		留出
in the habit of		有……的习惯

 *Notes*

1. Life insurance is not something that any individual with insurable interests can decide to do away with. 人寿保险并不是任何具有保险利益的个人可以决定放弃的。

2. In any case, there is an absolute undeniable guarantee that your insurance premium, once locked at a particular amount (comparatively lower when you are young) is going to stay the same and not increase. 不管怎样，这是一个不争的事实，你的保费一旦锁定在一个特定的数额(在年轻时相对较低)，它就会一直保持不变且不会上涨。

3. Either premiums get reduced or the coverage of the policy modifies conditional to the loyalty of the customer with that particular insurer. 降低保费或给具有特定保险人的忠实顾客修改保单条款。

4. If you can save some amount from even such a nominal amount, you'll definitely be able to save up for the bigger things in life. 如果你可以从如此微薄的收入中存些钱，那么你肯定能为生活中更大的事情做好准备。

5. Death is, of course, certain and while there is nothing that can be done to bring somebody back to life, leaving a protective cover for the deceased's loved ones is some form of comfort and solace. 当然，死亡是必然的，没有什么能使人复活。但给已故者的爱人留下一笔有保障的保险也是某种安慰。

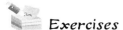 *Exercises*

I. Read the following statements and decide whether they are True (T) or False (F).

1. Life insurance is for old people and that we could invest in it about thirty-odd years later.　　　　　　　　　　　　　　　　　　　　　　　　　　　　　　(　　)

2. Life insurance is something that any individual with insurable interests cannot give up.　　　　　　　　　　　　　　　　　　　　　　　　　　　　　　　　(　　)

3. Life insurance companies are willing to provide many loyalty benefits to their customers.　　　　　　　　　　　　　　　　　　　　　　　　　　　　　　　(　　)

4. Although insurance premium locked at a particular amount, it is going to increase with your age.　　　　　　　　　　　　　　　　　　　　　　　　　　　　　　(　　)

5. Having a life insurance policy means that you have some stability in life.　　(　　)

II. Choose the correct answer according to Passage I.

1. What thought do people often have for life insurance? (　　)
   A. We could invest it about thirty years later.
   B. Young people could not buy life insurance.
   C. Life insurance is for old people.

D. Everyone should buy life insurance.

2. Why does the author say life insurance sounds morbid? (   )

A. Because individuals with insurable interests can decide to do away with it.

B. Because a life insurance policy goes into effect only after the certainty of death.

C. Because it will make people think of death.

D. Because death is a bad thing.

3. Why are insurance companies reluctant to lower the premiums for older people? (   )

A. Because older people are not much healthier than young people.

B. Because older people may have more health ailments and problems.

C. Because it will influence life insurance industry.

D. Because people have realize the importance of life insurance.

4. What advantage do people buy a life insurance policy at their early ages? (   )

A. They may set aside a monthly or periodical amount to pay off their life insurance premiums.

B. They may save up for the bigger things in life.

C. It helps to ensure that they are constantly saving a certain amount every month.

D. It helps to get them in the habit of saving at their early ages

5. What can you get from the passage? (   )

A. We know about some importance and benefits of buying a life insurance.

B. We could put some money to invest in life insurance.

C. We should buy a life insurance when we are in our twenties.

D. Life insurance is an absolute necessity in one's life.

III. Fill in the missing information.

Another advantage of _____ a life insurance policy at an _____ is that one can _____ a monthly or periodical amount to pay one's_____, which helps to_____ that one can constantly_____ a certain amount every month or at _____intervals. In short, when one has just begun_____ paying a premium at regular periods helps to get one _____at a very early age. If you can save some amount from even such a nominal amount, you'll definitely be able to_____ for the bigger things in life.

Passage II

Auto Insurance Market

Within 25 years, the private passenger automobile insurance industry will shrink by as much as 60 percent, according to a report by the consulting firm KPMG. That's the bad news. The good news is it will be smaller because there will be fewer car accidents and fatalities largely thanks to "radically safer" vehicles, according to KPMG in its report, "Marketplace of Change: Automobile Insurance in the Era of Autonomous Vehicles."

A rise in on-demand car services and the adoption of autonomous vehicles will also reduce the need for auto insurance, KPMG says. According to KPMG, accident frequency could decline by 80 percent by the year 2040 — when millennials will be ages 44 to 58. While the cost per accident may rise substantially because the new cars and their parts will be more expensive, the frequency decline will be dramatic and result in sizable reductions in loss costs and premiums, the report says. More than 90 percent of accidents each year are caused by driver error, according to the report. Combining the accident frequency and severity assumptions, the personal auto sector will cover less than US$50 billion in loss costs by 2040.

Transformation

The personal auto insurance landscape is already feeling the effects of safe car technology with the growing popularity of accident-prevention features such as traffic jam assistance and lane departure warnings that partially remove the human element from driving. The report cites David Zuby, executive vice president and chief research officer of the industry-supported Insurance Institute for Highway Safety, who points to research showing that vehicles equipped with front crash prevention technology have a 7–15 percent lower claim frequency under property damage liability coverage than comparable vehicles without it. "Further automation, if successful, could lead to even further reduction of insurance claims," says Zuby.

KPMG estimates that severity incurred in each accident is likely to rise considerably. There will still be auto accidents because of weather, road conditions and animal collisions. Also, technology failures will cause problems. The authors also note that drivers will likely have the option to turn off the safety technology at times and drive manually instead. Other experts and consultants have also weighed in on the effect of safer cars, car-sharing and autonomous cars on the insurance business.

Implications for Insurers

The implications for the auto insurance industry are enormous, according to the KPMG report authors, who predict extensive consolidation among insurers and sweeping changes in how auto insurers operate.

Joe Schneider, managing director at KPMG Corporate Finance, believes the continued proliferation of automated vehicles will put considerable strain on carriers. "Many insurers don't have a profitability cushion to erode and lack the structural agility to shed costs quickly in an environment of rapid change," Schneider said. "Once the massive market disruption begins and traditional insurance business models are flipped upside down, we expect significant turmoil."

KPMG surveyed insurance executives to gauge their awareness of industry issues around autonomous vehicles and concluded that the industry is not prepared for what's coming. More than half of respondents (55 percent) told KPMG they believe that regulators will impede the adoption of autonomous vehicles. The KPMG report identifies four possible business strategies for insurers looking to address the changes it says are coming:

Consolidate: For those existing carriers with scale, consider acquisition opportunities to leverage large existing platforms.

Diversify: Move into other products that could potentially shield from challenges across the personal and commercial auto lines of business.

Innovate: With new areas of risk, identify new areas to provide insurance protection and launch new products to meet needs.

Partner and ally: Consider new business models, which will likely require partnering with others, where insurance could be embedded into the cost of a vehicle or part of usage fees.

Exercises

I. Choose the correct answer according to Passage II.

1. According to KPMG, accident frequency could decrease by _____ by the year 2040 — when millennials will be ages 44 to 58. (   )

   A. 60%
   B. 80%
   C. 20%
   D. 90%

2. Combining the accident frequency and severity assumptions, the personal auto sector will cover less than _____ in loss costs by 2040. (   )

   A. 5,000,000,000
   B. 50,000,000,000
   C. 500,000,000,000
   D. 500,000,000

3. Which vehicles have a 7–15 percent lower claim frequency under property damage liability coverage than comparable vehicles without it? (   )

   A. Vehicles with traffic jam assistance
   B. Vehicles with lane departure warnings
   C. Vehicles equipped with front crash prevention technology
   D. Autonomous vehicles

4. There will still be auto accidents because of _____. (   )

   A. weather
   B. road conditions
   C. technology failures
   D. All of the above

5. According to authors prediction of the KPMG report, what change will auto insurers take place? (   )

   A. Extensive consolidation among insurers
   B. Innovation
   C. Partner
   D. Alliance

II. Choose the best translation.

1. 结合事故发生频率和责任承担的严重性，到 2040 年个人汽车行业在损失成本上将会减少五百亿美元。（   ）

   A. Combining the accident frequency and severity assumptions, the personal auto sector will cover less than US$50 billion in loss costs by 2040.

   B. Combining the accident frequency and serious responsibility, the personal auto sector will cover less than US$5 billion in loss costs by 2040.

   C. Integrating the accident frequency and serious responsibility, the personal auto sector will cover less than US$50 billion in loss costs by 2040.

   D. Integrating the accident frequency and severity assumptions, the personal auto sector will cover less than US$500 billion in loss costs by 2040.

2. 事故发生频率的急剧下降将导致损失成本和保费的极大减少，但每一事故产生的费用可能会大大增加，因为这些新车和其部件会更贵。（   ）

   A. While the cost per accident may rise substantially because the new cars and their parts will be more expensive, the frequency decline will be dramatic and result in sizable reductions in loss costs and premiums.

   B. While the cost per accident may raise substantially because the new cars and their parts will be more expensive, the frequency will be declined dramatically which result in sizable reductions in loss costs and premiums.

   C. The cost per accident may rise substantially because the new cars and their parts will be more expensive, but the frequency will be declined dramatically which cause sizable reductions in loss costs and premiums.

   D. The cost per accident may raise substantially, so the new cars and their parts will be more expensive, the frequency decline will be dramatic and cause sizable reductions in loss costs and premiums.

3. 随着事故预防功能的日益普及，个人汽车保险业已受到安全汽车技术的影响。（   ）

   A. With the growing popularity of accident-prevention features, safe car technology affects the personal auto insurance industry.

   B. With the growing popularity of accident-prevention functions, safe car technology has a feeling of affecting the personal auto insurance industry.

   C. The personal auto insurance landscape is already feeling the effects of safe car technology with the growing popularity of accident-prevention features.

   D. The personal auto insurance landscape has been already feeling the role of safe car technology with the growing popularity of accident-prevention functions.

4. 其他专家和顾问们对安全汽车的效果、汽车共享及无人驾驶汽车的保险业务发表高见。（   ）

   A. Other experts and consultants give remarks on the effect of safer cars and insurance business about car-sharing and autonomous cars.

   B. Other experts and consultants give remarks in the effect of safer cars and insurance business about car-sharing and autonomous cars.

C. Other experts and consultants have comments on the effect of safer cars, car-sharing and autonomous cars on the insurance business.

D. Other experts and consultants have weighed in on the effect of safer cars, car-sharing and autonomous cars on the insurance business.

5. 考虑新的业务模式，这些可能需要与其他公司合作，可将保险嵌入车辆成本中或部分的使用费用中。（　　）

A. Consider new business models, which will likely need partners with others, where insurance could be embedded into the premiums of a vehicle or part of usage fees.

B. Consider new business models, which will likely require partnering with others, where insurance could be embedded into the cost of a vehicle or part of usage fees.

C. Considering new business models, which will likely require partnering with others, where insurance could be embedded into the cost of a vehicle or part of usage fees.

D. Considering new business models, which will likely need partners, where insurance could be embedded into the cost of a vehicle or part of usage fees.

Special Terms

social insurance	社会保险
pension	养老金
unemployment insurance	失业险
maternity insurance	生育险
occupational injury insurance	工伤险
housing fund	住房公积金
mandatory benefits	强制性福利
dependency ratio	抚养比例
life insurance	人寿险
insurance premium	保费
auto insuranc market	汽车保险市场
traffic jam assiastance	交通堵塞援助
lane departure warnings	车道偏离警告

Chapter Nine

Marketing

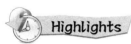

Text
Marketing
Reading Skills (9)
Note-taking and Thinking
Further Development
Passage I
Marketing in the Digital Age——A Brand-new Game
Passage II
Classic Cases of SWOT Analysis

This is the 9th chapter of the book. In the first section, you will learn a text, and you will have some information about marketing. In the second section, you will have a deeper understanding about marketing. In this section, you will learn two passages about marketing in the digital age and classic cases of SWOT analysis and they will help you have a further development on mastering reading skills of note-taking and thinking.

Starter

Do you know what marketing mix is? How does marketing help a company to make profits?

Text

Marketing

Introduction

What does the term marketing mean? Many people think of marketing only as selling and advertising. And no wonder, for every day we are bombarded with television commercials, newspaper ads, direct mail campaigns, Internet pitches and sales calls. Although they are important, they are only two of many marketing functions and are often not the most important ones. Today, marketing must be understood not in the old sense of making a sale but in the new sense of satisfying customer needs. Selling occurs only after a product is produced. By contrast, marketing starts long before a company has a product. Marketing can be defined as below.

Marketing is the management process responsible for identifying, anticipating, and satisfying customer requirements profitably.

This is the definition preferred by the UK's Chartered Institute of Marketing (CIM). From this definition, we can get the following points.

1. Marketing is a management process

Marketing has just as much legitimacy as any other business function, and involves just as much management skill. It requires planning and analysis, resource allocation, control and investment in terms of money, appropriately skilled people and physical resources. It also, of course, requires implementation, monitoring and evaluation. Marketing continues throughout the product's life, trying to find new customers and keep current customers by improving product appeal and performance, learning from product sales results and managing repeat performance. As with any other management activity, it can be carried out efficiently and successfully, or it can be done poorly, resulting in failure.

2. Marketing is about giving customers what they want

Marketing is the homework that managers undertake to assess needs, measure their extent and intensity, and determine whether a profitable opportunity exists. All marketing activities should be geared towards this. It implies a focus towards the customer or end consumer of the product or service. If customer requirements are not satisfactorily fulfilled, or if customers do not obtain what they want and need, then marketing has failed both the customer and the organization.

Marketing Mix

The major marketing management decisions can be classified in one of the following four categories: product, price, place (distribution) and promotion.

These variables are known as the marketing mix or the 4Ps of marketing. They are the variables that marketing managers can control in order to best satisfy customers in the target market.

The firm attempts to generate a positive response in the target market by blending these four marketing mix variables in an optimal manner.

1. Product

The product is the physical product or service offered to the consumer. In the case of physical products, it also refers to any services or conveniences that are part of the offering. Product decisions include aspects such as function, appearance, packaging, service, warranty, etc.

2. Price

Pricing decisions should take into account profit margins and the probable pricing response of competitors. Pricing includes not only the list price, but also discounts, financing, and other options such as leasing.

3. Place

Place (or distribution) decisions are those associated with channels of distribution that serve as the means for getting the product to the target customers. The distribution system performs transactional, logistical, and facilitating functions. Distribution decisions include market coverage, channel member selection, logistics, and levels of service.

4. Promotion

Promotion decisions are those related to communicating and selling to potential consumers. Since these costs can be large in proportion to the product price, a break-even analysis should be performed when making promotion decisions. It is useful to know the value of a customer in order to determine whether additional customers are worth the cost of acquiring them. Promotion decisions involve advertising, public relations, media types, etc.

Marketing Communications

Marketing is a broad topic that covers a range of aspects, including advertising, public relations, sales and promotions. People often confuse sales with marketing, when in fact the two are very different. The former involves getting a product or service into the market, promoting it, influencing behavior, and encouraging sales. Marketing communications break down the strategies involved with marketing messages into categories based on the goals of each message. There are distinct stages in converting strangers to customers that govern the communication medium that should be used.

1. Advertising

The many forms of advertising make it hard to generalize about its unique qualities. However, several qualities can be noted.

(1) Advertising can reach masses of geographically dispersed buyers at a low cost per exposure. For example, TV advertising can reach huge audiences.

(2) Beyond its reach, large-scale advertising by a seller says something positive about the seller's size, popularity and success.

(3) Because of advertising's public nature, consumers tend to view advertised products as standard and legitimate — buyers know that purchasing the product will be understood and accepted publicly.

(4) Advertising enables the seller to repeat a message many times, and lets the buyer receive and compare the messages of various competitors.

(5) Advertising is also very expressive, allowing the company to dramatize its products through the artful use of visuals, print, sound and color.

(6) On the one hand, advertising can be used to build up a long-term image for a product (such as Mercedes-Benz car ads). On the other hand, advertising can trigger quick sales (as when department stores like Debenhams and Selfridges advertise a weekend sale).

2. Personal selling

Personal selling is the most effective tool at certain stages of the buying process, particularly in building up buyers' preferences, convictions and actions. Compared with advertising, personal selling has several unique qualities.

(1) It involves personal interaction between two or more people, so each person can observe the other's needs and characteristics and make quick adjustments.

(2) Personal selling also allows all kinds of relationships to spring up, ranging from a matter-of-fact selling relationship to a deep personal friendship. The effective salesperson keeps the customer's interests at heart in order to build a long-term relationship.

(3) Finally, with personal selling the buyer usually feels a greater need to listen and respond, even if the response is a polite "no, thank you".

3. Sales promotion

Sales promotion includes a wide assortment of tools — coupons, contests, price reductions, premium offers, free goods and others — all of which have many unique qualities.

(1) They attract consumer attention and provide information that may lead to a purchase.

(2) They offer strong incentives to purchase by providing inducements or contributions that give additional value to consumers.

(3) Moreover, sales promotions invite and reward quick response. Whereas advertising says "buy our product", sales promotion offers incentives to consumers to "buy it now".

4. Marketing Public Relations (MPR)

Public relations or PR offers several unique qualities. It is all those activities that the organization does to communicate with target audiences which are not directly paid for.

(1) PR is very believable: news stories, features, sponsorships and events seem more real and believable to readers than ads do.

(2) Public relations can reach many prospects who avoid salespeople and advertisements, since the message gets to the buyers as "news" rather than as a sales-directed communication.

(3) Like advertising, PR can dramatize a company or product. The Body Shop is one of the few international companies that have used public relations as a more effective alternative to mass TV advertising.

The Importance of Marketing

Marketing plays an important role in an economy, because it provides the means for competition to take place. In a competitive marketplace, businesses try to create new or improved products at lower prices than their competitors. Companies without a marketing mindset are at a disadvantage in today's business world. Those who are still centered around their products, rather than their customers, are doomed to fail.

 Words and Terms

bombard [bɔm'bɑːd]	v.	炮轰；轰击；大肆批评
commercial [kə'mɜːʃəl]	n.	(电台或电视播放的)商业广告
anticipate [æn'tɪsɪpeɪt]	v.	预见，预期
legitimacy [lɪ'dʒɪtɪməsɪ]	n.	合法(性)，合理(性)
implementation [ɪmplɪmen'teɪʃən]	n.	执行实现
classify ['klæsɪfaɪ]	v.	分类
distribution [dɪstrɪ'bjuːʃən]	n.	分配，分销
variable ['veərɪəbl]	n.	可变因素；变量
optimal ['ɔptɪməl]	adj.	最佳的，最优化的
warranty ['wɔrəntɪ]	n.	(商品的)保修证书
discount ['dɪskaʊnt]	n.	折扣
lease [liːs]	v.	租赁
logistics [lə'dʒɪstɪks]	n.	物流
promotion [prə'məʊʃən]	n.	促销

convert [kən'vɜ:t]	v.	使转变，转换
dispersed [dɪs'pɜ:st]	adj.	散布的
exposure [ɪks'pəʊʒə]	n.	(在电视、报纸等上的)亮相
expressive [ɪks'presɪv]	adj.	富有表现力的
trigger ['trɪɡə]	v.	引发，触发
preference ['prefərəns]	n.	偏好，偏爱
coupon ['ku:pɔn]	n.	优惠券
incentive [ɪn'sentɪv]	n.	动机，动力
genuine ['dʒenjʊɪn]	adj.	真正的
sponsorship ['spɔnsəʃɪp]	n.	赞助
prospect ['prɔspekt]	n.	潜在顾客

marketing mix	营销组合
marketing manager	营销经理
target market	目标市场
marketing communication	营销传播

1. Marketing has just as much legitimacy as any other business function, and involves just as much management skill. It requires planning and analysis, resource allocation, control and investment in terms of money, appropriately skilled people and physical resources. 市场营销与任何其他企业职能一样有存在的必要，并需要一定的管理技能它需要计划与分析、资源分配、资金的投入及控制、有适当技能的员工和物质资源。

2. Marketing continues throughout the product's life, trying to find new customers and keep current customers by improving product appeal and performance, learning from product sales results and managing repeat performance. 市场营销活动贯穿于产品的整个生命周期，它包括两方面的活动：一是设法寻找新顾客，二是通过提高产品的吸引力与性能，从产品的销售结果中获取信息和重复绩效管理等方式留住现有的顾客。

appeal 吸引力

e. g.: a city with appeal for tourists 对游客有吸引力的城市

3. Marketing is the homework that managers undertake to assess needs, measure their extent and intensity and determine whether a profitable opportunity exists. 市场营销是管理人员负责的工作，包括评估消费者需求、衡量需求的范围和强度，以及确定是否存在利润空间。

在这个句子中，that managers undertake to assess needs, measure their extent and intensity and determine whether a profitable opportunity exists 是 homework 的定语从句。

4. The firm attempts to generate a positive response in the target market by blending these four marketing mix variables in an optimal manner. 企业努力以最优的方式融合这四种营销组合变量，目的是为了引起目标市场的积极回应。

5. Pricing decisions should take into account profit margins and the probable pricing response of competitors. Pricing includes not only the list price, but also discounts, financing, and other options such as leasing. 在做出定价决策时，应当考虑两方面的因素，即利润率和竞争对手的定价回应。定价的项目不仅包括价目单上所列的价格，还包括折扣、赊货以及其他项目，如租赁。

discount 折扣

e. g. : discount of 30% 七折

They give 10% discount for cash payment. 如现金付款，他们给予九折优惠。

6. Place (or distribution) decisions are those associated with channels of distribution that serve as the means for getting the product to the target customers. The distribution system performs transactional, logistical, and facilitating functions.

地点(或分销)决策与分销渠道相关，分销渠道就是商品顺利到达消费者手中的途径和方式。分销体系具有交易、物流以及提供便利等功能。

在这个句子中，channels 是定语从句 that serve as the means for getting the product to the target customers 的先行词，它在从句中充当主语。

7. Advertising can reach masses of geographically dispersed buyers at a low cost per exposure. For example, TV advertising can reach huge audiences. 广告可以通过一定形式的媒体，以较低的成本向各地的消费者传递信息。例如，电视广告可以向大量的观众传递信息。

disperse 散布，散开

e. g. : A group of children dispersed. 一群孩子散开了。

8. Public relations can reach many prospects who avoid salespeople and advertisements, since the message gets to the buyers as "news" rather than as a sales-directed communication. 公共关系营销活动可以影响许多回避销售人员和广告的顾客，因为它所传递的信息对于顾客来说是一种新闻而非以销售为导向的信息。

在这个句子中，prospects 是定语从句 who avoid salespeople and advertisements 的先行词，在句子中充当主语。

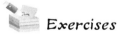

Exercises

I. Answer the following questions according to the text.

1. What does marketing mean?
2. What is marketing mix?
3. What are the common forms of marketing communication?
4. What tools does sales promotion include?
5. Why is marketing important in an economy?

II. Identify the key words or main ideas of the following parts.

Part 1	1. Marketing is a _____
	2. Marketing is about_____

Part 2	Marketing Mix or 4Ps of marketing _____, _____, _____, _____
Part 3	Marketing is a broad topic that covers a range of aspects, including _____, _____, _____ and _____.
Part 4	The _____ of Marketing

III. Match the words or phrases in Column A to the words or phrases in Column B.

    A   B
1. _____ distribution   A 促销
2. _____ logistics   B 折扣
3. _____ preference   C 物流
4. _____ commercial   D 营销组合
5. _____ promotion   E 赞助
6. _____ discount   F (电视或电台播放的)广告
7. _____ sponsorship   G 偏好，偏爱
8. _____ marketing mix   H 分配
9. _____ coupon   I (商品的)保修证书
10. _____ warranty   J 优惠券

IV. Choose the best translation.

1. Because of advertising's public nature, consumers tend to view advertised products as standard and legitimate — buyers know that purchasing the product will be understood and accepted publicly. (　　)

 A. 由于广告具有独特性，消费者往往认为广告中的服务是符合标准及合法的——顾客们知道购买这种服务会被公众所理解和接受。

 B. 由于广告具有通用性，消费者偏偏认为广告中的产品是符合要求及合法的——顾客们知道购买这种产品会被公众所理解和相信。

 C. 由于广告具有公众性，消费者往往认为广告中的产品是符合标准及合适的——顾客们知道购买这种产品会被家人所理解和相信。

 D. 由于广告具有公众性，消费者往往认为广告中的产品是符合标准及合法的——顾客们知道购买这种产品会被公众所理解和接受。

2. Personal selling also allows all kinds of relationships to spring up, ranging from a matter-of-fact selling relationship to a deep personal friendship. (　　)

 A. 人员销售活动也使得许多关系得以建立，包括从一般的购买关系到深入的个人友谊等一系列关系。

 B. 团体销售活动也使得各种各样的关系得以建立，包括从一般的同事关系到深入的个人友谊等一系列关系。

 C. 人员销售活动也使得各种各样的关系得以建立，包括从一般的销售关系到深入的个人友谊等一系列关系。

D. 团体销售活动也使得许多关系得以建立，包括从一般的销售关系到深入的亲戚关系等一系列关系。

3. Sales promotion effects are usually short-lived, however, and are often not as effective as advertising or personal selling in building long-run brand preference. (　　)
   A. 但是，促销活动的效果通常是短暂的，而且通常在建立长期的品牌偏好方面不如广告或人员销售有效。
   B. 但是，销售活动的效果通常是短暂的，而且通常在建立长期的品牌偏好方面不如广告或人员销售有效。
   C. 但是，促销活动的效果通常是长期的，而且通常在建立短期的产品偏好方面不如广告或人员销售有效。
   D. 但是，销售活动的效果通常是短暂的，而且通常在建立长期的产品偏好方面不如广告或人员促销有效率。

4. Marketing is the management process responsible for identifying, anticipating, and satisfying customer requirements profitably. (　　)
   A. 市场营销是为了组织自身和利益相关者的收益而辨认、预见以及满足顾客需求的管理过程。
   B. 市场销售是为了组织自身和利益相关者的利益而发现、预见以及满足顾客要求的管理过程。
   C. 市场营销是为了组织自身和利益相关者的收益而分解、预报以及满足顾客需求的商业过程。
   D. 市场营销是为了组织自身和利益相关者的利益而发现、预见以及满足顾客需求的管理过程。

5. Companies without a marketing mindset are at a disadvantage in today's business world. Those who are still centered around their products, rather than their customers, are doomed to fail. (　　)
   A. 在当今的商业世界中，缺乏营销意识的企业是处于有利地位的。那些仍然以其商品而非顾客为中心的企业注定要成功。
   B. 在当今的商业世界中，缺乏营销意识的企业是处于不利地位的。那些仍然以其产品而非顾客为中心的企业注定会失败。
   C. 在当今的经济世界中，缺乏销售意识的企业是处于不利地位的。那些仍然以其商品而非顾客为中心的企业注定会失败。
   D. 在当今的经济世界中，缺乏营销意识的企业是处于有利地位的。那些仍然以其产品而非消费者为中心的企业注定会失败。

Reading Skills (9)
Note-taking and Thinking

It is said that over 50 percent of the material read or heard in class is forgotten in a matter of minutes. Taking notes can trigger recall and overcome forgetting, so it is a very important learning tool and useful not only in reading, writing but also in studying. For your course work, you will often need to look back at what you've learned from your reading. If you had the time and energy, you could just reread all the material from beginning to end. But reviewing the material is easier and quicker if you identify and mark important information the first time you read it.

Features of Good Notes

Efficient and effective notes generally display the following features.

1. They are organized into key points and minor points.

2. They record relevant source/bibliographical details, eg. author, title, publisher, date of publication, page number.

3. They use visual techniques, eg. highlighting, graphics, colors, and underlining to identify main points.

4. They use abbreviations and symbols to show connections between key points and minor points.

5. They have line spaces so that you can add to your notes later, eg. for revision.

You need to adapt your note-taking style to suit your purpose. To do this, you will need to think critically, and be prepared, so that your notes are systematic, organized, and help you to effectively recall, understand and apply information. Note making is also an important step in developing your understanding.

Before Reading

Ask questions before you read.

1. Why am I reading this?

2. What do I need to understand?

3. How does this information relate/compare to other topics and information?

4. What do I need to remember?

5. What are the main points?

During Reading

Read actively and effectively.

1. Clarify your purpose.

2. Consult study guides and subject outlines.

3. Keep the main subject headings firmly in mind.

4. Turn chapter headings into questions.

5. Seek answers to these questions through your reading.

6. Always keep pen and paper handy — for note taking, and for highlighting main points.

After Reading

Evaluate the relevance and validity of what you have read.

1. Who is the author and what is their motive for writing this?

2. Who is the target audience? Is bias apparent?

3. What methodology has been used?

4. What conclusions are reached?

5. Does the author justify these conclusions?

6. How does the study relate to broader issues?

Note-taking Strategies

1. Be selective and systematic

As you take notes from a written source, keep in mind that not all of a text may be relevant to your needs. Think about your purpose for reading.

(1) Are you reading for a general understanding of a topic or concept?

(2) Are you reading for some specific information that may relate to the topic of an assignment?

Before you start to take notes, skim the text. Then highlight or mark the main points and any relevant information you may need to take notes from. Finally—keeping in mind your purpose for reading—read the relevant sections of the text carefully and take separate notes as you read.

2. Identify the purpose and function of a text

Whether you need to make notes on a whole text or just part of it, identifying the main purpose and function of a text is invaluable for clarifying your note-taking purposes and saving time.

(1) Read the title and the abstract or preface (if there is one).

(2) Read the introduction or first paragraph.

(3) Skim the text to read topic headings and notice how the text is organized.

(4) Read graphic material and predict its purpose in the text.

Your aim is to identify potentially useful information by getting an initial overview of the text (chapter, article, pages) that you have selected to read. Ask yourself: will this text give me the information I require and where might it be located in the text?

3. Identify how information is organized

Most texts use a range of organizing principles to develop ideas. While most good writing will have a logical order, not all writers will use an organizing principle. Organizing principles tend to sequence information into a logical hierarchy, some of which are:

(1) Past ideas to present ideas.

(2) The steps or stages of a process or event.

(3) Most important point to least important point.

(4) Well known ideas to least known ideas.

(5) Simple ideas to complex ideas.

(6) General ideas to specific ideas.

(7) The largest parts to the smallest parts of something.

(8) Problems and solutions.

(9) Causes and results.

An Example: Look at the text on underwater cameras and then look at how the text is presented in note form. The most important words to include in notes are the information words. These are usually nouns, adjectives and verbs.

4. Record your thoughts

When taking notes for an assignment, it is also helpful to record your thoughts at the time. Record your thoughts in a separate column or margin and in a different color to the notes you took from the text.

(1) What ideas did you have about your assignment when you read that information?

(2) How do you think you could use this information in your assignment?

Further Development

Passage I

Marketing in the Digital Age
——A Brand-new Game

As people spend more time on social media, advertisers are following them.

Earlier this year BMW advertised on WeChat, a popular messaging app in China with around 550million monthly users. But its ads were shown only to those whose profiles suggested they were potential buyers of expensive cars. Others were shown ads for more affordable stuff, such as smartphones. The campaign bruised a few egos. Some of those not shown the BMW ad complained, referring to themselves as Diaosi, or (putting it politely) losers.

The carmaker's experience shows the complexities of advertising today, when it is so easy for dissatisfied customers to make their voices heard. But it was also an example of how marketing chiefs are struggling to find the right way to reach consumers on new digital platforms, where they are spending ever more of their time.

Not long ago social-media marketing was something that brand managers might ask their summer interns to deal with. Today it has become a pillar of the advertising industry. Social networks like Facebook, Twitter and LinkedIn have cultivated vast audiences: 2 billion people worldwide use them, says eMarketer, a research firm. Online advertising of all sorts continues to grow, and within that category, spending on social-media ads has gone from virtually nothing a few years ago to perhaps US$20 billion this year.

Advertisers like social-media platforms because they gather all sorts of data on each user's age, consumption patterns, interests and so on. This means ads can be aimed at them with an accuracy that is unthinkable with analogue media. For example, Chevrolet, an American car brand, has sent ads to the Facebook pages and Twitter feeds of people who had expressed an interest in, or signed up to test-drive, a competitor's vehicle.

Such fine-tuned targeting means that the distinction between advertising and e-commerce is becoming blurred. Facebook, Twitter, Instagram and other platforms are selling ads containing "buy now" buttons, which let users complete a sale on the spot. It is too early to tell how many consumers want such a convenience, but the social platforms foresee a future in which they get paid by advertisers to provide instant-shopping services that make the platforms more useful to their members, and get them to spend more time on them.

To wring the most out of the ability to target consumers precisely on social media, ad agencies are making big changes to their campaigns. Instead of creating a single, broad-brush message that will run across television, radio, print and outdoor, they are producing many variations on a theme, matching each to the subset of consumers they judge most likely to respond to it. Last month Lowe's, an American home-improvement retailer, ran a campaign on Facebook in which users were sent one of several dozen versions of its ad, depending on which part of their homes they had mentioned on social media.

The iterative nature of digital marketing has meant lots of work for ad agencies and public-relations firms. However, the brands that hire them must weigh the "production-cost trade-offs" that come with personalisation on social media, says Pete Blackshaw of Nestlé, a food manufacturer,"You can target too much."

Marketing chiefs also need to think through efforts to give their brands "online personalities". Twitter has been the main place where brands try to sound authentic and clever. When Apple announced its gold iPhone in 2013, Denny's, a restaurant chain, sent out a gently mocking tweet showing a photo of its pancakes, which are "always available in golden". It seemed to go down well with consumers.

But in attempting to ride social-media trends, companies can easily fall flat on their faces. DiGiorno, a frozen-pizza maker, noticed that a number of people were using the hashtag "Why I Stayed" on Twitter and sent out a jocular tweet that they had stayed for the pizza. It turned out that the comment thread was about domestic violence and why women remained in abusive relationships. DiGiorno took to social media again—this time to apologise.

In spite of such pitfalls, social platforms are likely to receive an ever larger part of marketers' budgets. But the digital-media business is still young and volatile, and it is hard to predict which social networks are destined to become the new-media equivalents of America's big four broadcast-TV networks. For a time, Twitter seemed to be the place to be for advertisers; more recently it has been dogged by management turnover and slowing user growth. Now Facebook is the favourite among marketing folk: it claims nearly five times as many users and nine times as much revenue as Twitter. Facebook has bought several nascent social-media services that might have grown to become challengers, such as Instagram, a photo-sharing app, and WhatsApp, a messaging app. It has been rolling out ads cautiously on Instagram, to see how users react, but has yet to start doing so on WhatsApp.

Some old media have yet to feel much pain from the loss of ad revenue to digital rivals. TV advertising has until now kept growing. But as time goes on, and as TV audiences both decline and shift to services that do not have ads, such as Netflix, the competition will be more keenly felt.

However, social networks, and TV advertisers interested in switching to them, have yet to work out what is the optimal format for video ads. In 2012 Twitter acquired Vine, which lets people post six-second videos; several months ago, Periscope, an app for live video also owned by Twitter, was all the rage. Advertisers have experimented with both services, but as yet neither has taken off as a marketing medium.

It still makes sense for marketers to try these new services out, because there is something of a first-mover advantage in digital advertising. Brands that are early to use new platforms benefit disproportionately, explains Linda Boff, a marketing chief at General Electric, because their users have not yet become saturated with marketing messages.

The latest social platforms to get the attention of marketing types are a bunch of messaging apps, such as Snapchat, WeChat and Kik, where young users send messages, photos and videos directly to friends. Brands are also starting to do more with Pinterest, where users can "pin up" images of things that appeal to them. It seems a fair assumption that users may want to buy the things they are pinning up, although the platform, which has 70million users, may never achieve the scale of Twitter (300million), let alone Facebook (1.5 billion).

Even if marketers master social media without coming across as clumsy, grating or intrusive, there will surely be a limit to how much advertising will shift to the platforms. Television ads are still great for reaching big audiences with simple messages. Print ads can lend brands an air of credibility (we would say that, wouldn't we?). Like fund managers, advertisers will always want a balanced portfolio.

(From:http://www.24en.com)

Words and Terms

bruise [bru:z]	vt.	擦伤，戳伤
complexity [kəmˈpleksətɪ]	n.	复杂，复杂性
intern [ˈɪntɜ:n]	n.	实习生
platform [ˈplætfɔ:m]	n.	平台
analogue [ˈænəlɒg]	adj.	类似的
distinction [dɪˈstɪŋ(k)ʃ(ə)n]	n.	区别
blurred [blɜ:d]	adj.	模糊不清的
authentic [ɔ:ˈθentɪk]	adj.	真正的，真实的
hashtag [ˈhæʃˈtæg]	n.	标签
jocular [ˈdʒɒkjʊlə]	adj.	爱开玩笑的，滑稽的
abusive [əˈbju:sɪv]	adj.	辱骂的，滥用的
pitfall [ˈpɪtfɔ:l]	n.	陷阱，圈套
volatile [ˈvɒlətaɪl]	adj.	不稳定的
nascent [ˈnæs(ə)nt]	adj.	初期的
saturated [ˈsætʃəreɪtɪd]	adj.	饱和的

Chapter Nine Marketing

clumsy ['klʌmzɪ]	adj.	笨拙的
credibility [kredɪ'bɪlɪtɪ]	n.	可信性
portfolio [pɔːt'fəʊlɪəʊ]	n.	投资组合

social-media marketing	社交媒体营销
trade-offs	权衡，交易
fall flat	失败
broad-brush	粗略的，粗枝大叶的
iterative nature	迭代性质
domestic violence	家庭暴力

Notes

1. The campaign bruised a few egos. Some of those not shown the BMW ad complained, referring to themselves as Diaosi, or (putting it politely) losers. 这个案例戳到一些人的痛点。那些没有收到宝马广告的人，称自己为屌丝，失败者。

2. But it was also an example of how marketing chiefs are struggling to find the right way to reach consumers on new digital platforms, where they are spending ever more of their time. 但是这也使市场营销主管能够找到如何通过新媒体平台将广告推送给消费者的好方法，消费者在新媒体上花费更多的时间。

where 引导定语从句修饰 digital platforms。

3. Online advertising of all sorts continues to grow, and within that category, spending on social-media ads has gone from virtually nothing a few years ago to perhaps US$20 billion this year. 各种线上广告持续增长，其中社交媒体广告在几年之内从零增长到 200 亿美元。

4. Chevrolet, an American car brand, has sent ads to the Facebook pages and Twitter feeds of people who had expressed an interest in, or signed up to test-drive, a competitor's vehicle. 美国汽车品牌雪佛兰通过脸书网页及推特回复将广告发送给关注或申请竞品汽车试驾的用户。

5. Facebook, Twitter, Instagram and other platforms are selling ads containing "buy now" buttons, which let users complete a sale on the spot. 脸书、推特、照片墙和其他平台在广告中加入"立即购买"按钮，使用户能立刻购买广告商品。脸书是创办于美国的一个社交网络服务网站，于 2004 年 2 月 4 日上线。主要创始人为美国人马克·扎克伯格。脸书还是世界排名领先的照片分享站点，截至 2013 年 11 月，每天上传约 3.5 亿张照片。截至 2012 年 5 月，脸书拥有约 9 亿用户。

脸书(Facebook)的总部在旧金山的加利福尼亚大街。截至 2012 年，F 公司有 3500 名雇员。而从 2006 年 9 月 11 日起，任何用户输入有效电子邮件地址和自己的年龄段，即可加入。用户可以选择加入一个或多个网络，比如中学、公司或地区。2014 年 12 月 17 日脸书为收购色拉布(Snapchat)开出的报价超过了 30 亿美元。

推特(Twitter)是一个社交网络(Social Network Service)及微博客服务的网站，是全球互联网上访问量最大的十个网站之一。它利用无线网络、有线网络、通信技术进行即时通讯，是微博客的典型应用。它允许用户将自己的最新动态和想法以短信形式发送给手机和个性化网站群，而不仅仅是发送给个人。

照片墙(Instagram)是一款最初运行在 iOS 平台上的移动应用，以一种快速、美妙和有趣的方式将你的随时抓拍下的图片分享，它还内置了很多种的滤镜效果，用户可以在自己的智能设备上完成拍摄照片、修改照片、发布照片的全过程。

6. Instead of creating a single, broad-brush message that will run across television, radio, print and outdoor, they are producing many variations on a theme, matching each to the subset of consumers they judge most likely to respond to it. 取消通过电视、广播、平面及户外传播的单一粗放的信息，广告公司制作同一主题下不同变体的创意形式，来适应各种消费群体，这种定制推送使消费者更愿意做出回应。

7. It turned out that the comment thread was about domestic violence and why women remained in abusive relationships. 结果却是该评论主题是关于家庭暴力以及为什么妇女仍处在虐待关系中。

turn out 结果是。

8. But the digital-media business is still young and volatile, and it is hard to predict which social networks are destined to become the new-media equivalents of America's big four broadcast-TV networks. 但是数字媒体公司仍很年轻且不稳定，很难预测哪个社交网络能与美国四大广播电视网络抗衡。

Exercises

I. Read the following statements and decide whether they are True(T) or False(F).

1. BMW's ads were shown only to those whose profiles suggested they were potential buyers.　　　　　　　　　　　　　　　　　　　　　　　　　　　　　　　(　　)

2. The carmaker's experience shows the complexities of advertising today, when it is so difficult for dissatisfied customers to make their voices heard.　　　(　　)

3. Today social-media marketing has played a vital role in the advertising industry.　(　　)

4. Advertisers favor social-media platforms in that they collect all sorts of data on each user's age, consumption patterns, interests and so on.　　　　　　　　　　　(　　)

5. The digital-media business is well developed now, so it is easy to predict which social networks are destined to become the new-media equivalents of America's big four broadcast-TV networks.　　　　　　　　　　　　　　　　　　　　　　　　　(　　)

II. Choose the correct answer according to Passage I.

1. BMW's ads on WeChat were shown only to those whose profiles suggested they were potential buyers of_____. (　　)

　　A. expensive houses　　　　　　　　　　B. expensive cars
　　C. expensive cellphones　　　　　　　　D. cheap cameras

2. Advertisers like social-media platforms because _____. ( )

A. they gather all sorts of data on each user's age, consumption patterns, interests and so on

B. they are very cheap and convenient

C. they can collect more accurate information on each user's age

D. they knows the consumption patterns of users

3. Facebook, Twitter, Instagram and other platforms are selling ads containing "buy now" buttons, which let users complete a sale on the spot. Here the phrase "on the spot" means _____. ( )

A. instantly   B. conveniently
C. immediately   D. significantly

4. In spite of such pitfalls, social platforms are likely to receive an ever larger part of marketers' budgets. Here "pitfalls" means_____. ( )

A. 跌落   B. 洞穴
C. 缺点   D. 陷阱

5. Now what is the favourite among marketing folk?

A. Facebook   B. Wechat
D. Twitter   D. Instagram

III. Fill in the missing information.

As people spend more time on_____ , advertisers are following them. Earlier this year BMW advertised on WeChat, a popular messaging app in China with around 550million monthly users. But its ads were shown only to those whose profiles suggested they were_____ of expensive cars. The carmaker's experience shows the _____ of advertising today, and it was also an example of how marketing chiefs are struggling to find the right way to reach consumers on new _____. _____of all sorts continues to grow, and within that category, spending on_____ ads has gone from virtually nothing a few years ago to perhaps US$20 billion this year.

Passage II

Classic Cases of SWOT Analysis

Case I   Wal-Mart SWOT Analysis

Strengths

Wal-Mart is a powerful retail brand. It has a reputation for value for money, convenience and a wide range of products all in one store.

Wal-Mart has grown substantially over recent years, and has experienced global expansion (for example, its purchase of the United Kingdom based retailer ASDA).

The company has a core competence involving its use of information technology to support its international logistics system. For example, it can see how individual products are performing country-wide, store-by-store at a glance. IT also supports Wal-Mart's efficient procurement.

A focused strategy is in place for human resource management and development. People are key to Wal-Mart's business and it invests time and money in training people, and retaining a developing them.

Weaknesses

Wal-Mart is the world's largest grocery retailer and control of its empire, despite its IT advantages, could leave it weak in some areas due to the huge span of control.

Since Wal-Mart sells products across many sectors (such as clothing, food, or stationary), it may not have the flexibility of some of its more focused competitors.

The company is global, but has a presence in relatively few countries worldwide.

Opportunities

To take over, merge with, or form strategic alliances with other global retailers, focusing on specific markets such as Europe or China.

The stores are currently only in a relatively small number of countries. Therefore there are tremendous opportunities for future business in expanding consumer markets, such as China and India.

New locations and store types offer Wal-Mart opportunities to exploit market development. They diversified from large super centres, to local and mall-based sites.

Opportunities exist for Wal-Mart to continue with its current strategy of large, super centres.

Threats

Being number one means that you are the target of competition, locally and globally.

Being a global retailer means that you are exposed to political problems in the countries that you operate in.

The cost of producing many consumer products tends to have fallen because of lower manufacturing costs. Manufacturing cost have fallen due to outsourcing to low-cost regions of the world. This has led to price competition, resulting in price deflation in some ranges. Intense price competition is a threat.

Wal-Mart Stores, Inc. is the world's largest retailer, with US$256.3 billion in sales in the fiscal year ending Jan. 31, 2004. The company employs 1.6 million associates worldwide through more than 3,600 facilities in the United States and more than 1,570 units . . .more? Go to Wal-Mart Facts.

Case II Starbucks SWOT Analysis

Strengths

Starbucks Corporation is a very profitable organization, earning in excess of US$600 million in 2004. The company generated revenue of more than US$5000 million in the same year.

It is a global coffee brand built upon a reputation for fine products and services.

It has almost 9000 cafe shop in almost 40 countries.

Starbucks was one of the Fortune Top 100 Companies to Work For in 2005.

The company is a respected employer that values its workforce.

The organization has strong ethical values and an ethical mission statement as follow, "Starbucks is committed to a role of environmental leadership in all facets of our business."

Weaknesses

Starbucks has a reputation for new product development and creativity.

However, it remains vulnerable to the possibility that its innovation may falter over time.

The organization has a strong presence in the United States of America with more than three quarters of its cafe shop located in the home market.

It is often argued that it need to look for a portfolio of countries, in order to spread business risk.

The organization is dependant on a main competitive advantage, the retail of coffee.

This could make it slow to diversify into other sectors should the need arise.

Opportunities

Starbucks is very good at taking advantage of opportunties.

In 2004 the company created a CD-burning service in its Santa Monica (California USA) cafe with Hewlett Packard, where customers create their own music CD.

New products and services that can be retailed in their cafe shop, such as low price products.

The company has the opportunity to expand its global operations.

New markets for coffee such as India and the Pacific Rim nations are beginning to emerge.

Co-branding with other manufacturers of food and drink, and brand franchising to manufacturers of other goods and services both have potential.

Threats

Who knows if the market for coffee will grow and stay in favour with customers, or whether another type of beverage or leisure activity will replace coffee in the future?

Starbucks is exposed to rises in the cost of coffee and dairy products.

Since its conception in Pike Place Market, Seattle in 1971, Starbucks' success has led to the market entry of many competitors and copy cat brands that pose potential threats.

"Starbucks" mission statement is "Establish Starbucks as the premier purveyor of the finest coffee in the world while maintaining our uncompromising principles while we grow."

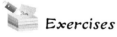 *Exercises*

I. Choose the correct answer according to Passage II.

1. What core competence does Wal-Mart have? (   )

A. The company has a core competence involving its abundant financial support.

B. The company has a core competence involving its use of information technology to support its international logistics system.

C. The company has a core competence involving a great deal of retail stores available.

D. Wal-Mart has grown substantially over recent years, and has experienced global expansion.

2. Wal-Mart's focused strategy is in place for_____. (   )

A. human resource management and development.

B. a reputation for value for money, convenience and a wide range of products all in one store.

C. the flexibility of some of its more focused competitors.

D. IT technologies

3. Starbucks is a global coffee brand built upon a reputation for_____. (   )

A. its advanced technologies

B. luxurious decoration of the cafe shops

C. fine products and services

D. good taste of the coffee

4. What's the ethical mission statement of Starbucks? (   )

A. Starbucks is committed to a role of environmental leadership in all facets of our business.

B. The company is a respected employer that values its workforce.

C. It is a global coffee brand built upon a reputation for fine products and services.

D. It has almost 9000 cafe shop in almost 40 countries.

5. Starbucks has a reputation for new product development and creativity. Here the word "reputation" means _____. (   )

A. chance

B. advantage

C. shortcoming

D. fame

II. Choose the best translation.

1. 沃尔玛是著名的零售商品牌，它以物美价廉、货物繁多和一站式购物而闻名。(   )

A. Wal-Mart is a powerful retail brand. It has a reputation for value for money, convenience and a wide range of products all in one store.

B. Wal-Mart retail brand is famous, it is famous for its good and inexpensive, goods is various and one-stop shopping.

C. Wal-Mart is famous for value for money, convenience and a wide range of products all in one store.

D. Wal-Mart retail brand is famous, it is famous for its good but inexpensive, various and one-stop shopping.

2. 沃尔玛的一个核心竞争力是由先进的信息技术所支持的国际化物流系统。(   )

A. Wal-mart is a core competence by advanced information technology supported by the international logistics system.

B. Wal-mart is has a core competence by advanced information technology supported by the international logistics system.

C. Wal-Mart has a core competence involving its use of information technology to support its international logistics system.

D. Wal-mart is a core competence by advanced information technology supporting by the international logistics system.

3. 星巴克公司是一个盈利能力很强的企业，它在 2004 年盈利超过六亿美元。（   ）

A. Starbucks Corporation is an organization that profit ability strong, it earned more than six hundred million in 2004.

B. Starbucks Corporation is a very profitable organization, earning in excess of $600 million in 2004.

C. Starbucks Corporation is an organization that profit ability strong, it earned more than six hundred billion in 2004.

D. Starbucks Corporation is a very profitable organization, earned in excess of $600 million in 2004.

4. 它对于美国市场的依赖度过高，超过四分之三的咖啡店都开在自己的老家。（   ）

A. It too dependent for the US market, more than three in four coffee shops are open in my own home.

B. It is too dependent for the US market, more than three in four coffee shops are open in their domestic market.

C. The organization has a strong presence in the United States of America with less than three quarters of their cafe shop in the home market.

D. The organization has a strong presence in the United States of America with more than three quarters of their cafe shop located in the home market.

5. 该组织依赖于一个主要的竞争优势，即零售咖啡。（   ）

A. The organization is dependent on a main competitive advantage, the retail of coffee.

B. The organization has a main competitive advantage, the retail of coffee.

C. The organization is selling the retail of coffee, it is a main advantage.

D. It is a main advantage that the organization sells the retail of coffee.

Special Terms

marketing mix	营销组合
marketing manager	营销经理
target market	目标市场
marketing communication	营销传播
social-media marketing	社交媒体营销
iterative nature	迭代性质
Portfolio	证券投资组合

Chapter Ten

New Economy and New Business

Text
Introduction to E-business Technology and E-business
Reading Skills (10)
Recognizing Important Facts or Details
Further Development
Passage I
Alipay to Launch in Europe as Alibaba Steps Up Payments Game
Passage II
It's So Hard to Get Cash in India That Some People Are Ordering It Online

This is the 10th Chapter of the book. In the first section, you will learn a text, and you will have some information about the benefit of E-business technology. In the second section, you will have a deeper understanding about E-business. In this section, you will learn two passages about E-business and they will help you have a further development on mastering reading skills of recorgnizing important facts or details.

Chapter Ten New Economy and New Business

Starter

When it comes to e-business, "e" stands for experience, endeavor and energy, and definitely not for easy. What does e-business really mean to you?

Text
Introduction to E-business Technology and E-business

The Benefits of E-Business Technology

The Internet has changed the way the world does business, and your company can take advantage of the technology for its own benefit. E-business is the process of exchanging date or information over the Internet while taking orders, placing orders or interacting with your own staff, according to online business resource to achieve e-commerce optimization. By understanding the benefits of e-commerce technology, your company can be better equipped to use the Internet as a business tool.

Everyone is Equal

When you are interacting with your clients or vendors using e-business, it is difficult for them to tell how big your business is. With a professionally developed and maintained website, any small business can look as impressive on the Internet as the large corporations do. It is a level playing field that helps create opportunity for small businesses.

Order Entry

An Internet order interface that is hooked directly into your real-time inventory software can allow customers to order products from your company 24 hours a day, seven days a week. You can save money on hiring a sales staff by opening up an order-entry section on your website for clients that want to make smaller orders, or for those that only order a few times a year. That frees up your sales professionals to go out and find new business.

Customer Service

E-Business can save you money on your customer service as well. By making your client's account information available on the Internet, customers can check their accounts whenever they want. By creating a customer service section on your website that allows customers to request return product authorizations, you can increase your customer service levels while lowering your cost of doing business.

Marketing

In the first quarter of 2010, consumers bought US$34 billion worth of products and services on the Internet, according to Antone Gonsalves writing for Information Week.com. There was also 1.1 trillion online advertisements created in the same period, according to Information Week.com. More consumers are using the Internet to get their product information, find vendors and buy products. An e-business presence can help put your company in touch with this growing retail sector.

The Advantages of E-Business

The Internet has been a door to a myriad of new business opportunities. Business owners of e-businesses and their customers find advantages in Internet transactions as opposed to brick-and-mortar operations. If you are thinking about starting an e-business or adding an online component to your existing business, discover some of the advantages an e-business offers.

Cost-Effective Marketing

With an e-business, all of your marketing efforts end with one goal to drive target traffic to your business website. With one central place to send customers, your e-business website allows you to use many online marketing tactics including email marketing, article marketing, social media networking and e-newsletters. Most of these online marketing efforts are very low cost or free, so an e-business allows for highly cost-effective marketing strategies.

Flexible Business Hours

E-business breaks down the time barriers that location-based businesses encounter, according to E-commerce Education. Because the Internet is available 24 hours a day, seven days a week, your business never closes. An e-business can literally be making money while you are fast asleep.

Eliminates Geographic Boundaries

An e-business also allows you to broaden your reach. An online business can reach customers in the four corners of the Earth. As long as someone has an Internet connection, you may be able to reach and sell your product or service to these visitors to your business website.

Reduces Transaction Cost

Running an online business reduces the cost per transaction because it takes less manpower to complete an online transaction. Once you get your website up and running, the customer places the order online, which removes the need for a salesperson. The customer payment goes through your online payment processing software or system eliminating the need for a store clerk. Someone has to download the order and ship it, which is probably you, but an e-business transaction has less burden of cost on the business, making each transaction more cost effective than a brick-and-mortar business.

Low Overhead Costs

Running an e-business cut back or out most of the costs involved in running a physical location. E-businesses have less expensive phone, rent and utility bills than businesses with physical locations. An e-business also reduces the cost of paying employees because you do not need someone to your website during business hours. Some e-businesses do not require any additional space and can be run out of your home, which you are already paying rent for or your mortgage payment. Even housing inventory may not be an issue because you may be able to establish a drop-shipping situation, where your wholesaler ships orders for you on behalf of your business.

E-Commerce Business Models

E-Commerce or Electronics Commerce business models can generally categorized in following categories.

Business-to-Business (B2B)
Business-to-Consumer (B2C)
Consumer-to-Consumer (C2C)
Consumer-to-Business (C2B)
Business-to-Government (B2G)
Government-to-Business (G2B)
Government-to-Citizen (G2C)

财经英语阅读（第2版）

Words and Terms

optimization [ˌɒptɪmaɪˈzeɪʃən]	n.	最佳化，最优化
interact [ɪntərˈækt]	v.	交流；相互作用
vendor [ˈvendə]	n.	供应商
interface [ˈɪntəfeɪs]	n.	界面；相互作用
hook [hʊk]	v.	用钩挂
trillion [ˈtrɪljən]	n.	万亿
myriad [ˈmɪrɪəd]	adj.	无数的
component [kəmˈpəʊnənt]	n.	成分；零件
tactic [ˈtæktɪk]	n.	战术；策略
barrier [ˈbærɪə]	n.	障碍
encounter [ɪnˈkaʊntə]	v.	相遇，碰见
take advantage of		利用
retail sector		零售部门
brick-and-mortar		实体的

Notes

1. E-business is the process of exchanging date or information over the Internet while taking orders, placing orders or interacting with your own staff, according to online business resource to achieve e-commerce optimization. 电子商务是通过在网上交换数据或信息接收订单，订货或与自己的员工进行互动，根据网上电子商务业务实现资源优化。

2. It is a level playing field that helps create opportunity for small businesses. 这个公平竞争的环境，会为小型企业创造机会。

3. By creating a customer service section on your website that allows customers to request return product authorizations, you can increase your customer service levels while lowering your cost of doing business. 通过创建网站客服部，客户有退货的权利，你可以在提升你的客户服务水平的同时降低经营成本。

4. Business owners of e-businesses and their customers find advantages in Internet transactions as opposed to brick-and-mortar operations. 电子商务企业和他们的客户发现与实体店不同的网上交易的优势。

5. With an e-business, all of your marketing efforts end with one goal to drive target traffic to your business website. 有了电子商务，你为营销做出的所有努力，都是为了驱动目标流量流向你的网站。

6. Someone has to download the order and ship it, which is probably you, but an e-business

transaction has less burden of cost on the business, making each transaction more cost effective than a brick-and-mortar business. 有人下载订单和装运，这个人也许是你，但一桩电子商务的交易成本对企业负担少，比实体店更符合成本效益。

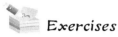

Exercises

I. Answer the following questions according to the text.

1. What benefit can e-business technology bring?
2. What are the advantages of e-business?
3. How many categories can e-business models be categorized?
4. How can e-business make everyone equal?
5. How can e-business serve customers better?

II. Identify the key words or main ideas of the following parts.

Part 1	The _____ of e-business technology: 1. _____ 2. _____ 3. _____ 4. _____
Part 2	The _____ of e-business: 1. _____ 2. _____ 3. _____ 4. _____ 5. _____
Part 3	E-commerce business models can be categorized in _____ categories.

III. Match the words or phrases in Column A to the words or phrases in Column B.

A		B
1. _____	interact	A. 供应商
2. _____	vendor	B. 授权
3. _____	brick-and-mortar	C. 互动
4. _____	authorization	D. 实体的
5. _____	encounter	E. 技巧
6. _____	tactic	F. 遭遇，遇见
7. _____	retail sector	G. 零售部门
8. _____	trillion	H. 利用
9. _____	interface	I. 万亿
10. _____	take advantage of	J. 界面

IV. Choose the best translation.

1. By understanding the benefits of e-commerce technology, your company can be better equipped to use the Internet as a business tool. (　　)

   A. 通过了解电子商务技术的好处，你的公司可以更好地利用互联网作为一种商业工具。
   B. 了解了电子商务的好处，你的公司可以更好地配备互联网作为工具。
   C. 了解了电子商务的好处，你的公司会有更好的设备，把互联网当作商务工具。
   D. 通过了解电子商务技术的好处，你的公司互联网工具设备会更好。

2. An e-business presence can help put your company in touch with this growing retail sector. (　　)

   A. 电子商务的出现让零售部门不断增加与你的公司的联系。
   B. 电子商务的存在可以帮助你的公司与这个不断增长的零售部门联系。
   C. 电子商务的出现可以帮助贵公司在这个增长的零售部门的触摸。
   D. 电子商务的出现让你的公司不断地与零售部门取得联系。

3. Running an online business reduces the cost per transaction because it takes less manpower to complete an online transaction. (　　)

   A. 跑一个网上业务可以减少交易成本，因为它需要花费很少的力气去完成。
   B. 因为网上交易需要很少的人，所以在线交易可以省成本。
   C. 经营在线交易可以降低成本，因为需要很少的人去完成网上交易。
   D. 运行一个在线业务降低了每次交易的成本，因为它需要较少的人力完成在线交易。

4. An Internet order interface that is hooked directly into your real-time inventory software can allow customers to order products from your company 24 hours a day, seven days a week. (　　)

   A. 一个网上订单的界面，直接连接进入你的实时库存软件，能让客户一天 24 小时从你的公司订购产品，一周七天。
   B. 一个网上订单的界面，勾住你的实时库存软件，让客户一天 24 小时从你的公司订购产品，一周七天。
   C. 一个网上订单的界面能让客户直接从你的实时库存软件一天 24 小时订购产品，每周七天。
   D. 一个网上订单的界面能让客户直接从你的实时库存软件每周七天，每天 24 小时订购你的产品。

5. When you are interacting with your clients or vendors using e-business, it is difficult for them to tell how big your business is. (　　)

   A. 当你与客户或者供应商使用电子商务联系时，一般很难向他们描述你的业务的大小。
   B. 当你用电子商务与你的客户或供应商互动，一般很难跟他们描述你的业务到底有多大。
   C. 你在用电子商务互动时，会很难向客户或者卖主描述你的业务量大小。
   D. 当你与客户和卖主互动时，你很难说业务是做得有多大。

Chapter Ten New Economy and New Business

Reading Skills (10)
Recognizing Important Facts or Details

  Being able to recognizing the important facts or details is the key to reading comprehension. Then, what are facts or details? Facts are statements that tell what really happens or what the case is, and they are usually based on direct evidences. When you read an article, the question you should always bears in mind is: What facts are presented in the article? What evidence does the author include to support statements of fact? Usually you can find them by answering the 5 Ws (who, what, where, when and why).

  Besides these, to understand the main idea thoroughly, you must go even further to recognize the important facts or details within a context. These facts and details give you a deeper understanding of the passage you read. They may establish a point, show a relationship between ideas, or serve as examples to help you understand the main idea more fully. If adding up the facts or details does not lead logically to the main idea, you have failed either to identify the main idea or to recognize the important supporting details.

  Details are of little value unless they support the main idea, help to draw some conclusion, or answer a need for the reader. On the other hand, they are necessary in order to explain thoroughly the ideas the author is trying to get across. There is no way to remember all the details you read; therefore, it is advisable to separate the major and minor details. A major detail is is one that supports the main idea. If a major detail were omitted, the meaning could be changed or would be incomplete. Minor details are interesting and make the material more readable, but they do not alter the essence of what the writer is trying to get across. You should select details in accordance with the main idea or to fit the purpose for which you are reading.

  Here are some ways to help you recognize important facts or details:

  Bears the 5 Ws (who, what, where, when and why) in mind and try to find out the keys to these questions.

  After reading the following paragraph, please circle the most important fact and check the least important detail.

  Keep it in mind that not all facts or details are equally important. Look only for the facts related to the main idea.

  To check on your understanding of the material you have read, review the facts or details which you have decided are the most important. Consider if they support what you have identified as the main idea. If adding up the facts or details does not lead logically to the main idea, you have failed either to identify the main idea or to select the important supporting details.

Further Development

Passage I

Alipay to Launch in Europe as Alibaba Steps Up Payments Game

Alipay, the payment app run by Alibaba's affiliate Ant Financial, is launching in Europe to allow Chinese tourists to pay for things abroad, in its biggest push out of Asia yet.

The app will recognize where the Chinese Alipay user is in Europe and send notifications about where to eat, shopping offers and places to see. There are also user reviews on the app. When a user attempts to pay, a barcode will be shown on a person's device which the merchant can scan.

Alipay is one of China's biggest payment services and competes with Tencent's WeChat Payment. Alipay is deeply ingrained in the lives of Chinese consumers and is used to pay for items in-store and online for goods and services ranging from taxis to restaurants and clothing.

Alibaba is hoping that its active Alipay users, which now total 450 million, according to the company, will continue to use the app abroad allowing the company to take advantage of the increasing number of Chinese tourists who are spending more.

"The vision is targeting two billion people within next five to ten years, not only in China but other countries too," Sabrina Peng, president of Alipay International, told CNBC at the Money 2020 fintech conference in Copenhagen on Tuesday.

Partnerships Key

Chinese tourists spent US$215 billion abroad last year, a 53 percent rise from 2014, according to the World Travel & Tourism Council. Alipay is hoping that much of this spending will be through its app.

Ant Financial said that Alipay was used by 120 million users abroad last year and told CNBC that globally, it now processes 170 million transactions per day.

Alipay has been expanding out of China in recent times. Alibaba and Ant Financial upped their stake in Indian payments firm Paytm last year as it looks to expand into India. Peng revealed to CNBC that the company is "actively looking" for more partners in Asia as it looks to go deeper into the region.

But the firm does not plan to invest heavily in payment firms in Europe just yet. Ant Financial is talking to a number of partners from financial institutions to restaurants and theatres across Europe to get them on board with Alipay. Merchants will be able to view the shopping habits on Chinese consumers spending in their stores through Alipay's dashboard.

Last year, it struck a deal with Wirecard, a German payment processing company, which will let merchants using Wirecard's point-of-sales terminals accept Chinese visitors' purchases made with Alipay.

Partnerships will be key for the platform in order to get merchants sending through offers and deals. Alipay does not compete directly with the likes of Samsung Pay and Apple Pay as both services just allow people to purchase items with their phone. Instead, with the focus on allowing merchants to use Alipay to help market to customers and learn their behavior, Ant Financial sees it as a tool to drive revenues.

"Merchants are not crying for another payment solution. What they want is more business. We are not a payment service, we are more than payments. Payment is very critical part of the circle, it is not the only part of the circle," Peng told CNBC. "For merchants it's the same story, they want to know Chinese consumers, Asian consumers, Japanese, Korean, Indians, but it's hard for them to know their overseas customer because they lack a platform. That's what we are doing: connecting consumers and merchants together to help them connect better."

Peng did admit that finding local partners was "a bit challenging" given the scale of customers the company needs to get on board.

Chinese consumers will be able to use Alipay in the U.K., Germany, France and Italy to begin with starting in the summer.

 Words and Terms

affiliate [əˈfɪlieɪt]	n.	分支机构
barcode [bɑːˈkəʊd]	n.	条形码
ingrain [ˈɪnˈɡreɪn]	v.	使根深蒂固
transaction [trænˈzækʃn]	n.	交易
stake [steɪk]	n.	赌注，股份
dashboard [ˈdæʃbɔːd]	n.	仪表盘
revenue [ˈrevənjuː]	n.	收入
Alipay		支付宝
Ant Financial		蚂蚁金融
WeChat Payment		微信支付

Samsung Pay　　　　　　　　三星支付
Apple Pay　　　　　　　　　苹果支付

 *Notes*

1. The app will recognize where the Chinese Alipay user is in Europe and send notifications about where to eat, shopping offers and places to see. There are also user reviews on the app. When a user attempts to pay, a barcode will be shown on a person's device which the merchant can scan. 该应用程序将识别中国的支付宝用户在欧洲的地址，将发送就餐、优惠购物和景点通知。该应用上也有用户评论。用户想要支付的话，只要让商家扫描用户手机上的条形码就可以了。

2. Alipay is deeply ingrained in the lives of Chinese consumers and is used to pay for items in-store and online for goods and services ranging from taxis to restaurants and clothing. 支付宝已经深入中国消费者的生活。人们不管是乘车、餐馆就餐还是购物都用它来支付。

3. "The vision is targeting two billion people within next five to ten years, not only in China but other countries too," Sabrina Peng, president of Alipay International, told CNBC at the Money 2020 fintech conference in Copenhagen on Tuesday. "在未来的五到十年，不仅在中国，其他国家也一样，预计目标是二十亿人使用支付宝，"支付宝国际主席塞布丽娜·彭在星期二哥本哈根的 Money2020 会议上告诉美国全国广播公司财经频道记者。

CNBC 为美国全国广播公司(NBC)环球集团所持有的全球性财经有线电视卫星新闻频道，是全球财经媒体中公认的佼佼者，其深入的分析和实时报道赢得了全球企业界的信任。

4. Last year, it struck a deal with Wirecard, a German payment processing company, which will let merchants using Wirecard's point-of-sales terminals accept Chinese visitors' purchases made with Alipay. 去年，它与德国银行软件公司 Wirecard 达成协议，让商家通过使用 Wirecard 销售点终端接受中国游客使用支付宝。

 Exercises

I. Read the following statements and decide whether they are True(T) or False (F).

1. Chinese tourists will be allowed to pay for things in Europe in the future. 　　(　　)

2. The app will not recognize where the Chinese Alipay user is in Europe and can't send notifications about where to eat, shopping offers and places to see. 　　(　　)

3. But the firm does plan to invest heavily in payment firms in Europe. 　　(　　)

4. Alipay is one of China's biggest payment services and competes with Tencent's WeChat Payment. 　　(　　)

5. Alipay does not compete directly with the likes of Samsung Pay and Apple Pay as both services just allow people to purchase items with their phone. 　　(　　)

Chapter Ten New Economy and New Business

II. Choose the correct answer according to Passage I.

1. Alipay is launching in _____ to allow Chinese tourists to pay for things abroad, in its biggest push out of Asia yet. (   )
   A. India
   B. Africa
   C. America
   D. Europe

2. Alipay is one of China's biggest payment services and competes with _____ . (   )
   A. Apple Pay
   B. Tencent's WeChat Payment
   C. Samsung Pay
   D. QQ Payment

3. According to the World Travel & Tourism Council, Chinese tourists spent US$215 billion abroad last year, a _____ rise from 2014. (   )
   A. 53 percent
   B. 54 percent
   C. 55percent
   D. 56 percent

4. _____ will be key for the platform in order to get merchants sending through offers and deals. (   )
   A. Opportunities
   B. Partnerships
   C. Money
   D. Consumers

5. Chinese consumers will be able to use _____ in the U.K., Germany, France and Italy to begin with starting in the summer. (   )
   A. Tencent's WeChat
   B. Alipay
   C. Apple Pay
   D. Samsung Pay

III. Fill in the missing information.

Alipay, the payment app run by Alibaba's affiliate Ant Financial, is _____ in Europe to allow Chinese tourists to pay for things abroad, in its biggest push out of Asia yet.

The _____ will recognize where the Chinese Alipay user is in Europe and send _____ about where to eat, shopping offers and places to see. There are also user reviews on the app. When a user attempts to pay, a _____ will be shown on a person's device which the _____ can scan.

167

Passage II

It's So Hard to Get Cash in India
That Some People Are Ordering It Online

As millions of Indians line up to try and get their hands on cash, an e-commerce company has started delivering it to their doorsteps.

It's a response to the Indian government's sudden ban on 500 and 1,000 rupee notes six weeks ago, which removed 86% of the country's cash and has left people struggling to get money for their daily needs.

Snapdeal, one of India's biggest online retailers, has added rupee notes to the hundreds of products it already offers. Users can get up to 2,000 rupees (US$30) in cash by swiping their debit cards through a machine carried by the company's couriers and paying a one rupee commission.

The pilot program debuted Thursday in the cities of Gurgaon and Bangalore. Snapdeal is using the rupee notes it receives from cash-on-delivery transactions, a popular method of paying even for online goods in India.

A company spokeswoman declined to give exact figures, but told CNN Money that it has already received a "significant number" of requests for cash.

Many Indians are switching to digital payment methods, but those who can't have few options but to spend hours waiting in line at banks or ATMs. And for a country where more than 90% of daily transactions are estimated to take place in cash, the shift away from paper currency is a huge task.

Snapdeal's initiative is the latest inventive workaround to the cash shortage. Some banks have provided ATM buses, and one company even let people hire helpers that will stand in line for them.

"The launch of the cash on demand service is intended to further help our consumers tide over any cash crunch that they might face in addressing their daily needs," Snapdeal co-founder Rohit Bansal said in a statement.

Chapter Ten New Economy and New Business

The company said it plans to expand the cash delivery service to other Indian cities in the coming weeks.

Exercises

I. Choose the correct answer according to Passage II.

1. An e-commerce company has started_____ it to their doorsteps. (   )
A. giving
B. delivering
C. transporting
D. shipping

2. Many Indians are _____ to digital payment methods. (   )
A. switching
B. using
C. determined
D. going

3. Snapdeal, one of India's biggest online _____, has added rupee notes to the hundreds of products it already offers. (   )
A. company
B. corporation
C. retailers
D. wholesaler

II. Choose the best translation.

1. 数百万印度人为了取现金而大排长龙，为此一家电子商务公司开始提供现金快递上门服务。(   )
   A. Millions of Indians line up to try and get cash, an e-commerce company has started to deliver it to their customers.
   B. As millions of Indians line up to try and get their hands on cash, an e-commerce company has started delivering it to their doorsteps.
   C. Millions of Indians go out to queue for cash, an e-commerce company has started to deliver it to their customers.
   D. As millions of Indians line up to try and get cash, an e-commerce company supplies money door to door.

2. 这一试点计划已于周四在古尔冈和班加罗尔推行。(   )
   A. The trial plan started on Tuesday in Gurgaon and Bangalore.
   B. The plan try to started on Tuesday in Gurgaon and Bangalore.
   C. The trial plan started on Thursday in Gurgaon and Bangalore.
   D. The pilot program debuted Thursday in the cities of Gurgaon and Bangalore.

3. Snapdeal 的计划是为解决现金短缺问题而发明的最新变通方案。（　　）
A. Snapdeal's initiative is the latest inventive workaround to the cash shortage.
B. Snapdeal's plan is to solve the problem of cash shortage and to invent new method.
C. Snapdeal plans to invent new method to solve the problem of cash shortage.
D. Snapdeal's initiative is the latest method to solve cash shortage.

4. 该公司一位发言人拒绝透露确切的数字。（　　）
A. Spokeswoman from the company rejected the exact numbers.
B. A company spokeswoman declined to tell the specific numbers.
C. A company spokeswoman declined to give exact figures.
D. Spokeswoman from the company didn't want to show the exact figures.

5. 该公司表示，他们计划在未来几周内将现金快递服务扩展至印度其他城市。（　　）
A. The company demonstrated that they will expand the cash delivery service to other Indian cities in a few weeks.
B. The company expressed that they will deliver service of cash to other cities in India in some weeks.
C. The company said it is going to extend their cash service of delivery to other India cities in a few weeks.
D. The company said it plans to expand the cash delivery service to other Indian cities in the coming weeks.

Special Terms

interface	界面
trillion	万亿
Alipay	支付宝
barcode	条形码
transaction	交易
tactic	战术；策略
stake	赌注，股份
retail sector	零售部门
affiliate	分支机构
brick and mortar	实体的
Ant Financial	蚂蚁金融
WeChat Payment	微信支付
Samsung Pay	三星支付
Apple Pay	苹果支付
online retailers	网上零售商
cash-on-delivery	货到付款

Chapter Eleven

Multinational Companies

Text
The US-based Multinational Company Wal-Mart
Reading Skills (11)
Note-taking and Thinking
Further Development
Passage I
An American Hamburger and Fast Food Restaurant Chain——McDonald's
Passage II
Toyota-Suzuki Alliance Marks Auto Industry Fight for Survival

This is the 11th chapter of the book. In the first section, you will learn a text, and you will have some information about the US-based multinational company Wal-Mart. In the second section, you will have a deeper understanding about multinational companies. In this section, you will learn two passages and they will help you have a further development on mastering reading skills of note-taking and thinking.

Starter

The world's 500 largest companies generated US$27.6 trillion in revenues and US$1.5 trillion in profits in 2015. Together, 2016 Fortune Global 500 companies employ 67 million people worldwide and are represented by 33 countries. Do you know which company is the world's No.1 in the Forbes Fortune 500 list in 2016?

Text
The US-based Multinational Company Wal-Mart

The Introduction to Wal-Mart

A multinational corporation (MNC) has facilities and other assets in at least one country other than its home country. Such companies have offices and/or factories in different countries and usually have a centralized head office where they coordinate global management. Nearly all major multinationals are either American, Japanese or Western European, such as Nike, Coca-Cola, Wal-Mart, AOL, Toshiba, Honda and BMW.

Wal-Mart is an American multinational retail corporation that operates a chain of Hypermarkets, discount department stores and grocery stores. Headquartered in Bentonville, Arkansas, the company was founded by Sam Walton in 1962. As of September 30, 2016, Wal-Mart has 11,573 stores and clubs in 28 countries, under a total of 63 banners.

Wal-Mart is the world's largest company by revenue, according to the Fortune Global 500 list in 2016, as well as the largest private employer in the world with 2.2 million employees. Wal-Mart is a family-owned business, as the company is controlled by the Walton family. Sam Walton's heirs own over 50 percent of Wal-Mart through their holding company, Walton Enterprises, and through their individual holdings. It is also one of the world's most valuable companies by market value, and is also the largest grocery retailer in the U.S. In 2016, 62.3 percent of Wal-Mart's US$478.614 billion sales came from its U.S. operations.

Wal-Mart's investments outside North America have seen mixed results: its operations in the United Kingdom, South America and China are highly successful, whereas ventures in Germany and Korea failed.

Wal-Mart as we know it today evolved from Sam Walton's goals for great value and great customer service. "Mr. Sam," as he was known, believed in leadership through service. This belief that true leadership depends on willing service was the principle on which Wal-Mart was built, and drove the decisions the company has made for the past 50 years. So much of Wal-Mart's history is tied to the story of Sam Walton himself, and so much of our future will be rooted in Mr. Sam's principles.

The Road to Wal-Mart

Sam Walton was born in 1918 in Kingfisher, Oklahoma. In 1942, at the age of 24, he joined the military. He married Helen Robson in 1943. When his military service ended in 1945, Sam and Helen moved to Iowa and then to Newport, Arkansas. During this time, Sam gained early retail experience, eventually operating his own variety store.

In 1950, the Waltons left Newport for Bentonville, where Sam opened Walton's 5&10 on the downtown square. They chose Bentonville because Helen wanted small-town living, and Sam could take advantage of the different hunting seasons that living at the corner of four states had to offer.

Inspired by the early success of his dime store, and driven to bring even greater opportunity and value to his customers, Sam opened the first Wal-Mart in 1962 at the age of 44 in Rogers, Arkansas.

Changing the Face of Retail

Sam's competitors thought his idea that a successful business could be built around offering lower prices and great service would never work. As it turned out, the company's success exceeded even Sam's expectations. The company went public in 1970, and the proceeds financed a steady expansion of the business. Sam credited the rapid growth of Wal-Mart not just to the low costs that attracted his customers, but also to his associates. He relied on them to give customers the great shopping experience that would keep them coming back. Sam shared his vision for the company with associates in a way that was nearly unheard of in the industry. He made them partners in the success of the company, and firmly believed that this partnership was what made Wal-Mart great.

As the stores grew, so did Sam's aspirations. In addition to bringing new approaches and technologies to retail, he also experimented with new store formats—including Sam's Club and the

Wal-Mart Supercenter—and even made the decision to take Wal-Mart into Mexico. Sam's fearlessness in offering lower prices and bringing Wal-Mart's value to customers in the U.S. and beyond set a standard for the company that lives on to this day. His strong commitment to service and to the values that help individuals, businesses and the country succeed earned him the Presidential Medal of Freedom, awarded by President George H. W. Bush in 1992. Today, "saving people money so they can live better" is the driving force behind everything we do.

Every Day Low Price (EDLP)

Every Day Low Price (EDLP) is the cornerstone of our strategy, and our price focus has never been stronger. Today's customer seeks the convenience of one-stop shopping that we offer. From grocery and entertainment to sporting goods and crafts, we provide the deep assortment that our customers appreciate — whether they're shopping online at Wal-Mart.com, through one of our mobile apps or shopping in a store. We currently operate three primary store formats in the U.S., each custom tailored to its neighborhood.

Our Stores

Wal-Mart has stores in 50 states and Puerto Rico offering low prices on the broadest assortment of products through a variety of formats including the supercenter, discount store and neighborhood market.

Wal-Mart Supercenter

Wal-Mart began building supercenters in 1988 and are around 182,000 square feet employing about 300 associates. Wal-Mart Supercenters offer a one-stop shopping experience by combining a grocery store with fresh produce, bakery, deli and dairy products with electronics, apparel, toys and home furnishings. Most supercenters are open 24 hours, and may also include specialty shops such as banks, hair and nail salons, restaurants, or vision centers.

Words and Terms

retail [ˈriːteɪl]	n.	零售
hypermarket [ˈhaɪpəmɑːkɪt]	n.	特大型超级市场
revenue [ˈrevənjuː]	n.	收益
principle [ˈprɪnsəpl]	n.	原则
expectation [ekspekˈteɪʃ(ə)n]	n.	期待，预期
finance [ˈfaɪnæns]	v.	供给……经费，筹措资金
associate [əˈsəʊʃɪeɪt]	n.	同事，伙伴
partnership [ˈpɑːtnəʃɪp]	n.	合伙，合作关系
aspiration [æspəˈreɪʃ(ə)n]	n.	渴望、抱负
approach [əˈprəʊtʃ]	n.	方法
commitment [kəˈmɪtm(ə)nt]	n.	承诺，保证

Chapter Eleven　Multinational Companies

multinational company	跨国公司
global management	全球管理
customer service	客户服务
grocery store	杂货店
store format	商店模式
one-stop shopping	一站式购物
supercenter	超级购物中心
discount store	折扣商店
neighborhood market	社区超市

 Notes

1. Wal-Mart is the world's largest company by revenue, according to the Fortune Global 500 list in 2016, as well as the largest private employer in the world with 2.2 million employees. 根据2016年"《财富》世界500强"排行榜，沃尔玛是全球最大的盈利公司，也是拥有220万员工的世界最大的私营雇主。Fortune Global 500 list:《财富》世界500强排行榜是美国财富杂志每年评选的"全球最大五百家公司"排行榜。它一直是衡量全球大型公司的最著名、最权威的榜单，由《财富》杂志每年发布一次。

2. Sam Walton's heirs own over 50 percent of Wal-Mart through their holding company, Walton Enterprises, and through their individual holdings. It is also one of the world's most valuable companies by market value, and is also the largest grocery retailer in the U.S. 山姆·沃尔顿的继承人通过他们的持股公司(沃尔顿企业有限公司)和个人股份，拥有超过50%的沃尔玛股份。沃尔玛还是全世界市场价值最高的公司和全美国最大的食品零售商。

3. The company went public in 1970, and the proceeds financed a steady expansion of the business. Sam credited the rapid growth of Wal-Mart not just to the low costs that attracted his customers, but also to his associates. 1970年，这家公司公开上市，所获得的收益为其稳定的扩张提供了资金。山姆认为，沃尔玛的快速发展不仅仅是低价格吸引了顾客，主要还是归功于他的同事们。

4. Every Day Low Price (EDLP) is the cornerstone of our strategy, and our price focus has never been stronger. 天天低价是我们的基本策略，我们最关注的就是价格。
Every Day Low Price (EDLP)：天天低价是美国沃尔玛首先提出来的促销口号，但已广泛被各商家使用。它是指折扣零售业者(例如综合超市)所采取的价格策略，亦即每天都保持较低的价格及毛利来运作，目的是吸引大量客流前来消费。

5. Wal-Mart has stores in 50 states and Puerto Rico offering low prices on the broadest assortment of products through a variety of formats including the Supercenter, Discount Store and Neighborhood Market. 沃尔玛在50个州和波多黎各以低价格提供最广泛种类的产品，经营模式多样包括超级购物中心、折扣商店和社区超市。

Puerto Rico：波多黎各(Puerto Rico)是美国在加勒比海地区的一个自治领地，正式名称是

财经英语阅读（第 2 版）

波多黎各自由邦(英语：The Commonwealth of Puerto Rico，西班牙语：Estado Libre Asociado de Puerto Rico)，圣胡安为其首府。波多黎各是大安的列斯群岛四个大岛中最小的一个岛，位于多米尼加共和国东面，在小安的列斯群岛西北。它包含一个主岛和若干小岛。整个地区分为 78 个市级行政区。

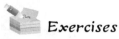 *Exercises*

I. Answer the following questions according to the text.

1. What is a multinational company?
2. What was the principle on which Wal-Mart was built?
3. How did Sam share his vision for the company with his associates?
4. Why did Sam Walton get the Presidential Medal of Freedom?
5. What kind of shopping experience do Wal-Mart Supercenters offer?

II. Identify the key words of main ideas of the following parts.

Part 1	The _____ to Wal-Mart
Part 2	The _____ to Wal-Mart
Part 3	Changing the Face of _____
Part 4	Every Day _____
Part 5	Our _____
Part 6	Wal-Mart _____

III. Match the words or phrases in Column A to the words or phrases in Column B.

A　　　　　　　　　　　　　　　B

1. _____ partnership　　　　A. 全球管理
2. _____ multinational company　B. 资产
3. _____ store format　　　　C. 一站式购物
4. _____ global management　　D. 合作关系
5. _____ asset　　　　　　　　E. 跨国公司
6. _____ one-stop shopping　　F. 经营形式
7. _____ customer service　　G. 供给……经费
8. _____ hypermarket　　　　　H. 收益
9. _____ finance　　　　　　　I. 特大型超级市场
10. _____ revenue　　　　　　J. 客户服务

IV. Choose the best translation.

1. Wal-Mart is an American multinational retail corporation that operates a chain of hypermarkets, discount department stores and grocery stores. (　　)

Chapter Eleven　Multinational Companies

A. 沃尔玛是总部位于法国的跨国零售企业，经营连锁的特大型超市、折扣百货商店和杂货店。
B. 沃尔玛是总部位于美国的跨国批发企业，经营连锁的特大型超市、折扣百货商店和杂货店。
C. 沃尔玛是总部位于英国的跨国零售企业，经营着分散的特大型超市、百货商店和杂货店。
D. 沃尔玛是总部位于美国的跨国零售企业，经营连锁的特大型超市、折扣百货商店和杂货店。

2. Sam Walton's heirs own over 50 percent of Wal-Mart through their holding company, Walton Enterprises, and through their individual holdings. (　　)

A. 山姆·沃尔顿的后裔通过他们的下属公司(沃尔顿企业有限公司)和个人股份，拥有超过50%的沃尔玛股份。
B. 山姆·沃尔顿的继承人通过他们的持股公司(沃尔顿企业有限公司)和个人股份，拥有超过50%的沃尔玛股份。
C. 山姆·沃尔顿的后裔通过他们的持股公司(沃尔顿企业有限公司)和个人股份，拥有少于50%的沃尔玛股份。
D. 山姆·沃尔顿的继承人通过他们的连锁公司(沃尔顿企业有限公司)和个人股份，拥有超过50%的沃尔玛股份。

3. The company went public in 1970, and the proceeds financed a steady expansion of the business. (　　)

A. 1970年，这家公司公开上市，所获得的收益为其稳定的扩张提供了资金。
B. 1970年，这家公司公开出售，所获得的收益为其稳定的扩张提供了资金。
C. 1970年，这家公司公开上市，所获得的资产为其稳定的扩张提供了资金。
D. 1970年，这家公司公开上市，所获得的收益为其稳定的发展提供了资金。

4. Sam's fearlessness in offering lower prices and bringing Wal-Mart's value to customers in the U.S. and beyond set a standard for the company that lives on to this day. (　　)

A. 山姆无惧提供高价并让利于美国的顾客，除此之外，他还为公司设计了一个使之存活至今的标准。
B. 山姆惧怕提供低价并让利于美国的顾客，除此之外，他还为公司选择了一个使之存活至今的标准。
C. 山姆无惧提供低价并让利于美国的顾客，除此之外，他还为公司设定了一个使之存活至今的标准。
D. 山姆惧怕提供低价并让利于美国的顾客，除此之外，他还为公司设定了一个使之存活至今的规定。

5. We currently operate three primary store formats in the U.S., each custom tailored to its neighborhood. (　　)

A. 我们现在在美国有五种主要的商店形式，每一种都是根据附近社区的特点量身定制的。
B. 我们现在在美国有三种主要的分销模式，每一种都是根据附近社区的特点量身定制的。

177

C. 我们现在在美国有三种主要的经营模式，每一种都是根据附近社区的特点量身定制的。

D. 我们现在在中国有六种主要的企业模式，每一种都是根据附近小区的特点量身定制的。

Reading Skills (11)
Note-taking and Thinking

It is said that over 50 percent of the material read or heard in class is forgotten in a matter of minutes. Taking notes can trigger recall and overcome forgetting, so it is a very important learning tool and useful not only in reading, writing but also in studying. For your course work, you will often need to look back at what you've learned from your reading. If you had the time and energy, you could just reread all the material from beginning to end. But reviewing the material is easier and quicker if you identify and mark important information the first time you read it.

Features of Good Notes

Efficient and effective notes generally display the following features.

(1) They are organized into key points and minor points.

(2) They record relevant source/bibliographical details, eg. author, title, publisher, date of publication, page number.

(3) They use visual techniques, eg. highlighting, graphics, colors, and underlining to identify main points.

(4) They use abbreviations and symbols to show connections between key points and minor points.

(5) They have line spaces so that you can add to your notes later, eg. for revision.

You need to adapt your note taking style to suit your purpose. To do this, you will need to think critically, and be prepared, so that your notes are systematic, organized, and help you to effectively recall, understand and apply information. Note making is also an important step in developing your understanding.

Before Reading

Ask questions before you read.

(1) Why am I reading this?

(2) What do I need to understand?

(3) How does this information relate/compare to other topics and information?

(4) What do I need to remember?

(5) What are the main points?

During Reading

Read actively and effectively.

(1) Clarify your purpose.

(2) Consult study guides and subject outlines.

(3) Keep the main subject headings firmly in mind.

(4) Turn chapter headings into questions.

(5) Seek answers to these questions through your reading.

(6) Always keep pen and paper handy – for note taking, and for highlighting main points.

After Reading

Evaluate the relevance and validity of what you have read.

(1) Who is the author and what is their motive for writing this?

(2) Who is the target audience? Is bias apparent?

(3) What methodology has been used?

(4) What conclusions are reached?

(5) Does the author justify these conclusions?

(6) How does the study relate to broader issues?

Note-taking Strategies

1. Be selective and systematic

As you take notes from a written source, keep in mind that not all of a text may be relevant to your needs. Think about your purpose for reading.

(1) Are you reading for a general understanding of a topic or concept?

(2) Are you reading for some specific information that may relate to the topic of an assignment?

Before you start to take notes, skim the text. Then highlight or mark the main points and any relevant information you may need to take notes from. Finally — keeping in mind your purpose for reading — read the relevant sections of the text carefully and take separate notes as you read.

2. Identify the purpose and function of a text

Whether you need to make notes on a whole text or just part of it, identifying the main purpose and function of a text is invaluable for clarifying your note-taking purposes and saving time.

(1) Read the title and the abstract or preface (if there is one).

(2) Read the introduction or first paragraph.

(3) Skim the text to read topic headings and notice how the text is organized.

(4) Read graphic material and predict its purpose in the text.

Your aim is to identify potentially useful information by getting an initial overview of the text (chapter, article, pages) that you have selected to read. Ask yourself: will this text give me the information I require and where might it be located in the text?

3. Identify how information is organized

Most texts use a range of organizing principles to develop ideas. While most good writing will have a logical order, not all writers will use an organizing principle. Organizing principles tend to sequence information into a logical hierarchy, some of which are:

(1) Past ideas to present ideas.

(2) The steps or stages of a process or event.

(3) Most important point to least important point.

(4) Well known ideas to least known ideas.

(5) Simple ideas to complex ideas.

(6) General ideas to specific ideas.

(7) The largest parts to the smallest parts of something.

(8) Problems and solutions.

(9) Causes and results.

An Example: Look at the text on underwater cameras and then look at how the text is presented in note form. The most important words to include in notes are the information words. These are usually nouns, adjectives and verbs.

4. Record your thoughts

When taking notes for an assignment, it is also helpful to record your thoughts at the time. Record your thoughts in a separate column or margin and in a different color to the notes you took from the text.

(1) What ideas did you have about your assignment when you read that information?

(2) How do you think you could use this information in your assignment?

Further Development

Passage I

An American Hamburger and Fast Food Restaurant Chain—McDonald's

McDonald's is an American hamburger and fast food restaurant chain. Today, McDonald's is one of the world's largest restaurant chains, serving approximately 68 million customers daily in 119 countries across approximately 36,615 outlets. McDonald's primarily sells hamburgers, cheeseburgers, chicken products, French fries, wraps, breakfast items, soft drinks, milkshakes, and desserts. In response to changing consumer tastes, the company has expanded its menu to include salads, fish, smoothies and fruit. A McDonald's restaurant is operated by either a franchisee, an affiliate, or the corporation itself. The McDonald's corporation revenues come from the rent, royalties, and fees paid by the franchisees, as well as sales in company-operated restaurants. According to a BBC report published in 2012, McDonald's is the world's second largest private employer (behind Walmart with 1.9 million employees), 1.5 million of whom work for franchises.

Chapter Eleven Multinational Companies

The History of McDonald's

In 1917, 15-year-old Ray Kroc lied about his age to join the Red Cross as an ambulance driver, but the war ended before he completed his training. He then worked as a piano player, a paper cup salesman and a multimixer salesman. In 1954, he visited a restaurant in San Bernardino, California that had purchased several multimixers. There he found a small but successful restaurant run by brothers Dick and Mac McDonald, and was stunned by the efficiency of their operation. They produced a limited menu, concentrating on just a few items — burgers, fries and beverages — which allowed them to focus on quality and quick service.

They were looking for a new agent and Kroc saw an opportunity. In 1955, he founded McDonald's System, Inc., a predecessor of the McDonald's Corporation, and six years later bought the exclusive rights to the McDonald's name. By 1958, McDonald's had sold its 100 millionth hamburger.

Ray Kroc wanted to build a restaurant system that would be famous for providing food of consistently high quality and uniform methods of preparation. He wanted to serve burgers, buns, fries and beverages that tasted just the same in Alaska as they did in Alabama. To achieve this, he chose a unique path: persuading both franchisees and suppliers to buy into his vision, working not for McDonald's but for themselves, together with McDonald's. He promoted the slogan, "In business for yourself, but not by yourself." His philosophy was based on the simple principle of a 3-legged stool: one leg was McDonald's franchisees; the second, McDonald's suppliers; and the third, McDonald's employees. The stool was only as strong as the three legs that formed its foundation.

The Roots of Quality

McDonald's passion for quality meant that every single ingredient was tested, tasted and perfected to fit the operating system. Kroc shared his vision of McDonald's future, selling his early suppliers on future volumes. They believed in him and the restaurant boomed.

Again, Ray Kroc was looking for a partnership, and he managed to create the most integrated, efficient and innovative supply system in the food service industry. These supplier relationships have flourished over the decades. In fact, many McDonald's suppliers operating today first started business with a handshake from Ray Kroc.

McDonald's International Franchising

McDonald's is the world's leading global food service retailer with over 36,000 locations in over 100 countries. More than 80% of McDonald's restaurants worldwide are owned and operated by independent local business men and women.

The strength of the alignment among the company, its franchisees and suppliers (collectively referred to as the "System"), has been key to McDonald's long-term success. By leveraging our System, we have been able to identify, implement and scale ideas that meet customers' changing needs and preferences. In addition, our business model enables McDonald's to consistently deliver locally-relevant restaurant experiences to customers and be an integral part of the communities we serve.

McDonald's Business Model

The power of our franchisees, suppliers and employees working together toward a common goal is what makes McDonald's the world's leading quick-service restaurant brand.

Franchisees bring the spirit of entrepreneurship and commitment to communities.

Suppliers are dedicated to highest levels of quality and safety.

The company facilitates learning and sharing across McDonald's more than 36,000 restaurants.

McDonald's Corporate Governance

McDonald's success is built on a foundation of integrity. Hundreds of millions of people around the world trust McDonald's. We earn that trust everyday by serving safe food, respecting our customers and employees and delivering outstanding Quality, Service, Cleanliness and Value (QSC&V).

McDonald's Board of Directors is entrusted with and responsible for the oversight of McDonald's Corporation in an honest, fair, diligent and ethical manner. The Board has long believed that good corporate governance is critical to fulfilling the Company's obligation to shareholders. We have and will continue to strive to be a leader in this area.

McDonald's Board believes that good governance is a journey, not a destination. Accordingly, we are committed to reviewing our governance principles at least annually with a view to continuous improvement. One thing that will not change, however, is our commitment to ensuring the integrity of the McDonald's System in all its dealings with stakeholders.

Words and Terms

chain [tʃeɪn]	n.	连锁
consumer [kənˈsjuːmə]	n.	消费者
franchisee [ˌfræntʃaɪˈziː]	n.	加盟商，特许经营商
franchise [ˈfræn(t)ʃaɪz]	n.	特许经营权
purchase [ˈpɜːtʃəs]	v.	购买
beverage [ˈbev(ə)rɪdʒ]	n.	饮料
predecessor [ˈpriːdɪsesə]	n.	前身；前辈，前任
supplier [səˈplaɪə]	n.	供应商
slogan [ˈsləʊɡ(ə)n]	n.	标语，口号
ingredient [ɪnˈɡriːdɪənt]	n.	(烹调的)原料，组成部分
alignment [əˈlaɪnm(ə)nt]	n.	结盟，联盟
private employer		私营雇主
exclusive right		专有权

international franchising	国际连锁经营
customer's need	顾客的需求
customer's preference	顾客的偏好
business model	商业模式
quick-service restaurant	快餐馆
corporate governance	企业管理
Board of Directors	董事会

Notes

1. McDonald's primarily sells hamburgers, cheeseburgers, chicken products, French fries, wraps, breakfast items, soft drinks, milkshakes, and desserts. 麦当劳主要销售汉堡、芝士汉堡、鸡肉产品、炸薯条、肉卷、早餐、软饮料、奶昔还有甜品。

2. In 1955, he founded McDonald's System, Inc., a predecessor of the McDonald's Corporation, and six years later bought the exclusive rights to the McDonald's name. 1955 年，他成立了麦当劳系统公司，这是麦当劳公司的前身，六年后他买下了麦当劳这个名字的专利权。

3. McDonald's passion for quality meant that every single ingredient was tested, tasted and perfected to fit the operating system. 麦当劳对质量的热切追求意味着每一种原料都是经过测试、品尝、完善以适应操作系统的。

4. The strength of the alignment among the Company, its franchisees and suppliers (collectively referred to as the "System"), has been key to McDonald's long-term success. 公司中的这种强大联盟，即它的加盟商和供应商(统称为系统)，是麦当劳长期繁荣发展的关键。

5. McDonald's Board of Directors is entrusted with and responsible for the oversight of McDonald's Corporation in an honest, fair, diligent and ethical manner. 麦当劳的董事会被授权以一种诚实、公平、勤勉、道德的方式监管公司。

Exercises

I. Read the following statements and decide whether they are True(T) or False (F).

1. All McDonald's restaurants are operated by the corporation itself.　　　(　)
2. By 1958, McDonald's had sold its 100 millionth hamburger.　　　(　)
3. More than 60% of McDonald's restaurants worldwide are owned and operated by independent local business men and women.　　　(　)
4. McDonald's success is based on integrity.　　　(　)
5. McDonald's Board believes that good governance is a destination.　　　(　)

II. Choose the correct answer according to Passage I.

1. McDonald's is the world's second largest_____(behind Wal-Mart with 1.9 million

employees), 1.5 million of whom work for franchises. (   )

  A. public employer   B. private employer

  C. private employee   D. public employee

  2. According to the passage, the McDonald's corporation revenues come from_____. (   )

  A. its own assets, liabilities

  B. the sales in restaurants operated by the franchisees

  C. the rent, royalties, and fees paid by the franchisees and the sales in company-operated restaurants

  D. the current assets and fixed assets of the franchisees

  3. Which of the following companies was a predecessor of the McDonald's Corporation? (   )

  A. McDonald's Food, Inc.

  B. McDonald's Franchise, Inc.

  C. McDonald's Restaurant, Inc.

  D. McDonald's System, Inc.

  4. McDonald's passion for quality meant that every single ingredient was tested and perfected to fit_____. (   )

  A. the distribution system

  B. the management system

  C. the accounting system

  D. the operating system

  5. How often does McDonald's Board review its governance principles? (   )

  A. At least once a month

  B. At most once a season

  C. At least annually

  D. At most monthly

III. Fill in the missing information.

  McDonald's is one of the world's largest restaurant chains, serving about _____ customers daily in_____countries across approximately outlets. McDonald's mainly offers hamburgers, _____, chicken products, _____, wraps, breakfast items, soft drinks, _____, and desserts. 1.5 million people work for McDonald's franchises. The power of franchisees, _____and employees working together toward makes McDonald's the world's leading quick-service restaurant brand.

Passage II

Toyota-Suzuki Alliance Marks Auto Industry Fight for Survival

  Toyota Motor Corp. sees the technological revolution shaking up the auto industry as a serious enough threat to its survival that the world's most valuable carmaker will consider partnering with one of its fiercest Japanese rivals.

In exploring collaboration between Toyota and Suzuki Motor Corp., chieftains Akio Toyoda and Osamu Suzuki seek to tie together companies with a history of failed alliances. The two would overlook Toyota's short-lived partnership with Tesla Motors Inc. and Suzuki's breakup with Volkswagen AG due to the daunting financial demands of keeping up with technological advances in areas such as electrification and autonomous driving.

"Toyota is not really good at creating alliances and in the past was fixated on the need to be able to cover all of our own bases," Toyoda, 60, said at a press conference Wednesday in Tokyo. "However, as the surrounding environment is changing drastically, we need to have capability to respond to changes in order to survive."

Toyoda and Suzuki, 80, said they began talking with one another last week and will slowly consider a potential capital alliance. While the two also haven't decided on specific fields for joint research and development, it's clear which company would stand to gain most in this regard. Toyota City, Japan-based Toyota has budgeted 1.07 trillion yen (US$10.3 billion) this fiscal year, more than seven times Suzuki's planned R&D spending.

India Domination

What Suzuki brings to the table is a leading position in India. Its Maruti Suzuki India Ltd. unit has long dominated the market with inexpensive cars like the Alto and Swift. Though Toyota has introduced budget models such as the Etios compact, its market share remains well behind the 47 percent reached by Maruti Suzuki last fiscal year.

"There are great changes centering in the automotive industry and in that case we have to share things, otherwise we won't be able to survive," Suzuki said. "That's the trigger for making the proposal."

Toyota completed a buyout earlier this year of Daihatsu Motor Co., which is now taking on more responsibility for developing compact vehicles for its parent in emerging markets. Daihatsu's top competitor in Japan's minicar segment is Hamamatsu-based Suzuki.

Japan Tie-ups

Joining with Suzuki would add to a multitude of tie-ups Toyota's forged with Japanese car and truck makers. Toyota said last year it would broaden technology-sharing with Mazda Motor Corp. It's the majority owner of Hino Motors Ltd., the largest shareholder in Subaru maker Fuji Heavy Industries Ltd. and has a stake in Isuzu Motors Ltd. The automaker also owns stakes in a web of suppliers making everything from engines to car seats.

Carmakers are forging partnerships as an industry under pressure to curtail pollution struggles with major self-inflicted scandals. Mitsubishi Motors Corp.'s improper testing for fuel economy dating back decades led the automaker to seek a rescue by Nissan Motor Co., while Volkswagen has earmarked 18 billion euros (US$19.9 billion) to cover the fallout of rigging its diesel engines with software to cheat emissions tests.

Nissan's plans to buy a stake in Mitsubishi Motor—already its partner for Japanese minicars—are centered on gaining a better foothold in Southeast Asia, where Toyota has a commanding presence.

Just before Volkswagen's emissions scandal broke, the German automaker parted ways with Suzuki following a years-long alliance that failed to yield a single joint project. Toyota, meanwhile, is about two years removed from winding down sales of the RAV4 EV, a plug-in sport utility vehicle developed with Tesla.

"The competition in R&D is very, very fierce," said Koji Endo, an auto analyst at SBI Securities Co. With regards to electrification, autonomous driving and other fields, Suzuki lags behind its peers, he said. "Without a partnership with a giant carmaker, it will be very challenging for them to stay in the race."

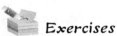

Exercises

I. Choose the correct answer according to Passage II.

1. Suzuki broke up with Volkswagen AG due to the daunting financial demands of keeping up with_____. (   )

   A. corporate development   B. technological advances

   C. corporate mergers   D. corporate acquisitions

2. Toyota has budgeted_____ this fiscal year, more than seven times Suzuki's planned R&D spending. (   )

   A. US$22.3 billion   B. 3.07 trillion yen

   C. US$11.3 billion   D. 1.07 trillion yen

3. Maruti Suzuki India Ltd. has long dominated the market with _____ like the Alto and Swift. (   )

   A. expensive cars   B. sports cars

   C. inexpensive cars   D. compact vehicles

4. Which of the following companies is Daihatsu's top competitor in Japan's minicar segment? (   )

   A. Suzuki   B. Toyota

   C. Honda   D. Nissan

5. _____ is the largest shareholder in Subaru maker Fuji Heavy Industries Ltd. and the majority owner of Hino Motors Ltd. (   )

   A. Benz   B. Volkswagen

   C. Mazda   D. Toyota

II. Choose the best translation.

1. 尽管历史上曾经有过失败的联盟，为了拓展丰田和铃木之间的合作，丰田公司的领头人丰田章男和铃木公司的领头人铃木修，希望两个公司能紧密联系在一起。(   )

Chapter Eleven Multinational Companies

A. In exploring operation between Toyota and Honda Motor Corp., chieftains Akio Honda and Osamu Suzuki seek to tie together companies with a history of successful alliances.

B. In exploring collaboration between Toyota and Suzuki Motor Corp., chieftains Akio Toyoda and Osamu Suzuki seek to tie together companies with a history of failed alliances.

C. In developing collaboration between Mazda and Suzuki Motor Corp., chieftains Akio Mazda and Osamu Suzuki seek to tie together companies with a history of failed alliances.

D. In developing negotiation between Toyota and Suzuki Motor Corp., chieftains Akio Toyoda and Osamu Suzuki seek to tie together companies with a history of successful alliances.

2. 尽管丰田已经引入预算车型(如紧凑型 Etios)，在上一财年，其市场份额仍然低于马鲁蒂铃木所达到的 47%。(   )

A. Even though Toyota has introduced compact models such as the Etios compact, its market share remains well behind the 47 percent reached by Maruti Suzuki last year.

B. Although Toyota has contributed budget models such as the Etios compact, its market share remains well behind the 47 percent reached by Maruti Suzuki last fiscal year.

C. Although Mitsubishi has contributed budget models such as the Etios compact, its market capital remains well behind the 47 percent reached by Maruti Suzuki last year.

D. Though Toyota has introduced budget models such as the Etios compact, its market share remains well behind the 47 percent reached by Maruti Suzuki last fiscal year.

3. 丰田今年早些时候完成了对大发汽车有限公司的收购，其主要责任更多是为母公司在新兴市场开发紧凑车型。(   )

A. BMW completed an acquisition earlier this year of Daihatsu Motor Co., which is now taking on more responsibility for controlling compact vehicles for its parent in emerging markets.

B. Toyota finished a buyout last year of Daihatsu Motor Co., which is now taking on more responsibility for developing inexpensive vehicles for its parent in emerging markets.

C. Porsche completed a merger earlier this year of Daihatsu Motor Co., which is now taking on more responsibility for planning compact vehicles for its parent in emerging markets.

D. Toyota completed a buyout earlier this year of Daihatsu Motor Co., which is now taking on more responsibility for developing compact vehicles for its parent in emerging markets.

4. 与铃木的联盟会促进丰田与日本的轿车和货车制造商的大量合作。(   )

A. Joining with Suzuki would add to a multitude of tie-ups Toyota's forged with Japanese car and truck makers.

B. Joining with Nissan would add to a lot of tie-ups Toyota's forged with Japanese car and plane makers.

C. Joining with Suzuki would add to a multitude of breakups Toyota's forged with Japanese car and truck makers.

D. Joining with Ford would add to a lot of tie-ups Toyota's forged with Japanese car and train makers.

5. 就在大众公司的排放丑闻爆出之前，这家德国汽车制造商结束了与铃木长达几年的合作，原因是无法开展一个单一的联合项目。(   )

A. Just before Volkswagen's emissions project broke, the German automaker parted ways with Suzuki following a years-long cooperation that failed to yield a single joint project.
B. Just before Volkswagen's emissions scandal broke, the American automaker parted ways with Suzuki following a years-long alliance that succeeded to yield a single joint project.
C. Just before Volkswagen's emissions scandal broke, the German automaker parted ways with Suzuki following a years-long alliance that failed to yield a single joint project.
D. Just before Audi's emissions scandal broke, the French automaker parted ways with Suzuki following a years-long cooperation that failed to yield a double-win project.

Special Terms

global management	全球管理
customer service	客户服务
multinational company	跨国公司
private employer	私营雇主
exclusive right	专有权
international franchising	国际连锁经营
customer's need	顾客需求
customer's preference	顾客偏好
business model	商业模式
corporate governance	企业管理
Board of Directors	董事会

Chapter Twelve

Accounting

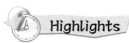 **Highlights**

Text
What is Accounting?
Reading Skills (12)
Drawing a Conclusion
Further Development
Passage I
Management Accounting Information
Passage II
Could an Accounting Change Destroy Jobs?

 **Preview**

    This is the 12th chapter of the book. In the first section, you will learn a text, and you will have some information about accounting. In the second section, you will have a deeper understanding about management accounting information. In this section, you will learn two passages and they will help you have a further development on mastering reading skills of drawing a conclusion.

Starter

Accounting is the study of how businesses track their income and assets over time. Accountants are often in short supply. Accounting jobs are plentiful even in the current weak economy and the salary for well-trained accountants is high. Do you want to choose accountant as your future career?

Text

What is Accounting?

What is Accounting?

Accounting is the systematic and comprehensive recording of financial transactions pertaining to a business, and it also refers to the process of summarizing, analyzing and reporting these transactions to oversight agencies and tax collection entities. Accounting is one of the key functions for almost any business; it may be handled by a bookkeeper and accountant at small firms or by sizable finance departments with dozens of employees at large companies. Accounting, which has been called the "language of business", measures the results of an organization's economic activities and conveys this information to a variety of users, including investors, creditors, management, and regulators. Practitioners of accounting are known as accountants. Accounting can be divided into several fields including financial accounting, management accounting, external auditing, and tax accounting. Accounting information systems are designed to support accounting functions and related activities.

Breaking Down "Accounting"

The reports generated by various streams of accounting, such as cost accounting and management accounting, are invaluable in helping management make informed business decisions.

Chapter Twelve Accounting

While basic accounting functions can be handled by a bookkeeper, advanced accounting is typically handled by qualified accountants who possess designations such as Certified Public Accountant (CPA) in the United States, or Chartered Accountant (CA), Certified General Accountant (CGA) or Certified Management Accountant (CMA) in Canada.

Creating Financial Statements

The financial statements that summarize a large company's operations, financial position and cash flows over a particular period are concise statements based on thousands of financial transactions. As a result, all accounting designations are the culmination of years of study and rigorous examinations combined with a minimum number of years of practical accounting experience.

Generally Accepted Accounting Principles

Accounting is facilitated by accounting organizations such as standard-setters, accounting firms and professional bodies. Financial statements are usually audited by accounting firms, and are prepared in accordance with generally accepted accounting principles (GAAP). In most cases, accountants use GAAP when preparing financial statements. GAAP is a set of standards related to balance sheet identification, outstanding share measurements and other accounting issues, and its standards are based on double-entry accounting, a method which enters each expense or incoming revenue in two places on a company's balance sheet.

Example of Double Entry Accounting

To illustrate double-entry accounting, imagine a business issues an invoice to one of its clients. An accountant using the double-entry method enters a credit under the accounts receivables column and a debit under the balance sheet's revenue column. When the client pays the invoice, the accountant debits accounts receivables and credits revenue. Double-entry accounting is also called balancing the books, as all of the accounting entries are balanced against each other. If the entries aren't balanced, the accountant knows there must be a mistake somewhere in the ledger.

Financial Accounting versus Management Accounting

Financial accounting refers to the processes accountants use to generate the annual accounting statements of a firm. Financial accounting focuses on the reporting of an organization's financial information to external users of the information, such as investors, regulators and suppliers. Management accounting uses much of the same processes but utilizes information in different ways. Management accounting focuses on the measurement, analysis and reporting of information that can help managers in making decisions to fulfill the goals of an organization. Namely, in management accounting, an accountant generates monthly or quarterly reports that a business's management team can use to make decisions about how the business operates.

Financial Accounting versus Cost Accounting

Just as management accounting helps businesses make decisions about management, cost accounting helps businesses make decisions about costing. Essentially, cost accounting considers all of the costs related to producing a product. Analysts, managers, business owners and accountants use this information to determine what their products should cost. In cost accounting, money is cast as an economic factor in production, whereas in financial accounting, money is considered to be a measure of a company's economic performance.

Tax Accounting

Tax accounting in the United States concentrates on the preparation, analysis and presentation of tax payments and tax returns. The U.S. tax system requires the use of specialized accounting principles for tax purposes which can differ from the generally accepted accounting principles (GAAP) for financial reporting. U.S. tax law covers four basic forms of business ownership: sole proprietorship, partnership, corporation, and limited liability company. Corporate and personal income are taxed at different rates, both varying according to income levels and including varying marginal rates (taxed on each additional dollar of income) and average rates (set as a percentage of overall income).

Accounting Information System

Many accounting practices have been simplified with the help of accounting computer-based software. An enterprise resource planning (ERP) system is commonly used for a large organization and it provides a comprehensive, centralized, integrated source of information that companies can use to manage all major business processes, from purchasing to manufacturing to human resources. Accounting information systems have reduced the cost of accumulating, storing and reporting managerial accounting information and have made it possible to produce a more detailed account of all data that is entered into any given system.

 Words and Terms

process ['prəuses]	n.	过程，程序
function ['fʌŋ(k)ʃ(ə)n]	n.	功能
accountant [ə'kaʊnt(ə)nt]	n.	会计师
investor [ɪn'vestə]	n.	投资者
creditor ['kredɪtə]	n.	债权人
culmination [kʌlmɪ'neɪʃ(ə)n]	n.	完成，成就
rigorous ['rɪgərəs]	adj.	严格的，严厉的，严密的
invoice ['ɪnvɔɪs]	n.	发票

sole proprietorship	独资企业
financial transaction	财务往来
tax collection	税收
finance department	财务部门

Chapter Twelve Accounting

economic activities	经济活动
financial accounting	财务会计
management accounting	管理会计
accounting information	会计信息
cost accounting	成本会计
Certified Public Accountant	注册会计师
financial statement	财务报表
cash flow	现金流
balance sheet	资产负债表
double-entry accounting	复式记账法

Notes

1. Accounting, which has been called the "language of business", measures the results of an organization's economic activities and conveys this information to a variety of users, including investors, creditors, management, and regulators. 会计被称为"企业的语言",衡量一个组织经济活动的结果,向一系列使用者传递这一信息,这些使用者包括投资者、债权人、管理层和监管者。

2. While basic accounting functions can be handled by a bookkeeper, advanced accounting is typically handled by qualified accountants who possess designations such as Certified Public Accountant (CPA) in the United States, or Chartered Accountant (CA), Certified General Accountant (CGA) or Certified Management Accountant (CMA) in Canada. 尽管记账员可以行使基本的会计职能,但是高等级的会计业务通常由具有以下资质的会计处理,如美国的注册会计师、加拿大的特许会计师、注册会计师或注册管理会计师。

美国注册会计师的英文简称是USCPA,它是被美国各州承认的唯一注册会计师资格。从1917年第一次实施考试起,至今已有近100年的历史,可以说它是最具价值及国际商业公信力的资格之一。

3. As a result, all accounting designations are the culmination of years of study and rigorous examinations combined with a minimum number of years of practical accounting experience. 因此,所有会计专业资质都是经过多年的学习和严格的考试,并且拥有最低年限的会计实践经验才能获得的。

4. Financial statements are usually audited by accounting firms, and are prepared in accordance with generally accepted accounting principles (GAAP). 财务报表通常由会计事务所进行审计,并且根据公认会计原则进行编制。

Generally Accepted Accounting Principles (GAAP)是一般公认会计原则,1937年美国会计程序委员会(CAP)发表第一号会计研究公告,开创了由政府机关或行业组织颁布"一般通用会计"的先河。

5. Double-entry accounting is also called balancing the books, as all of the accounting entries are balanced against each other. 复式记账也被称为平衡账簿,因为所有的会计科目都必须相互平衡。

Exercises

I. Answer the following questions according to the text.

1. What is accounting?
2. What fields can accounting be divided into?
3. What is GAAP?
4. What does financial accounting refer to?
5. What are the four basic forms of business ownership according to U.S. tax law?

II. Identify the key words of main ideas of the following paragraphs.

Part 1	What is_____
Part 2	_____ "Accounting"
Part 3	Creating_____
Part 4	Generally Accepted Accounting_____
Part 5	Example of_____
Part 6	Financial Accounting versus_____
Part 7	Financial Accounting versus_____
Part 8	_____ Accounting
Part 9	Accounting _____ System

III. Match the words of phrases in Column A to the words or phrases in Column B.

    A   B

1. _____ investor   A. 资产负债表
2. _____ sole proprietorship   B. 财务会计
3. _____ financial accounting   C. 独资企业
4. _____ balance sheet   D. 投资者
5. _____ invoice   E. 管理会计
6. _____ management accounting   F. 发票
7. _____ cash flow   G. 成本会计
8. _____ cost accounting   H. 债权人
9. _____ creditor   I. 复式记账法
10. _____ double-entry accounting   J. 现金流

IV. Choose the best translation.

1. Accounting is one of the key functions for almost any business; it may be handled by a bookkeeper and accountant at small firms or by sizable finance departments with dozens of employees at large companies. ( )

A. 会计是几乎任何一个企业的重要功能之一；在小型公司，它可能由一位记账员兼会计

Chapter Twelve Accounting

   处理，在大型公司，它可能由相当大的财务部门来处理。
B. 会计是几乎任何一个企业的基本功能之一；在小型公司，它可能由一位记账员兼出纳处理，在大型公司，它可能由相当大的财务部门来处理。
C. 会计是几乎任何一个企业的关键功能之一；在小型公司，它可能由一位簿记员兼会计处理，在大型公司，它可能由相当大的行政部门来处理。
D. 会计是几乎任何一个企业的关键功能之一；在小型公司，它可能由一位记账员兼会计处理，在大型公司，它可能由相当大的财务部门来处理。

2. The financial statements that summarize a large company's operations, financial position and cash flows over a particular period are concise statements based on thousands of financial transactions. (   )
   A. 财务报表总结一定时期内，一家大公司的管理、财务状况和现金流，是建立在成千上万的生意往来基础上的复杂报表。
   B. 财务报表分析一定时期内，一家大公司的运营、财务状况和现金流，是建立在成千上万的财务往来基础上的复杂报表。
   C. 财务报表总结一定时期内，一家大公司的运营、财务状况和现金流，是建立在成千上万的财务往来基础上的简要报表。
   D. 财务报表总结一定时期内，一家大公司的运营、整体状况和现金流，是建立在成千上万的生意往来基础上的简要报表。

3. Financial accounting focuses on the reporting of an organization's financial information to external users of the information, such as investors, regulators and suppliers. (   )
   A. 管理会计的工作重点是向外部使用者(如投资者、监管者和经销商)报告组织的财务信息。
   B. 财务会计的工作重点是向外部使用者(如投资者、监管者和供应商)报告组织的财务信息。
   C. 成本会计的工作重点是向外部使用者(如债权人、监管者和供应商)报告组织的财务信息。
   D. 财务会计的工作难点是向内部使用者(如投资者、监管者和供应商)报告组织的财务信息。

4. Analysts, managers, business owners and accountants use this information to determine what their products should cost. (   )
   A. 分析师、管理人员、企业业主和会计师利用这些信息来决定他们的产品成本。
   B. 律师、管理人员、企业业主和会计师利用这些信息来决定他们的产品成本。
   C. 分析师、行政人员、企业业主和会计师利用这些信息来决定他们的产品成本。
   D. 分析师、管理人员、企业债主和会计师利用这些信息来决定他们的产品定价。

5. Tax accounting in the United States concentrates on the preparation, analysis and presentation of tax payments and tax returns. (   )
   A. 德国的税务会计重点在于对税务支出和税务申报的准备、分析和说明。
   B. 美国的税务会计重点在于对税务支出和税务申报的准备、分析和说明。
   C. 美国的税务会计重点在于对财政支出和税务申报的准备、归纳和说明。
   D. 中国的税务会计难点在于对税务支出和审计申报的准备、总结和说明。

Reading Skills (12)
Drawing a Conclusion

Drawing a conclusion means arriving at one decision justified by the stated evidence.

Most reading experts stress the importance of increasing the level of comprehension — the rate at which words and ideas they stand for can be truly understood. They believe that there has been overemphasis on the "numbers game" of increasing the number of words a person can "run through" per minute.

To draw an accurate conclusion usually depends on your ability to read critically, that is, to identify ideas first and then to evaluate these ideas. In order to draw reasonable conclusions, we have to build our conclusions upon facts or evidence and not upon our own opinions, likes, or dislikes. Of course, our experience may prove useful, but most of our conclusions must be based on what we read in the passage.

Further Development

Passage I

Management Accounting Information

Managerial accounting, or management accounting, is a set of practices and techniques aimed at providing managers with financial information to help them make decisions and maintain effective control over corporate resources. Professionals within an organization who perform the managerial accounting function generally support two primary purposes. First of all, they generate routine reports containing information regarding cost control and the planning and controlling of operations. Second, managerial accountants produce special reports for managers that are used for strategic and tactical decisions on matters such as pricing products or services, choosing which products to emphasize or de-emphasize, investing in equipment, and formulating overall policies and long-range planning.

Management accounting information is focused at internal managers and decision makers. Its intended use is to provide financial data relevant to a manager's operations in an effort to make sound business decisions. Management accounting information comes in the form of financial ratios, budget forecasts, variance analysis and cost accounting. Without management accounting practices, making these decisions would be more like gambling and less of a science.

Forecasting

All businesses must conduct strategic planning in order to stay competitive. This is the process of planning for future operations through the use of forecasts. The goal of the forecasting process is to try to predict the outcome of future operations through trend analysis. Trend analysis takes past revenue, sales and growth statistics and carries these calculations out into future periods. If the average revenue growth has been 10 percent per year, then the forecast model will use an annual growth rate of 10 percent.

Budgeting

The forecasting process allows a company to build a model of the anticipated future revenue figures. Once the forecast models are built, the budget process can begin. The budget process allots capital — money — for the future operations. Estimates of the future costs and liabilities are made. These dollar amounts are constructed from analyzing the past liability and cost trends. If the costs of materials have gone up an average of 20 percent year over year, then this same 20 percent will be used to create the budget for next year. The budget takes into account the current cash on hand and the projected revenue from sales.

Variance Analysis and Cost Accounting

Variance analysis is the process of comparing the actual realized expenses with the budgeted expenses. Any variations are examined and corrected, if correction is necessary. This can include man-hours, machine hours, raw material consumption and production time, among other input items. All of these factors can affect the company budget and, ultimately, the profitability of the company. For example, if the production of a product takes 20 percent more man-hours to produce than budgeted, then the labor costs are over budget. This can be said about many different input items as listed above. Variances that are over budgeted tolerances require immediate corrective action. However, if a positive variance occurs, it could be used to help offset a negative variance or to increase production in an effort to improve the profit margin of the operation. An example of a positive variance is when man-hours are 20 percent less than budgeted to produce a product. The result is a 20 percent reduction in labor costs.

Ratio Analysis

Ratio analysis is completed at the end of each accounting period — monthly, quarterly and annually — to determine the company's ability to pay its long- and short-term debts. These rations demonstrate a company's solvency and liquidity. These ratio analysis tools can be used to determine a company's effective use of inventory and raw material. This analysis tells the management team whether the company is operating within the overall guidelines that will promote profitability. Many other ratios can be used to determine what their receivable collections periods are like and whether they are using and maintaining proper levels of inventory.

Accounting for Decision Making

Managerial accounting is the process of using all of the accounting data available to make better business decisions—solid decisions based on trends, facts and projects. These decisions are critical to the future of any company. Effective managerial accounting takes much of the risk out of decision making and bases it more on fact. However, there is always financial risk in doing business. Analyzing past trends can create a clear picture of the future.

Words and Terms

routine [ruːˈtiːn]	adj.	日常的，例行的
strategic [strəˈtiːdʒɪk]	adj.	战略的
tactical [ˈtæktɪk(ə)l]	adj.	战术的
emphasize [ˈemfəsaɪz]	v.	强调，着重
predict [prɪˈdɪkt]	v.	预测，预报
statistics [stəˈtɪstɪks]	n.	统计，统计学，统计资料
calculation [kælkjʊˈleɪʃ(ə)n]	n.	计算
anticipate [ænˈtɪsɪpeɪt]	v.	预期
estimate [ˈestɪmeɪt]	v.	估计
solvency [ˈsɒlvənsɪ]	n.	偿还能力
liquidity [lɪˈkwɪdɪtɪ]	n.	资产折现力；流动性
financial ratio		财务比率
variance analysis		差异分析
raw material consumption		原材料消耗
production time		生产时间
labor cost		劳动力成本
profit margin		边际利润
ratio analysis		比率分析
long-term debt		长期负债
short-term debt		短期负债

Notes

1. Managerial accounting, or management accounting, is a set of practices and techniques aimed at providing managers with financial information to help them make decisions and maintain effective control over corporate resources. 管理会计是一系列实践操作与技术，其使用目的在于为管理人员提供财务信息，帮助他们做出决策，保持对公司资源的有效控制。

2. Trend analysis takes past revenue, sales and growth statistics and carries these calculations out into future periods. 趋势分析计入过去的收益、销售和增长等数据，并将这些运算计到未来周期中。

3. Variance analysis is the process of comparing the actual realized expenses with the budgeted expenses. 差异分析是比较实际费用和预算费用的过程。

4. Ratio analysis is completed at the end of each accounting period — monthly, quarterly and

annually — to determine the company's ability to pay its long- and short-term debts. 比率分析是在每个会计周期结束时完成的—每月、每季度、每年—以决定公司偿还长期和短期债务的能力。

5. Effective managerial accounting takes much of the risk out of decision making and bases it more on fact. 有效的管理会计排除了决策过程中的很多风险，使决策更多地建立在事实基础上。

Exercises

I. Read the following statements and decide whether they are True (T) or False (F).

1. Management accounting information comes in the form of financial statements, budget forecasts, ratio analysis and management accounting. ( )

2. All companies must make strategic planning in order to stay competitive. ( )

3. The goal of the budgeting process is to try to predict the result of future operations through trend analysis. ( )

4. If a positive variance occurs, it could be used to help offset a negative variance or to decrease production. ( )

5. There is always financial risk in doing business. ( )

II. Choose the correct answer according to Passage I.

1. In an organization, professionals performing the managerial accounting function generally support two main _____. ( )
   A. functions   B. purposes
   C. operations   D. levels

2. If the average revenue growth has been 15 percent per year, the forecast model will use an annual growth rate of _____. ( )
   A. 30 percent   B. 25 percent
   C. 20 percent   D. 15 percent

3. If the production of a product takes 20 percent less man-hours than budgeted to produce, the result is a 20 percent reduction in _____. ( )
   A. raw material costs   B. labor costs
   C. machine costs   D. inventory costs

4. Managerial accountants produce special reports that are used to make strategic and tactical decisions on the following matters EXPECT _____. ( )
   A. pricing products or services
   B. investing in equipment
   C. analyzing customer preferences
   D. formulating overall policies

5. What factors can affect the company budget and the profitability of the company? (　　)
A. Man-hours, machine hours, raw material consumption and production time
B. Productivity and electricity consumption
C. Cash flow, long-term debts and short-term debts
D. Fixed assets, current assets and intangible assets

III. Fill in the missing information.

Managerial accounting is the process of using accounting data to make better＿＿＿＿＿. Management accounting information is used to provide＿＿＿＿＿relevant to a manager's＿＿＿＿＿to make sound business decisions. The forecasting process allows a company to build a model of the anticipated＿＿＿＿＿. Once the forecast models are built, the budget process can begin. The budget process＿＿＿＿＿for the future operations. Variance analysis is the process of comparing the actual realized expenses with the＿＿＿＿＿. Ratio analysis is completed to determine the company's ability to pay its long- and short-term＿＿＿＿＿.

Passage II

Could an Accounting Change Destroy Jobs?

US and international accounting boards are proposing to change how companies account for operating leases. These are contracts that are akin to extended rentals and don't transfer ownership of a property or piece of equipment. Although no date has been set for when the change would take effect, members of Congress (both Republicans and Democrats), the Chamber of Commerce and real estate professionals across the country are actively campaigning to stop the proposed rule. Opponents claim that changing the accounting companies use could "destroy" up to 3.3 million jobs and reduce annual average household income by more than US$1,000 per year.

Accounting rule changes can have real effects on the economy and better inform investors if they require companies to report more relevant information or to present existing information in a more visible form. In essence, the operating lease change would require disclosures that are currently done off-balance sheet to be reported more prominently.

Two Kinds of Leases

Under existing rules, companies must distinguish capital leases (which grant some claim to ownership of a building or machine to the entity leasing it) from operating leases (which do not, and are for shorter periods of use).

Capital leases are currently reported on the company's balance sheet, both as an asset — its value in producing revenue — and as a liability — the on-going obligation to make payments to the owner of the asset. Operating leases, on the other hand, are currently not shown on the balance sheet. They are reported as a rental expense on the company's income statement when payments are made. Significant additional detail about a user's operating lease contracts, however, is provided in notes to the financial statements.

The proposed accounting change requires operating leases with a term of more than a year to be reported like capital leases, that is as assets and liabilities on the balance sheet. As a result, the assets of leases will rise but so will their liabilities.

The new accounting rule, backed by investor groups and the US Securities and Exchange Commission, is intended to make the balance sheet more comprehensive and informative. It could also improve the comparability of financial statements for companies with different mixes of operating and capital leases, making it easier for lenders, investors, and regulators to assess their relative financial strength.

The Critics' Case

Their argument begins with an estimate that the accounting change will add US$1.5 trillion to balance sheet debt of US publicly traded companies. That's an increase of 1.2% over the current total of liabilities for these firms.

This increase would reduce the ratio of liquid assets to debt liabilities for affected companies. Opponents claim that debt ratios are treated by banks and other credit providers as critical measures of financial strength. A decrease in the ratio of liquid assets or cash flow to debt would be seen by lenders as a deterioration in credit quality, even though the company's true financial position remains unchanged — because the leases were always there, just accounted for differently.

To restore the debt ratio to the previous, apparently satisfactory level, companies would be forced to cut back on spending, and that would most likely mean laying off workers. In the meantime, their lower credit quality would raise borrowing costs, further reducing their ability to carry on business activity. Ultimately, the operating response of firms to the accounting change would mean lower employment and income for many and a decline in the price of leased commercial real estate.

Not So Fast

This narrative is not completely convincing because it uses assumptions about the unknown effects of current accounting and how people will respond to the change. In fact, the estimated effects of the proposal are highly uncertain and depend on the assumptions used. How uncertain? Depending on the choice of assumptions, estimated job losses range from 190,000 to 3.3 million and the decline in annual household earnings could be as low as US$68 or as high as US$1,180. The range includes dramatically high numbers and others close to zero.

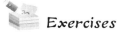 *Exercises*

I. Choose the correct answer according to Passage II.

1. Opponents claim that changing the accounting companies use could reduce annual average household income by more than _____ . (   )

   A. US$3,000 per year   B. US$2,000 per year

C. US$1,000 per year   D. US$500 per year

2. The new accounting rule is intended to make _____ more comprehensive and informative. (　　)

　A. tax returns   B. the balance sheet
　C. the income statement   D. the cash flow statement

3. Lenders would see a decrease in the ratio of _____ as a deterioration in credit quality, even though the company's true financial position remains unchanged. (　　)

　A. liquid assets to debt   B. fixed assets to debt
　C. cash flow to equity   D. debt to equity

4. In order to restore the debt ratio to the previous level, companies would be forced to reduce _____ . (　　)

　A. production   B. net loss
　C. spending   D. net income

5. Ultimately, the operating response of firms to the accounting change would mean the following consequences EXCEPT _____ . (　　)

　A. a decline in the price of leased commercial real estate
　B. lower employment
　C. lower income for many people
　D. higher employment

II. Choose the best translation.

1. 尽管这项改变何时生效尚未确定，国会议员们、商会和全国的房地产专业人士都积极地开展活动抵制这项提案。(　　)

　A. Even though the date has been set for when the change would take effect, members of Congress, the Chamber of Trade and real estate professionals across the country are actively campaigning to stop the proposed rule.

　B. Even though no date has been set for when the change would happen, members of Congress, the Chamber of Commerce and housing professionals around the country are actively campaigning to support the proposed rule.

　C. Although the date when the change would take effect has not been set, members of Congress, the Chamber of Trade and real estate professionals across the country are actively campaigning to stop the proposed rule.

　D. Although no date has been set for when the change would take effect, members of Congress, the Chamber of Commerce and real estate professionals across the country are actively campaigning to stop the proposed rule.

2. 实际上，经营性租赁记账方式的改变是要求公开那些目前没有记入资产负债表的项目，将它们清楚地呈现出来。(　　)

　A. In fact, the capital lease change would require disclosures that are currently done off-balance sheet to be reported more prominently.

　B. In essence, the operating lease change would require disclosures that are currently done

off-balance sheet to be reported more prominently.
C. In fact, the operating lease change would require exposures that are generally done off-balance sheet to be reported more prominently.
D. In essence, the operating lease change would require disclosures that are currently done within balance sheet to be reported more patently.

3. 在现有规则下，企业必须把资本租赁(承租的主体于支付租金后可获取厂房或设备的所有权)和经营性租赁(只是为了短期使用，不取得所有权)区别开来。( )
A. Under existing rules, companies must distinguish capital leases (which grant some claim to ownership of a building or machine to the entity leasing it) from operating leases (which do not, and are for shorter periods of use).
B. Under current rules, companies must distinguish capital leases (which grant some claim to liability of a building or machine to the entity leasing it) from operating leases (which do not, and are for shorter periods of use).
C. Under past rules, companies must differentiate capital leases (which permit some claim to ownership of a factory or machine to the entity leasing it) from operating leases (which do not, and are for shorter periods of use).
D. Under existing rules, companies must differentiate capital leases (which grant some claim to revenue of a building or machine to the entity leasing it) from operating leases (which do not, and are for longer periods of use).

4. 反对者们声称，负债率是银行和其他信贷提供者衡量企业财务实力的重要指标。( )
A. Supporters claim that equity ratios are treated by banks and other credit providers as important measures of financial strength.
B. Opponents think that revenue ratios are treated by banks and other credit providers as important measures of financial strength.
C. Opponents claim that debt ratios are treated by banks and other credit providers as critical measures of financial strength.
D. Supporters think that debt ratios are treated by loaners and other credit providers as critical measures of financial strength.

5. 同时，信用等级低会增加借贷成本，进一步降低开展经营活动的能力。( )
A. At the same time, their lower service quality would raise borrowing costs, further reducing their ability to carry on business activity.
B. In the meantime, their lower credit quality would raise borrowing costs, further reducing their ability to carry on business activity.
C. In the meantime, their lower product quality would raise borrowing expenses, further reducing their ability to keep on business activity.
D. At the same time, their higher credit quantity would raise borrowing costs, further reducing their ability to carry on business activity.

Special Terms

sole proprietorship	独资企业
financial transaction	财务往来
financial accounting	财务会计
management accounting	管理会计
accounting information	会计信息
cost accounting	成本会计
Certified Public Accountant	注册会计师
financial statement	财务报表
cash flow	现金流
balance sheet	资产负债表
double-entry accounting	复式记账法
financial ratio	财务比率
variance analysis	差异分析
labor cost	劳动力成本
profit margin	边际利润
ratio analysis	比率分析
long-term debt	长期负债
short-term debt	短期负债

参考译文

第一章 全球化的经济合作

课文

亚太经济合作组织

亚太经济合作组织(APEC)是一个经济体论坛,由太平洋地区 21 个经济体成员组成,旨在促进整个亚太地区的自由贸易。它成立于 1989 年,以应对日益增长并相互依存的亚太经济和在世界其他地方出现的区域贸易集团,化解因高度工业化的日本将在亚太地区主宰经济活动的担忧,并建立欧洲以外国家的农产品和原材料的新市场。

历史

1989 年 1 月,澳大利亚总理鲍勃·霍克呼吁更有效的环太平洋地区的经济合作。这促成了亚太经合组织于 11 月在澳大利亚首都堪培拉召开了第一次会议,该会议由澳大利亚外交部长加雷思·埃文斯主持。十二个国家的部长参加了会议,会议决定今后年度会议将在新加坡和韩国举行。

亚太经合组织第一次领导人非正式会议于 1993 年举行。美国总统比尔·克林顿在与澳大利亚总理保罗·基廷讨论后,邀请成员经济体的政府首脑参加在布莱克岛举行的峰会。他相信这将帮助陷入僵局的乌拉圭贸易谈判重回正轨。在会议上,一些领导人呼吁继续减少贸易和投资壁垒,在亚太地区构想一个共同体,通过合作促进繁荣。亚太经合组织秘书处设在新加坡,负责协调该组织的活动。

目前,亚太经合组织有 21 个成员,包括在太平洋海岸线的大部分国家。然而,会员的标准是,成员是一个独立的经济体,而不是一个国家。因此,亚太经合组织对于其成员使用的术语是"成员经济体"而非"成员国"。这一标准的一个结果是,论坛的会员包括中国台湾(以"中华台北"名义参与)以及中国香港,香港作为英国一个殖民地进入亚太经合组织,但现在是中华人民共和国的一个特别行政区。

亚太自由贸易区

　　2006年在河内举行的峰会上，亚太经合组织第一次正式讨论亚太自由贸易区的概念(自由贸易区)。然而，至少自1966年以来，为这一地区的建议就已经被提过，日本经济学家清小岛也提到过关于太平洋自由贸易协定的建议。虽然并未引起多少关注，但这一想法促进了太平洋贸易和发展会议的形成，以及促进了1980年成立了太平洋经济合作委员会，1989年成立了亚太经合组织。

　　在2006年峰会之后，经济学家弗雷德·伯格斯腾倡导亚太地区的自由贸易协定。他的想法说服亚太经合组织工商咨询理事会支持这一观点。相应地，作为区域全面经济伙伴关系(RCEP)，东盟和现有的自由贸易协定(FTA)伙伴进行谈判，该谈判没有正式包括俄罗斯。跨太平洋伙伴关系(TPP)成为该地区由美国推进的贸易谈判，中国和俄罗斯并未参与该谈判。在2014年北京举办的亚太经合组织峰会上，这三个计划都在讨论之列。在跨太平洋合作会议之前，奥巴马总统在美国驻北京大使馆主持了一个亚太经合组织会议。

　　在2014年北京亚太经合组织峰会上，亚太经合组织领导人同意启动关于亚太自由贸易区的"集体战略研究"，指示官员进行研究，咨询利益相关者，并于2016年底报告研究结果。亚太经合组织执行董事艾伦·博拉尔德在精英访谈节目透露，自由贸易区将成为亚太经合组织未来的大目标。

一年一度的亚太经合组织经济领导人会议

　　自1989年成立以来，亚太经合组织与所有成员经济体的代表举行了年度会议。前四年的年度会议由部长级官员出席。从1993年开始，年会被命名为亚太经合组织经济领导人会议，除中国台湾派部长级官员参加外，所有成员经济体政府首脑参加该会议。一年一度的领导人会议不叫作峰会。

　　在2001上海举行的领导人会议上，亚太经合组织领导人推动新一轮贸易谈判和支持贸易能力建设援助的计划，导致几周后多哈发展议程的开始。会议还同意美国提出的《上海协议》，强调实施开放市场、结构性改革和能力建设。作为协议的一部分，亚太经合组织会议致力于制定和实施透明度标准，在五年内亚太地区贸易的交易成本减少5%，并追求关于信息技术产品和服务贸易自由化的政策。

拓展阅读

第1篇

一带一路

　　丝绸之路经济带和21世纪的海上丝绸之路，也被称为"一带一路"。它是由中国领导人习近平提出的一个关于发展战略和框架的倡议，关注中华人民共和国和欧亚大陆其他国家紧密的连接和合作，主要包括两大部分，陆上"丝绸之路"经济带和远洋"海上丝绸之路"。战略凸显出中国在全球事务中发挥更大作用。

　　倡议的覆盖范围主要是亚洲和欧洲，包括约60个国家。大洋洲和非洲东部也包括在内。

"一带一路"已经与两个以美国为中心的贸易协议,即跨太平洋伙伴关系和跨大西洋贸易和投资合作,形成对比。

丝绸之路经济带

2013年9月和10月,中国领导人习近平访问中亚和东南亚,提出共同建设21世纪"丝绸之路"经济带和"海上丝绸之路"的倡议。从本质上讲,"带"包括位于原中亚的丝绸之路的国家,从中亚到西亚、中东和欧洲。该倡议呼吁通过基础设施建设,加强文化交流,扩大贸易区域,将该地区整合成一个紧密相连的经济区。

除了这一很大程度上类似于历史丝绸之路的区域,南亚和东南亚据说是"一带"的扩展区域。"一带"中的许多国家也是中国引领的亚洲基础设施投资银行(AIIB)的成员。"一带"的北部贯穿中亚,俄罗斯直到欧洲,中部穿过中亚、西亚、波斯湾和地中海,南部从中国到东南亚、南亚和印度洋。

海上丝绸之路

"海上丝绸之路"也被称为"21世纪海上丝绸之路"。它是一个互补的倡议,旨在投资和促进东南亚、大洋洲、和北非,贯穿几个连续的水域——南海、南太平洋以及更广泛的印度洋领域的协作。

2013年10月,习近平在印尼议会的讲话中首次提出"海上丝绸之路"计划。就像它的姐妹倡议—丝绸之路经济带一样,在这一领域的大多数国家已加入由中国引领的亚洲基础设施投资银行。

东非

东非,包括桑给巴尔岛,经过对当地港口的改进,以及内罗毕和坎帕拉之间的现代标准轨距铁路建设的完成,将形成海上丝绸之路的一个重要组成部分。

2014年5月,国务院副总理李克强访问肯尼亚,与肯尼亚政府签署了合作协议。在本协议下,将建设一条铁路线连接蒙巴萨岛和内罗毕。铁路建成后,将延伸约2700公里,耗资约2.5亿美元。

2015年9月,中国国机集团签署了一项,与通用电气公司合作的谅解备忘录。备忘录设定的目标是在撒哈拉以南非洲建造风力涡轮机,促进清洁能源项目和增加能源消费者的数量。

金融机构

亚洲基础设施投资银行

2013年10月,中国首次提出亚洲基础设施投资银行,它是一个致力于提供基础设施项目贷款的开发银行。截至2015年,中国宣布在基础设施项目规划或建设上投入超过一万亿元(1600亿美元)。

2015年6月29日,亚洲基础设施投资银行在北京签署了章程协议(AIIB),即法律框架。提出的多边银行具有1000亿美元的授权资本,其中75%来自亚洲和大洋洲的国家。中国将成为最大的股东,持有26%的投票权。银行计划在年底前开始操作。

丝绸之路基金

2014年11月,习近平宣布计划创建一个400亿美元发展基金,该基金有别于最初创建的银行。作为基金，其角色将是投资企业而不是贷款项目。巴基斯坦的卡洛特(Karot)水电站是丝绸之路的第一个投资项目基金。

2016年1月，三峡建设总公司开始建造从伊斯兰堡到卡洛特(Karot)水电站50公里的公路。这是丝绸之路基金的第一个外国投资项目。中国政府已经承诺，到2030年，向巴基斯坦提供至少3.5亿美元用以资助水电站的建设。

监督

"一带一路"发展工作推进领导小组于2014年年底成立，领导阵容于2015年2月1日公布。这个领导小组由重量级人物组成，涉及政府的重要项目并直接向中华人民共和国国务院报告。副总理张高丽被任命为领导小组组长，组员有王沪宁、汪洋和杨晶，杨洁篪为副组长。

2014年3月，中国国务院总理李克强在政府工作报告中，呼吁加快"一带一路"倡议，以及中国—印度—孟加拉国—缅甸经济走廊和中国—巴基斯坦经济走廊的进展。

第2篇

一带一路的倡议——想法来自中国，但属于全世界

北京——在当今世界处于不断上升的贸易保护主义和单边主义环境中，"一带一路"的倡议已经成为最受欢迎的公益事业和有着光明前景的国际合作平台，中国外交部长王毅在离开刚刚结束的中国两会会场时说。

该倡议由中国国家主席习近平于2013年提出，并见证了不断扩大的"朋友圈"，以及为该路线上的国家带来的实实在在的利益。

它将为加入该倡议的国家的经济和社会发展提供前所未有的机遇，正如"它是走向人类共命运的共同体之路"，内罗毕大学的高级讲师加里逊·伊提拉说道。

理想的开放性、包容性

该倡议具有广泛磋商、共同奉献和共享利益的指导性原则，已经成为"合唱"，而不是"独奏"。

受到古代长期以来的连接中国与亚洲、欧洲和非洲主要贸易通道的启发，该倡议旨在在这些地区创建共同的繁荣，将古代贸易路线建设成为现代化的贸易路线。

当保护主义和单边主义正趋于上升趋势，"一带一路"的倡议已经成为世界的共同事业，通过使其更具有普惠性和包容性将有助于平衡经济全球化，王毅表示。

"'一带一路倡议反对狭隘的保护主义和孤立主义，'俄罗斯科学院远东研究所主任塞奇·卢贾宁说道。"我们曾经只有九十年代的西方欧美经济一体化发展的选择，现在有一个来自中国的新选择。"

全球经济增长的刺激

"一带一路"倡议的建设不仅仅对中国有益，沿线国家同样受益。在全球需求不足的背景下，该蓝图将为世界经济增长做出贡献。

中国人民大学发布的一份报告说，中国已经开始协调该路线上许多国家进行该发展战略

倡议的签约，如哈萨克斯坦的光明路项目以及吉尔吉斯斯坦的可持续发展战略。

迄今为止，中国企业已经在20多个沿线国家建立了56个经贸合作区，累计投资超过180亿美元，创造了10亿美元的收入和160000个工作岗位。

去年，中国在沿路线53个国家的直接投资达到145.3亿美元，与61个相关国家签署合同的总价值达1260亿美元。

今年，"一带一路"的建设计划将继续成为全球经济的增长点，贸易交流将进一步扩大，基础设施连接和金融中介将推动生产能力合作、跨境电子商务等领域的发展。

全球化的新引擎

全球化目前正面临着各种问题和挑战，中国提出的"一带一路"倡议将成为未来全球化引擎，在雅加达公共会议发表演说的世界贸易组织的前首席帕斯卡尔·拉米说道。

过去的全球化基本上是由西方驱动，而现在新的全球化将更多地由东方而非西方推动，《美国的世界秩序》一书的作者阿米塔夫·阿查里雅在最近的一次采访中告诉新华社。

当西方竖起一面"墙"向后退时，东方通过中国提出的"一带一路"倡议，修建起通往外面世界的大门，拥抱全球化，马来西亚的《新海峡时报》在其网站上发表的一篇文章中如此说道。

2013年提出的该倡议迄今为止获得了超过100个国家和国际组织的支持，其中40多个国家和国际组织与中国签署了合作协议。

"中国共同构建"一带一路"的倡议拥抱一个多极化的世界、经济全球化、文化多元化和更大的信息化的趋势，旨在成为资源配置方面高效率，在实现有关国家之间的市场深度融合，"伦敦的48个俱乐部集团的副主席基思·班尼特说。

因此，它将共同创造一个所有人受益的开放、包容和平衡的区域经济合作架构，英国商界领袖告诉新华社。

第二章 金融市场

课文

金融市场

金融市场是一个以低交易成本交易买卖金融证券、商品以及其他有价值的可互换物品，所成交的价格反映金融市场供求关系的资金融通市场。有价证券包括股票和债券，商品包括贵重金属或者农产品。

在金融业，"金融市场"这个术语被常常用来指筹集资金(资金融通)的市场：为了长期融通资金——资本市场；为了短期融通资金——货币市场。金融市场吸引投资者投入资金，为企业提供融资渠道——它们以这种方式帮助企业为自己的运营筹措资金，实现增长。货币市场允许以短期的方式借入资金，而资本市场允许企业筹措长期资金以支持企业扩张。

金融市场的基本功能

金融市场有六个基本功能。这些功能简要罗列如下：

① 借贷：金融市场允许资金(购买力)从一个经纪人转移到另一个经纪人，以达到投资或消费的目的。

② 价格确定：新资产的价格以及金融资产的现有存量都由金融市场决定。决定价格是金融市场的主要功能。

③ 信息汇集和协调：金融市场充当有关金融资产价值信息的收集者与汇集整合者。

④ 风险分担：金融市场允许把风险从那些承担投资的人身上转移到那些提供资金的投资人身上。

⑤ 资产流动性：金融市场给金融资产持有者提供了转售或清理持有资产的机会。

⑥ 效率：金融市场减少交易成本和获取信息的成本。有助于提高金融市场的效率。

金融市场的种类

金融市场可被分为若干子类市场：

① 商品市场，促进商品交易。

② 货币市场，提供短期债务融资和投资。获取短期融资的主要手段是通过银行贷款或者透支，或者通过交易或国库券。

③ 金融衍生产品市场，为金融风险管理提供手段。

④ 期货市场，是参与者在未来某一特定的日期买卖日用品和交割期货合约的拍卖市场。

⑤ 外汇市场，促进外汇与国际货币的交易。

⑥ 现货市场，商品、外汇和有价证券即刻或现场交易，商品现金出售立即交割。(商品和有价证券7个工作日内交割完毕，外汇2个工作日内交割完毕)

⑦ 银行行间市场，是银行与金融机构之间交易货币的金融体系，不包括散户投资者和零售型股票券商规模较小的交易方。

⑧ 资本市场，包括股票市场和债券市场。股票市场通过发行股份或普通股提供融资。债券市场通过发行债券提供融资。

资本市场还可以分为初级市场和二级市场。初级市场是将新发行的证券销售给最初购买者的证券市场。金融产品包括在初级以及二级金融市场买卖信贷供给、抵押借款、公司股份和保险。二级市场是对已发行的现有证券进行转售，使得买卖方可以转售他们的产品和现有证券给第三方的有价证券市场。发行人只有通过初级市场筹措到所需资金。初级市场的交易存在于发行者和投资者之间，而二级市场交易存在于投资者和投资者之间。众所周知的二级金融市场是证券交易所，允许对过去已发行的公司股份进行交易。

资产流动性是二级市场交易有价证券的一个关键方面。资产流动性指的是投资者可以轻松地出售其购买的证券而不会损失资产的价值。投资者从流动性证券中获利，因为他们可以在任何时候出售他们的资产；流动性不强的证券会迫使卖方打折，清除他们的这些资产。

如何选择股票

证券交易所是金融市场的一个好例子。公司可以通过向投资者出售公司股票来募集资金，而这些现有股票还可以继续买卖。作为投资者，如何选择股票？由于存在多种选择，选股对于普通投资者来说是一个挑战。

选股的第一步是确定你的目标。你的投资组合是打算用来创收的吗？考虑行业中的低成长性公司，比如公用事业、房地产信托投资基金或业主有限合伙制。你想保留资本吗？稳定的蓝筹公司往往因承担风险小而受到投资者青睐。你想你的资本增长吗？瞄准一系列的市值和周期循环阶段。结合这些策略可以让你的股票投资组合多样化。

投资者需要留心，及时了解时事和观点。博客、杂志和在线财经新闻会告知投资者有关市场的重大发展，促使他们去查看并了解更多信息。这是每天可以做的被动式研究的一种简单形式。有时候，一篇新文章或博客帖子会产生潜在的投资理念基础。

然后，投资者需要找到他们感兴趣的公司。一旦你要在一个行业里出售，并且知道其主要参与者，寻找讨论该公司如何赚钱的投资者报告，该报告应该包括公司的资产负债表信息、收入和现金流业绩、增长机会。

遵循这些步骤，你可以发现一些自己感兴趣的股票，或者发现市场上没有你感兴趣的股票。如果答案是后者，你就避免了潜在的不良投资。

拓展阅读

第1篇

中国股票市场

中国股市近几周的崩溃已促使政府采取积极措施以阻止下滑。如果股票继续下跌，将损害中国消费者的信心并使已然减速的经济增长进一步放缓，而这对于全球经济的影响将是惨痛的。

发生了什么？

中国股市曾一路飙升，在6月12日之前的一年里上涨了超过一倍。数百万中国的工薪阶层和中产阶级对股市下了重注，经常借钱炒股，而这也进一步刺激了上涨。

但上涨与经济基本面并不相符，催生了对于泡沫的担忧。股票在中国经济增速放缓之时仍在上涨。当外国投资者和国内机构购买经营稳定的大型公司股票时，工薪阶层和中产阶级家庭购买价格较低的中小型公司股票，并因为这些股票的价格在上涨而不断购入。许多公司脆弱的资产负债表和长期的公司管理问题被搁置一边。

最近几个月，中国股市经历了短暂的虚弱期，因为投资者对于市场过热的忧虑开始增加。即便如此，政府仍频繁地安抚投资者以稳定市场。

现在，投资者失去了信心。在6月26日沪深两市大跌超过7%后，中国的中央银行在第二天以降息作为回应，称这是为了提振经济。但股市持续大规模下跌，促使政府采取积极的行动应对。

对于股价下跌，中国正在如何应对？

自6月25日起，中国政府已经采取了一系列政策措施以阻止下跌。政府降低了利率，增加了股票投资者可获得的贷款，并承诺调查任何涉嫌操纵市场的人。

政府在 7 月 4 日采取了最为勇敢的举措,策划了一项计划,21 家证券公司将出资 194 亿美元(1200 亿人民币)建立基金购买大型公司的股票。上海证券交易所和深圳证券交易所暂停了 28 只新股的发行计划,并称将向未来的购买者退还所有已支付的定金,以释放更多现金投入到现有的股票中。政府机构还在 7 月 5 日宣布将向证券公司提供贷款,之后证券公司将可以向有意愿购买股票的投资者提供资金。

救市举措之后,大部分大型公司的股票价格在 7 月 6 日止跌。但大量散户投资者持有的中小型公司股票仍持续下跌。

外国投资者受影响程度如何?

中国股市才刚刚向外国投资者开放,所以海外买家并未受到下跌的严重影响。这类投资者持有大约 4%的中国股票。而这些股票高度集中在并不像中小型公司那般不稳定的大型公司。

但是股市的下跌能够很快蔓延。香港股市抵挡住了此前的几轮抛售,但在 7 月 6 日中国政府的行动之后下挫。而外国投资者在经常作为内地股市代言人的香港股市中投入了大量资金。

中国股市的问题会影响全球经济吗?

这是有可能的。

中国是世界第二大经济体,也是澳大利亚和巴西等国家商品的最大进口国。中国也是德国以及其他国家重要的工厂设备和其他机械的买家。如果中国股市的下跌损害了消费者信心,这将导致此类采购的减缓。

股市的衰弱如果长期蔓延到整个中国经济,可能促使北京重新审视其海外贷款和投资。许多国家的行业和公司的发展都依赖中国的资金。但是如果公司和个人到海外寻求资金安全,中国的境外投资可能还会上升。

第 2 篇

中国债券市场危机显露

——情况使投资人惊慌

现在,在中国庞大且日趋复杂的金融市场中,另一个快速增长的部门正在显露出危机迹象:9 万亿美元规模的债券市场。

上周,国债和企业债券出现价格下跌,本周二抛售仍在继续。这种情况令投资者感到惊恐,他们敦促政府暂时限制一些交易,并向处于困境的金融机构提供紧急贷款。

当更多的中国企业需要货币来应对经济增长放缓时,债券价格下降导致了借款成本的增加。周二,债券收益率再次创下新高。

从一定程度上说,这也是中国正在对全球金融变化做出反应。随着美联储提高短期利率,以及很多人认为唐纳德·特朗普上任后会加大政府支出,全球投资者都在出手债券。

但中国在实施自己的平衡措施时步履维艰。中国债券下跌的另一个原因是北京力图从金融体系中挤压出超发的货币,防止潜在泡沫出现,这些泡沫可能藏在阴暗的、难以追踪的经济角落。如果北京继续这些努力,债券价格可能还会进一步下跌。

至少有 40 家企业表示,他们将推迟或取消债券发行,因为销售债券会有被迫支付高额利率的风险,或者根本就销不出去。江苏苏美达集团就是其中之一,这家工业贸易公司出口的商品五花八门,从园艺工具到汽车零部件都有。上周四,该公司取消了 1.3 亿美元短期债券的发行。

中国有特别的理由感到担心。作为仅次于美国的全球第二大经济体,它的金融体系相当脆弱,眼下深陷债务,容易受隐性压力的影响。海外利率升高也可能会促使更多的中国投资者将资金转移出国,以追求更高的回报,或者是避开一些人眼中中国正在日益加剧的问题。

健康的债市对中国的重组计划至关重要。中国一直指望其快速增长的债市可以成为一种途径,将市场约束机制引入其传统的、浪费资源的政府导向型经济。

美国的金融体系比较成熟,企业有很多种办法筹到资金。他们可以从银行借款、靠出售股票或债券筹资,或者直接从任意数量的投资者那里筹集资金。

但在中国,国有银行是迄今为止主要的资金来源。这有助于推动中国的经济增长,但它也使得贷款流入了有政治背景的借款人那里,而不是经济最需要它的地方。这就是中国经济如今陷在供过于求的钢铁、玻璃、水泥和汽车厂里的原因之一。

特别是在过去两年中,中国已采取措施,鼓励股市、债市以及私人贷款机构的健康发展,它需要一种方式来确保引导资金流向的是重视利润的投资者,而不是政界人士及其在国有银行的盟友。

去年股市崩盘,私人贷款发展缓慢。但在上周之前,中国债市一直走势良好。地方政府的投资部门和其他大型借款机构最近数月涌入债市,以低利率发行债券,偿还利率更高的银行贷款——这也正是政府的意图所在。今年前 11 个月,债券发行量比去年同期增长了 47%。

政府没有预见到的是,中国各家银行进行的投机性债券交易出现了爆炸式增长。

银行越来越多地通过出售理财产品筹集资金,这些产品看上去像是可靠的银行存款,通常出售给普通投资者。银行极少披露这些理财产品背后的内幕,而且通常也不把它们计入资产负债表。

然而,越来越清楚的是,很多理财产品都在以债券为支撑。理财产品的债券持有量在截至今年 6 月的 18 个月内翻了一番。除了这种风险之外,银行还使用大规模杠杆押注债券价格的走向。现在政府正在努力控制它。

周二,一年期的国债收益率从两周前的 2.35%上升到 3.11%,对于债券来说,这个涨幅已经很大。当债券价格下跌时,收益率就会上涨,导致发行债券的成本增加。

企业债券的收益率也在快速上升,对于将资金注入到常常不透明的中国公司,投资者已经开始要求获得更好的回报。这反转了今年早些时候的趋势:当时投资者对中国债券非常看好,他们也购买了企业债券,导致国债和企业债券之间的自然差距缩小。

FXM 兄弟基金合伙人苗作兴预测,企业债券将会继续遭到抛售,直到政府和企业债券收益率的差距再次拉大为止。

第三章　国　际　贸　易

课文

国际贸易——世界永恒的话题

贸易是商品和服务的交换，是最基本的社会活动。贸易几乎与人类几乎同时存在。没有贸易，就没有社会。

作为当今世界最重要的经济活动之一，国际贸易在一国经济的发展和全球的加速发展中发挥着越来越重要的作用。但什么是国际贸易？国际贸易又称世界贸易、对外贸易或海外贸易，是国家间商品和服务的交换。国际贸易有许多类型，具体如下：

从货物的流向来看，国际贸易可分为进口贸易、出口贸易和转口贸易。

出口贸易，指将国内市场生产加工的商品运输到国际市场进行销售。

进口贸易，指将商品从国外运到国内市场进行出售或使用的交易。

过境贸易(转口贸易)指的是通过第三方国家将商品从商品生产国运输到商品消费国，进行买卖商品的贸易。

从商品形态上看，国际贸易可分为有形商品贸易和无形商品贸易：

有形商品贸易　指的是实际有形商品的贸易。我们购买的东西常常是"实实在在"的东西，也就是我们能触摸到或看到并能够使用的东西。比如，汽车、酒、鞋子等。

无形商品贸易　有时，我们花钱购买的并非是触摸得到的实物，我们购买的商品是"无形的"，或者是看不见的，如公共汽车费、旅馆服务、保险及邮政服务。在这种情况下，我们购买的是"服务"，而不是"商品"。购买和销售服务被称为"无形商品贸易"。同样，在对外贸易中我们不仅进出口商品，也提供进出口服务。

产生国际贸易的原因

在当今复杂的经济领域中，没有任何个人或是国家能够做到自给自足。不同的国家利用不同的经济资源；不同的人民具有不同的技能，这就是国际贸易及经济活动的基础。国际贸易的发生有着诸多的原因。

1. 资源原因

气候条件和地形对农业生产非常重要。这些因素的不同使得一些国家能够种植某些植物，并使其他国家唯一的选择就是——进口他们生产的产品。例如，哥伦比亚和巴西有机会向世界各国出口咖啡豆。另一个例子是，美国这个大平原国家有着理想的气候和地形，(凭借这样的优势条件)可提高小麦的产量。这使得美国成为最大的小麦出口国。

2. 经济原因

除了获得他们所需的产品外，各国还希望通过相互交易来获得经济效益。世界各地的同一商品的不同价格也反映了生产成本的差异。例如，A国和B国在生产卡片和计算机方面可能具有相同的能力，但如果大规模生产商品，生产成本就会降低。这两个国家也明白，如果其中一个国家努力专注于生产其中的一类商品，同时去进口另一类商品，这将对双方有利。

3. 政治原因

政治目标有时会超过国家之间的经济考虑。一个国家可能会因某一国家持有相同的政治观念而与其进行贸易，同样，也会因另一个国家持有与他不一样的政治观念，禁止或限制与这些国家进行贸易，这对双方都是不利的。

国际贸易带来的好处

世界上大多数国家似乎都有强烈扩大贸易往来的愿望。乍一看，不同的国家似乎有许多不同的经济、政治和社会原因想要进行交易。然而，从表面上看，都有一个共同的财政优势，促使所有国家通过国际贸易获利。

1. 降低商品价格

一方面，国家贸易有着成本优势。这在国际贸易的"经济理性"部分中得到了解释。此外，世界市场的竞争是源源不断的，这促进了更低价格的出现。如果进口货物质量好，价格又不高于国内价格，就会有成本优势。

2. 商品和服务的多样化

国际贸易意味着各国可以为消费者提供更丰富的商品，从而提高人们的生活水平。国家贸易还因价格优势和国际市场竞争的存在而使商品的价格更低。

3. 扩大市场

国际贸易扩大了市场，市场的扩大促使制造商能够在调研和生产方面利用经济规模。此外，由于世界各地的市场往往处于不同的发展阶段，新扩展的市场也可以帮助延长产品的寿命。

4. 经济增长

国际贸易催化了经济的增长，为经济注入财富。它也给各国提供了发展的有益链接，促进了旅游、教育、提高了就业机会——这不仅促进了国家本身的经济发展，同时也催化了整个世界的经济发展和进步。

现今，原始的以"物换物"贸易在一些国家中依然存在。这些国家没有足够的外汇储备用于计算。这种贸易被称为易货贸易。另一种贸易方式为"以物换钱"，即用货物支付贷款，用于结算的货币主要有美元、英镑、瑞士法郎、欧元、港元及日元。

拓展阅读

第1篇

贸易均利化

——全球化能否使生活更美好？

过去二十年的经济形势使得多国的工薪阶层对全球化心存戒备。美国总统候选人、地产大亨，同时也是电视真人秀明星的唐纳德·特朗普(Donald Trump)承诺，若竞选成功，他将对中国的商品增收 45%的关税，此番言论部分是出于对全球化贸易的担忧。经济学家们大都对这种冒进的贸易保护措施嗤之以鼻，他们认为全球化贸易无疑是利大于弊的。然而，新的调查显示，很多短期成本和收益数据实际上比账本上显示的更加平衡，而不是偏向于本国。

麻省理工学院的大卫·奥拓，苏黎世大学的大卫·多恩和圣迭戈加利福尼亚大学的戈登·汉森提供的切实可信的证据表明，发达国家的工人们在中国崛起的现实中遭受的损失比经济学家预期的要多。他们在今年 1 月发表的文章上说，突然让外国竞争者进入国内市场，将会使得工资和就业率在至少十年内维持较低水平。

贸易带来的好处多多。有了贸易，消费者可以买到他们本来买不到的东西。而没有贸易，苏格兰人也只能喝苏格兰艾莱岛的威士忌了。商品种类越来越多：美国人能买的车就不仅是本土的福特，还可以是沃尔沃或者斯巴鲁。不过国际贸易最大的福利就是能够增加国家财富，这也是亚当·斯密以来的经济学家们一直秉承的观点。贸易使得市场更加广阔，专业分工更加细化，成本更低，收入更高。

经济学家长久以来认为，财富也许不能平均分配。沃尔夫冈·斯托尔帕和保罗·萨缪尔森在 1941 发表的一篇论文指出，在两个经济体之间的贸易中，如果一国劳动力相对稀缺(如美国)而另一国劳动力相对丰富(如中国)，可能导致劳动力相对稀缺的国家的工资水平下降。然而，许多人都认为这只是小概率事件。他们认为，受贸易影响的产业工人会在其他领域找到新的就业机会。

大多数研究认为贸易对工人的影响是积极的。但之后中国融入全球贸易，体量巨大。1991 年到 2013 年，其出口的制成品占全球制成品出口的份额从 2.3%激增到 18.8%。在美国，对于某些类别的商品，美国的国内消费几乎全靠从中国进口。

中国自改革开放以来，获得了巨大的收益。平均实际收入从相当于美国 1990 年的 4%到如今已经提升到了 25%。数以百万计的中国人因为贸易的发展走出了贫困。很多人认为，全球市场更大，供应成本降低，劳动实现了再分配，企业不再局限于萎缩的制造业而把目光转向了效益更多的其他行业，因此受益良多。

但这些好处在几十年后才能看到。同样的研究发现，在短期内，美国从贸易中获得的收益与中国相比微不足道。依赖于中国进口的行业成本太高，抵消了消费者以及免受冲击的企业获得的大部分利益。经济学家们的认知似乎有些错误，他们认为工人们很容易适应贸易的变动。生产活动往往具有地域集聚性。因此，中国进口造成的坏影响同样也就相对集中，比如美国中西部的枢纽地区。生产商受到的巨大竞争压力打乱了地区经济的节奏，梅斯尔·奥拓(Messrs Autor)、多恩(Dorn)和汉森(Hanson)在文中写道，这损害了供应商和本地的服务产业。这样的地方缺少新兴产业来吸纳失业工人，而失业者也不愿意(或不能)搬到更繁荣的地区去。劳动力市场对中国贸易的调整非常缓慢，并没有预期那样全面。

因此，作者在 2013 年的一篇研究报告中发现，1900 至 2007 年间，美国制造业就业率下降了 44%，这都归咎于进口的中国商品的竞争。对于任一行业，每个工人每年多增加 1000 美元的中国进口商品的消费，将导致一些产业集聚地区的工人收入平均下降 500 美元。政府福利上涨仅为每个工人抵消了 58 美元。2014 年，一篇由麻省理工学院的大龙·阿西莫格鲁和丹普莱斯共同撰写的文章研究了 21 世纪的美国的"就业凹陷"，计算出中国进口商品的竞争导致全美减少了 240,000 个工作岗位。

中国的巨额经常项目顺差似乎加重了同中国的贸易成本：中国从其他国家进口的进口量低于向其他国家的出口量。中国与美国的贸易尤其不平衡。在 1992 年到 2008 年期间，美国经常账户赤字中20%～40%都源于与中国的贸易，中国从美国进口的商品锐减不少，反之亦然。

国际贸易给全球带来了巨额的福利。所以，贸易调整援助、工作再培训以及其他旨在为全球贸易提供政治支持的政府花费，虽然数额巨大，但听起来也无可厚非。然而，为了政策效果，经济学家和政治学家不能再把这些政策看作是收买贸易反对者的政治好处。为了使人人都享受到贸易带来的好处，贸易反对者的看法必不可少。

第2篇

贸易保护主义无法拯救世界经济

对贸易保护主义来说，全球金融危机无疑是一针催化剂。近段时间，随着全球经济形势恶化，一些国家试图通过建立贸易壁垒来促进增长前景。中国的有识之士呼吁这些政府不要重蹈历史覆辙，回到贸易保护主义和经济孤立主义。

随着世界经济的恶化，历次全球经济危机往往都伴随着贸易争端的高发。1930年，美国政府大范围提高关税，引发了全球范围报复性贸易战。20世纪七八十年代两次石油危机时，主要国家放任货币贬值以扩大出口的做法引发了贸易摩擦。1997年亚洲金融危机之后，全球反倾销、反补贴和保障措施案件明显增多。

当前，金融危机已蔓延到制造业、服务业等实体经济领域，各国倒闭的工厂剧增，失业率上升，政治压力和社会问题接踵而至。越来越多国家以经济安全和保护本国虚弱产业为由，加强政府对经济的干预，阻挠其他国家，特别是新兴国家企业出口。

贸易保护主义不同于正当的贸易保护措施，它是对多边贸易规则中救济措施的滥用。从传统的关税和非关税壁垒，到技术性贸易壁垒、行业标准等，以及产业保护主义，当前贸易保护主义的形式更加复杂多样，隐蔽性更强。在危机加剧的背景下，即使符合WTO规则的保护措施也应慎用，这已成为各国共识。在2008年11月举行的G20金融峰会上，各国领导人共同呼吁抵制贸易保护主义，承诺在未来一年内，避免设置新的贸易和投资壁垒。年底的亚太经济合作组织领导人会议和今年初的世界经济论坛达沃斯年会上，再次发出了反对保护主义的强音。

历史告诉我们，任何针对他国的贸易保护举措，不仅会损害对方，最终也会伤及自身。经验告诉我们，大规模的贸易保护措施将使金融危机下本已严峻的经济形势更加困难。

1930年，美国为了应对经济危机，颁发了《斯姆特—霍利关税法》，大幅提高超过2万种外国商品的进口关税，结果引起了其他国家的贸易保护主义报复。面对危机，各国以邻为壑，全球贸易总额大幅缩减，从1929年的360亿美元缩小到1932年的120亿美元。美国自身也深受其害，出口总额从1929年的52亿美元左右缩减到1932年的12亿美元。这一法案即使在美国国内也被普遍认为是大萧条加剧的催化剂。

如今的全球贸易形势已相当严峻：经济危机导致外需衰退，各主要贸易国的出口增速已急剧下滑，甚至出现大幅萎缩。德国2008年11月份的出口额较前月大幅下滑10.6%，为1990年以来的最大单月降幅。中国2008年11月以来出口连续出现负增长，其中2009年1月出口下降了17.5%。如果未来贸易保护主义泛滥，会使严峻的形势雪上加霜，造成的后果很难预料。我们应该认真思索，这样的后果世界能否承受，又是否值得承受？

危机当头，重要的是各国携手共克时艰，而非互相指责，以邻为壑。金融危机是全球经济结构失衡、金融风险积聚长期积累的结果，解决问题也不可能一蹴而就。当前加强磋商、增强合作，保持国际贸易渠道畅通，才符合各国的根本利益。国际贸易的健康发展，是推动世界经济复苏的重要力量。当年罗斯福政府实行新政，与贸易保护主义决裂，带领美国经济走出低谷，推动了全球经济的增长。

在这场前所未有的世界金融危机中，中国与其他国家一样都受到严重冲击。去年第三季度以来，经济增速放缓，出口大幅下滑，就业压力加大。即便如此，中国仍坚定认为，贸易保护主义是条死胡同。在全球贸易萎缩的情况下，2008年中国从各国进口11331亿美元的商品，增长18.5%，促进了贸易伙伴的经济发展。危机爆发以来，中国政府果断出台了一系列扩大内需的措施。作为一个开放的大国，中国内需的提升可为其他国家提供更大的市场空间和更多的投资机会。今年，中国将继续扩大进口，积极组织企业采购团赴海外大规模采购，进口设备、商品和技术。

中国始终奉行互利共赢的开放战略，倡导国际经济合作。我们主张积极推进符合各国利益与多边贸易体制的多哈回合谈判。中国愿与世界各国一道，以开放迎接挑战，以合作应对危机，共克时艰，推动世界经济走向新的繁荣。

第四章 财务管理

课文

财务管理介绍

国际财务管理的重要性

国际财务管理处理国际业务上的财务决定。国际业务的发展，首先，最明显地体现在国际贸易范围的扩大。第二次世界大战后，为了促进贸易发展，制定了关贸总协定。在过去的这些年里，它很大地消除了贸易壁垒，国际贸易呈现多方面发展。自然而然地，进出口贸易中涉及的财务工作和跨国交易总量越来越多。

随着国际贸易的发展，出口国的产品在进口国变得越来越成熟。一旦产品在进口国变得成熟，出口国就会在当地生产产品以便避开关税，能够做到以最低成本提供该产品。

因此，跨国公司的出现是国际贸易扩大的副产品，这种说法并没有错。随着跨国公司业务的不断增长，财务决定也出现了复杂的情况。除了要考虑投资的地点、时间和金额，各子公司和总公司营运资金管理的决定越来越复杂，因为基本政策从一家跨国公司到另一家跨国公司是不同的。那些对全球财富价值最大化感兴趣的跨国公司采取中央集权的方法，而那些不干涉子公司的跨国公司则把权力下放。

资金流动的性质变得如此复杂，因此，正确的管理成为一种必需，也与国际财务管理的研究高度相关。事实上，为了规避风险，国际财务管理建议在特定的时刻对特定的案例采取最适合的方法。

财务经理三大主要财务决策作用

财务管理是对财务资源实行高效有效的计划与控制，目的是使利润最大化，保证个人(称为个人理财)、政府(称为公共财政)、盈利和非营利组织/公司(称为公司或管理财务)资金的流动性。总的来说，它涉及风险平衡和利润问题。

财务管理的决策性功能主要被分为以下三个部分。

A. 投资决策

这也是最重要的决定。它从公司确定所需的资产总额开始，有两种投资决策：

a. 资本投资决策

这项涉及大笔资金，影响也是重大的。比如需要新机器或去开设新厂。

b. 营运资本投资决策

这是更常规的或计划的决策形式。比如存货数量、现金、一定时间内的应收金额的决策。

B. 财务决策

这是第二大主要决策。在确定购买哪些资产或者投资哪些证券之后，财务经理得确定如何去管理这些财务。

C. 资产管理决策

这是第三个，也是最后一项决策。一旦得到资产并做出正确的财务决策，这些资产必须有效地被管理。通过高效有效地管理现有资产，公司会增加回报和降低非流动性的风险。

财务经理的角色

在财务和财务管理领域，财务经理有很大的权力。他不仅要提高公司的财务，还要做公司的其他工作。我们可以用下面的话来解释他的角色。

A. 财务经理在公司筹资中的作用

财务经理检查公司的不同资金来源。他不从所有来源获得资金。首先，他确定短期和长期的的需求，之后，他选择资金的最佳来源。他有权力改变公司的资金结构，给公司带来更多的利益。

B. 财务经理在杠杆收益最大化中的作用

财务经理利用经营和财务杠杆，使公司在杠杆中实现利益最大化。

C. 财务经理在国际金融决策中的作用

财务经理在国际财务决定上寻找机会。在这些机会中，他做信用违约互换、利率互换和货币互换合同。

D. 财务经理在投资决策中的作用

财务经理在真正投资项目之前，会检查每个投资项目的净现值。投资项目的净现值是指公司如果投资该项目应获得的折现率的净利润。公司接受高的净现值。因此，由于责任重大，财务经理的角色显得很重要。

E. 财务经理在风险管理中的作用

发生风险意味着面对不同的损失。财务经理在风险和管理上非常谨慎。他在寻找新的控制公司风险的方法上扮演着重要角色。就像其他的管理部分，他要估算风险、组织员工负责控制风险并计算出风险调整后的净现值。他会与所有风险控制机构见面，如保险公司和在普适水平的评级机构。他能把公司的不幸转变成财富。通过对不利情况的良好估计，他尽力维护公司的资金。

拓展阅读

第1篇

2016：上海金融业的一个大年

上海作为一个中国的大都市，现已成为一个国际金融中心。在过去的一年里，上海一直致力于发展一系列的金融部门措施。这些措施包括深化金融改革，提高行业的基础设施建设，深化金融体制创新，提高城市在金融行业的国际影响力。

中国金融信息中心、中国经济信息服务上海分公司分析2016金融业中的城市的努力并于1月9日发布以下十大事件：

1. 深化上海自贸区金融改革

2015年10月，上海自由贸易区引进40项创新金融改革措施。2016年先后发布了更详细的规则，进一步解释和指导各项措施的落实。

2. 投资贷款联动机制在上海试点

4月，张江国家自主创新示范区和三家商业银行——上海银行、华瑞银行和浦发硅谷银行——被选为投资贷款联动机制试行的试点银行。该机制的目的是让中小型科技企业更容易获得金融服务，有助企业的发展。

3. 上海保险交易所开幕

为扩大在世界第三大保险市场上的透明度和效率，2016年6月12日，中国的第一个保险资产交易平台，上海保险交易所开幕。其目的是吸引更多的国际保险和再保险巨头到上海。之后，一个国家保险投资基金也在上海自由贸易区建立。

4. 上海商业票据交换公司和中国信托登记有限开放

2016年12月见证了上海商业票据交换公司与中国信托登记有限公司的交流，此交流为集中式商业票据交易提供了一个全国性的平台，并拓宽现有的金融基础设施。该设施服务于日益增长的市场需求，提高市场监管。中国信托登记公司于12月26日开业，主要集中登记、发行信托产品以及监管信托业交易。

5. 全国互联网金融协会在中国上海成立

中国国家互联网金融协会于2015年3月25日在上海成立，对中国蓬勃发展的互联网金融业起着至关重要的作用。协会研究制定和引入行业规则和自律机制，更好地规范互联网金融领域并促进其进一步发展。

6. CCP12在上海登记

全球中央对手方协会(CCP12)作为一个非营利组织，于2016年6月8日在中国(上海)自由贸易试验区注册。该协会成立于2001年，一直致力于进一步对整个行业的最佳结算和风险管理的实践进行讨论。它也支持监管协调和全球标准成就战略发展。它在上海落户体现了中国的金融市场发展和风险防范的进步赢得了国际认可。

7. 上海黄金交易所推出以人民币计价的黄金基准价格

上海黄金交易所(SGE)是世界上最大的实物黄金交易所，于2016年4月19日在上海推出以人民币计价的基准价格。这一措施将有利于中国国内的黄金市场和全球贵金属市场。该所认为，上海黄金基准价格的推出对于充分反映中国黄金的供求情况和体现国家的黄金市场的价格趋势是有用的。该所也被认为是国际黄金市场的一个必要补充，将会让市场上实物黄金的价格更加公开。

8. "金砖四国"绿色新发展银行和上海浦东发展银行发行人民币计价债券

1月，上海浦东发展银行发行绿色债券200亿元(29亿美元)，这是中国国内首个绿色债券。

7月，金砖国家新开发银行首次发行以人民币计价的绿色金融债券30亿元，这是债券是首次由总部在中国的国际金融机构发行。发行债券表明国际金融机构对人民币国际化以及其对全球绿色经济增长和发展的贡献的信心。

9. 上海市财政局发行地方政府债券

上海财政局于11月通过政府债券发行系统发行了300亿元的地方政府债券，该政府债券发行系统是由上海证券交易所发展而来。此举被认为有利于扩大地方政府债券市场的发行渠道，优化投资者结构，提高债券的流动性。

12月，该局下发30亿元地方政府债券，目标客户为在上海保税区开立自由贸易账户的中国和外国的投资者。这是在中国自由贸易区首次发行债券，有助于拓宽境外人民币回流渠道，推动人民币国际化。

10. 中国发展银行开设上海代表处和陆家嘴金融城的管理机制改革

中国发展银行的分支机构于6月23日在上海开幕。该分行将支持上海自由贸易区的债券市场基础设施的发展。它也将参加当地的金融市场交易，推动人民币国际化。

第2篇

给父母的十条经济资助建议

想要寻找经济资助来付学费？遵循这10个技巧可以帮助你获得经济资助，你得记住，不要等到你的孩子上高三才开始考虑学生经济资助的事情。越早开始，你可能会得到越多的钱。

1. 尽早了解你的预期家庭贡献情况

孩子上初中时，你要估计你的预期家庭贡献。通过了解你的支付能力，你可以在你的经济范围内找到可以上的大学，并确定你可能需要奖学金和贷款来解决学费问题。你能收集越多的财政援助信息就越好。

2. 减少你孩子的储蓄

孩子20%的资产应该用在大学上，而不是只是你的5.6%。鼓励你的孩子存钱，但用保管账户保管大学资金。

3. 学习一点关于营销的知识

这是一个竞争择优奖励最重要的方面。突出孩子的成就，奖励委员会将更有可能考虑把奖学金给你的儿子或女儿。

4. 让财政援助成为参观校园的一部分

去跟学生资助办事处的人谈谈，这也是让你的家人在以校园为基础的奖励方面最好的方式。然后，做一些笔记！这些联系方式可能用得着。

5. 做一点侦探工作

查看一下你的孩子对经济资助的申请是否影响录用的可能性，如果是这样的话，找出方法。

6. 下决定申请提前录取

如果你的孩子想申请提前录取，确定它将如何影响学生经济援助的机会。接受提前录取可能阻碍获得奖项，如果你的孩子接受了提前录取，就不能够获得其他学校的经济支持了。(如果你的孩子已经被不具约束力提前录取，那就不是问题了。)

具有约束力的提前录取

具有约束力的提前录取政策是多数顶尖大学为那些还在高中三年级上学期的，已经选好第一志愿的学生准备的。它要求申请人在高中三年级的秋季学期(上学期)就提出入学申请。(DEADLINE 一般为 11/1 或 11/15)，该录取通知是一纸具有约束力的录取合同。实行该项招生政策的学校在接到申请材料的数月后，通知申请人录取与否的决定。申请人一旦被录取，就必须进入该校学习。一旦向一所学校提出了 ED 的申请，申请人就不再享有向其他学校申请 ED 或 EA 的权力了。例如，今年亚洲易网就通过 ED 为王同学成功申请到了纽约大学的录取。

不具约束力的提前录取

只有很少一部分学校实行不具约束力的提前录取的招生政策。它允许申请人提前提出入学申请，学校在一两个月后将评审结果通知申请人。与具有约束力的提前录取相比，该项招生政策不具有约束力。如果被申请学校录取，申请人并不一定就非要上该校不可，他仍可以等接到其他学校的录取结果(RD)后，再做决定。申请 EA 招生政策的申请人可以同时向另一学校提出同样的申请，但不可以再申请另一所学校的 ED。

7. 确定奖项之外的影响

如果你的孩子接受外界的奖学金，了解它将如何影响学生财政援助奖。一些学校会减少资助，其他将削减贷款。学校的政策会影响借款。

8. 注意期限

孩子申请得越早，就越可能接受援助。为协助学院形式的财政援助，尽早申报税费。记住，如果你申请的学校需要配置金融援助申请，要比 FAFSA 的期限要早。FAFSA 是 "The Free Application for Federal Student Aid "(自愿联邦奖学金)的缩写，是给美国公民或者绿卡持有者的资助。

9. 完成 FAFSA

填写此表格，即使你认为你不算很合格—富裕的家庭在一定的高学费的学校有时也符合援助。这一申请是你所有的联邦贷款、奖学金和工作研究奖中的唯一途径。

10. 让学校意识到特殊情况

如果你完成 FAFSA 或 PROFILE 后失去了工作，将你的情况通知学校。大多数标准的政策允许使用预期收入，这可能会增加金融援助。

参 考 译 文

第五章 企业管理

课文

管理人员和管理——职场永恒的话题

所有企业，不管规模大小，都特别需要管理和管理人员。他们是所有企业的特别组成部分。他们使得企业团结一致，运作正常。没有一个企业能够在脱离管理人员的情况下正常运行。但是，什么是管理人员？什么样的人才算是管理人员？管理人员又该具备什么样的职责？

企业的成员

管理人员在企业中工作，但不是每个在企业中工作的人都是管理人员。在一个企业中，我们可以把成员分为两大类：管理人员和作业人员。作业人员是那些直接从事工作任务并且没有监督他人工作权力的人，比如农场里的农夫、厂房里的工人、在街道作业的清洁工都属于作业人员的范畴。与此相反，管理人员是负责监督企业中他人活动的人。总之，管理人员和作业人员的本质区别是——管理人员有直接向他们汇报工作的下属员工。

管理人员的级别

管理人员是企业的基本资源。在一个全自动化工厂里，也许没有普通的作业人员，但必定有管理人员。管理人员是大多数企业最昂贵的资源，也是消耗最快、最需要经常补充的资源。建立一个管理团队需要花费数年，但是它有可能在短时间内因管理不善而消耗殆尽。

管理人员有三种级别，分别为基层管理人员、中层管理人员和高层管理人员。尽管管理职位和各种头衔有关，但确切地分辨出企业的管理人员并非难事。基层管理人员通常被称为主管，他们也有可能被称之为组长、指导员或是小组协调员。他们负责监督作业人员的日常活动。例如，在大学里，系主任就是基层管理人员，他们负责监督全体教员(作业人员)的日常教学活动。中层管理人员是指介于基层管理人员和高层管理人员之间的管理人员。这种管理人员管理和监督基层管理人员，可能还有对作业人员的管理。他们还负责把高层管理人员制定的目标转变成比他们级别低的管理人员的具体实施任务。在企业中，中层管理人员可能有这样的头衔，如项目经理、区域经理等。

处于或接近顶端的企业管理人员是高层管理人员。这些人负责制定企业和影响企业成员的大政方针。在企业中，高层管理人员通常以以下的头衔出现，比如，总裁、副总裁，财务总监、首席运营官、首席执行官、董事会主席。

管理的定义

管理是指通过计划、组织、领导、控制等环节来协调组织的资源，以便更有效益、更有效率地达到组织目标的过程。管理包括计划、组织、领导和控制一个组织或为达成目标所做的努力。

管理的职能

在二十世纪初,法国工业家亨利·法约尔在其著作中提出,所有的管理人员都从事五种管理活动。这五种活动称为"管理职能",它们包括计划、组织、指挥、协调和控制。但现在,它已被浓缩为四种管理活动,即计划、组织、领导和控制。

计划阐述的是组织未来的目标以及如何达成目标。计划是指为组织未来的业绩设置目标和确定为达成这些目标需要完成的任务和使用的资源。不管怎样,缺乏计划或计划不周就会影响企业的业绩。例如,服饰零售商旋转木马曾经遍布美国的各大商场,但由于计划不周,业绩下滑导致破产,最后消失在商界。该企业的高层管理者缺乏对市场趋势和人口发展趋势的洞察力,对如何获取利润和促进增长所做的计划不周详,另外,他们为管理继任所做的准备也失败了,这几个因素最终导致了这家拥有 1500 间店铺、市值 10 亿美元的全国性连锁企业的失败。

组织通常在计划之后实施,它反映了一个组织是如何设法实施计划的。组织包括布置任务、分配任务给各个部门,以及把资源分配给各个部门。例如,霍尼韦尔国际公司的管理人员重新组织了新产品开发活动,选拔擅长于市场营销、工程学和设计的员工组成"老虎队"来进行新产品的开发。新的结构设计将生产一个新的恒温器的时间从 4 年减少到 12 个月。现今,很多公司都效仿霍尼韦尔国际公司,重新组织能够更好地进行自我管理的团队。

领导是利用影响力来激励员工实现组织目标。领导意味着创造一个共享的文化和价值观,把目标传达给整个组织的员工,向员工灌输一种期望,希望他们能以高水平的表现实现组织目标。领导涉及激励整个部门和那些直接与部门经理一起工作的人。在这个充满不确定性、国际竞争日益激烈、劳动力日益多元化的时代,塑造文化、传达目标、激励员工的能力对于企业的成功来说至关重要。

控制指的是监督员工的活动,确定企业是否正在朝着目标前进,在必要时进行纠正。管理人员必须确保组织正朝着既定的目标前进。倾向于授权和信任员工的新趋势使得许多企业减少自上而下的控制力度,重视培训员工以期他们能够进行自我监督和自我纠正。

拓展阅读

第 1 篇

职场技能——成功经理人的十二条秘诀

作为一名经理、你有领导、监督,指导和激励他人的机会。而有能力这样做的你,将会对企业取得整体性的成功有着巨大的影响。下面是关于成为成功经理人的秘诀:

1. 不要去效仿别人

经不住去效仿以前经理人的诱惑,这点很不好,毕竟你不是以前的经理,你就是你。设想你所喜欢共事的经理以及他能够给你带来的那种感觉。同时,也设想你不喜欢的经理类型以及他给你带来的那种感觉。进行这两种设想的对比,你就可以开始你成功经理人的职业生涯。

2. 开始意味着坚持

设立一个明确的标准，然后以此为模板，人们对确定性的反应是积极的，

因为他们一般不喜欢惊喜。所以每个人都需要知道他们的期望和明确的标准是什么，这样才会让他们明白，自己将要做的事情是什么。所以为什么不把大家伙对目标标准的想法集中起来，这也是为你下一步让他们站在你这边，同意你工作的实施做好准备。这样的话，他们就有归属感，不需要时时激励他们，应以目标标准来求得生存。

3. 与员工分享企业目标

人们总会对赋予的责任做出回应。当然，你也总会碰到一两个对你所赋予的责任抱怨的人，他们也会尽最大能力去影响整个团队来反对你的工作，所以远离这些人或是给他们重新接受训练的机会，这样做会影响整个团队，并向他们展示你对工作职责甚至是他们的关心，以这样果断的方式是朝着成功经理人迈进关键的一步。

4. 定期进行团队评审，确保每个人都清楚期望目标

可以定期对团队和个人进行定期评审。一个月一次的员工评审是顺利展开工作的好方法。与员工交流他们的工作方向和能够利用的资源，对他们好的表现给予反馈，并表示对他们接下来的工作给予帮助和支持。

5. 为团队开启新仪式

团队仪式很重要，它会让团队成员有归属感。这样的仪式包括定期的社交活动、团建日和部门会议。

6. 公开反馈

对于一个成功的经理人，比起诚实，没有什么比信任更为重要的了。所以你要认真对待你做事的方式。但请记住，反馈不仅仅是对他人错误的反馈，也是对他人正确(表现好)的反馈。当你做出反馈时，要具体化。而不是说："你要好好地服务这个客户"。我比较喜欢你心平气和地安抚客户情绪的方式，你可以向她表明你能站在她的立场去理解她，但同时也应让她明白一个事实——造成事情发生的源头也有她的因素。

7. 对员工的专业技能给予肯定

你是经理也就意味着你负责管理他人的工作。如果你一味地独立完成工作，那你就不能成为一名成功的经理，而是一名高收入的工作人员。如果你能够对员工专业技能给予肯定，那么他们也会对你专业化的管理模式给予尊重。

8. 激励员工发挥创造性

向你的团队寻求解决问题的方法，而不是自己去解决。员工们喜欢解决问题，你可以通过参与来激励他们。创造就在我们身边，通过激励的方式来激励员工，会让他们想出比我们自己能想到的更好的解决方案。

9. 敢于承认错误

只要是人，都会犯错。敢于把错误公示于众，并向你的员工寻求帮助以免下次再犯同样

的错误。如果你把自己融入你的团队,他们也就没有任何顾虑地向你提出对今后避免犯错的反馈。

10. 管理和领导并非同一件事

一些成功的管理者并非好的领导。这门学问的奥妙就是知道何时下放权力。如果你能下放你的领导权力,这将对员工的发展是一个机会。而你依然保留对员工的整体控制,因为你依然有问责的权力。所以要选择相信你的员工,毕竟他们除了你没有任何的选择。

11. 不断提升自我

成为一名成功的经理人不是一个最终目标,而是开启你职业生涯的新方向。管理是需要不断学习和实践,然后慢慢提升的技能。你不可能不学习和实践就到达顶端,因此,你要通过参加优秀课程的学习,多阅读管理方面的书籍(不管相信与否,其中的一些还是很有趣的),甚至通过网络学习来不断提升自我。

12. 和员工成为朋友

不能仅仅因为你是一名成功的经理人,就可以改变你的员工。而是要让他们理解你对他们的工作负有责任。因此,有时候你不得不发号施令,但更多的时候,你必须依靠他们来帮助你完成工作任务。一个成功的经理人不会构筑一个人为的壁垒。

第 2 篇

面　　试

——和公司高管会面的 7 个要诀

恭喜你!你终于有机会和一位高管来一次面对面交谈了。他可能是公司的顶梁柱,所以这次交谈的机会太难得了,你要确保自己能抓住这次机会。

下面这些简单的事情可以帮到你:

1. 研究这个人

见面前,你先要研究这位高管的工作规划——他打算在公司里实现什么目标。之后,可以用你在公司里的人脉和自己的商业头脑了解他的个人规划,比如,他的职业目标是什么,他在期待什么工作机遇等。

2. 别假设他知道你是谁

高管们太繁忙了,他们常常不知道(也不记得)为什么自己的日程里有某个会议。见面时,你要先介绍自己,说明自己来的目的是什么——尽量把会议主题和他的公司业务联系起来,或者有可能的话,跟他的个人规划也沾点儿边。比如,你可以说:"我是 Acme 公司来的张三,我今天来的目的是为了和你讨论一下如何通过改进产品的质量控制,来提高公司的盈利能力。"

3. 迅速建立信任感

会面开始了,最开始的几分钟是你证明自己在见面前认真做功课的好机会。你要表现出来的是,你已经了解这个公司,比如,它这个行业里的地位是什么,面临的挑战又是什么。你们交谈的时候,把重点放在这位高管面对的业务问题上——别滔滔不绝地说些你的产品的那些花里胡哨的功能。公司高层们不会关心产品具体的特性和功能,他们更关心你做产品的底线是什么和你会怎样改变这种底线。

4. 问些聪明的问题

为你们的对话设计一些条条框框,只谈些跟公司业务相关的问题,或者聊聊这位高管使用的一些业务评估计策方面的事情。例如,如果你和一位首席财务官交谈的话,你可能想问一些关于公司对购买决策的投资回报率期望值方面的问题;如果你和一位首席技术官会面,你可以问一些有关公司对技术部绩效评估方面的问题。

5. 多倾听、少说话

如果你问了一个问题,那么就好好听听这位高管怎么回应你。当你在和一位客户对话的时候,只有当客户不断说话的时候,你们的对话才是最富有成效的。你的任务是对谈话的内容进行引导,以便你可以了解自己应该为客户提供什么样的服务。同理,在和高管说话的时候,在提出一个解决方案之前,你需要先充分了解公司现有的问题。

6. 让你们的谈话有价值

控制住自己,别急着一下子就把自己的解决方案说出来。如果你说出来的话像是推销,那么这位高管就会觉得你并没有认真听他说的话,或者更糟糕的是,他会觉得你一点儿也不在乎他刚告诉你的那些话。所以,千万不要这样做。你应该做的是,跟他聊聊你在解决一个类似问题时的经验,或者说说从另一个角度怎么看待这个问题。总之,你要为你们的谈话带来更多的价值。

7. 会面结束前做下一步计划

在你们即将结束谈话的时候,与这位高管一起为你的方案制定一些后续行动规划。大多数时候,你可能能够拿到为刚才讨论过的问题提供进一步定制方案的机会。不过,你要向这位高管建议怎么去实现这些计划,而不仅仅由他说了算。最理想的情况是,这位高管可以为你们的项目做出公开的承诺,即使他只是计划安排一个进一步讨论项目的小组会议。

第六章 投资与理财

课文

五种最愚蠢的投资理财方式

自己的钱该怎么打理才最明智,对此你一定心知肚明。但是你知道最糟糕的做法是什么吗？哪些是你应该避免的呢？

奇怪的是，那些应该避免的事情却有很多人仍然在做，而且人数之多让人瞠目——尽管这些人在内心深处可能很清楚自己的做法实际上有多愚蠢。

想把这些蠢事一个不落地全列出来恐怕不可能。不过我们可以试着列出其中的五件：

1. 追求高收益率

美国这个国家需要的是收益率能够达到 5%的定期存单。然而，这里有的只是利率的一降再降，以及联邦储备委员会尽量将利率维持在低位的政策，这样的现状逼得人们愈加疯狂——对于那些需要从投资中获取收益的人而言尤其如此。

在此环境下，人们在绝望地寻找着更高的收益率，并为此开始犯下着实愚蠢的错误。这其中包括为争取获得更高的收益率而不惜承担极高的风险或是投资那些他们毫不了解的复杂产品。美联储正在打造着一个各类阴谋、庞氏骗局和欺诈手段层出不穷的牛市。

美国证券交易委员会最近提醒投资者警惕，目前市场中有一种由骗子发行的虚假高收益"企业本票"在大量传播。

《华尔街日报》的杰森·茨威格指出了那些卖出"反向可转债"这一复杂产品的投资者所面临的困境，"反向可转债"是一种合法的金融产品，不过此类产品结构复杂，其本身存在着潜在的风险。加利福尼亚州洛斯阿尔托斯的 Bedrock 资产管理公司的首席投资官埃里克·刘易斯建议，如果你无法向自己的朋友解释清楚一项投资，包括这项投资可能会面临什么风险，那么你最好三思而行。

诸如安硕高收益率企业债交易所交易基金这样的高收益率债券基金为风险较高的企业提供贷款，这类基金的收益率约为 5%。这是你在不承担过高风险的情况下能够挣到的最高收益率。

2. 倾家荡产送孩子去私立大学读书

过去 40 年来，美国私立大学的学费以及各种开销增长了两倍——扣除了通货膨胀因素之后。公立大学的就读成本则是 40 年前的四倍。

在美国攻读一个本科学位所需开销数字之大，简直成了这个国家的耻辱。学生完成为期四年的学位攻读需要花费 16 万美元，而学习的效果往往还很成问题。

理财专家们强烈建议学生家长们不要将自己的养老积蓄用来为孩子付学费，这笔钱他们自己可能还用得着。

诚然，学位已经成为一种护身符——没有它，你可能找不到工作，不过即便有了学位，职场中能够提供的就业机会也少了。而对于预算开支不那么富裕的家庭而言，明智的选择是去公立大学读一个本科学位。读一所美国公立大学每年所需的学费和各种杂费平均不到 9 000 美元，而私立大学则需要 30 000 美元。

3. 持有自己所工作企业的股票

这大概是投资者能够做出的最愚蠢、最冒险的举动之一了。如果这家公司遇上麻烦，你将遭受双重打击。你可能会在丢了饭碗的同时，丢掉自己的积蓄——一杆子打翻一篮子的蛋。不信你去问问那些曾为安然或是雷曼兄弟工作过的人。

令人惊讶的是，美国的法律实际上在鼓励这种疯狂的举动。虽然企业的 401(k)计划受到监管部门监管，若企业让员工承担过高"风险"，则会受到惩罚，但是监管规定，允许企业向员工提供企业自己的股票作为投资选择之一。而实际上许多企业也在这么做。

员工福利研究所表示，自 2000 年以来，401(k)资产中雇主股票的占比已经减少了一半，不过目前的数字依然很惊人。而且，如今不愿意持有自己公司股票的员工是那些最年轻的人，而这些人其实是承担风险能力最高的人。

根据员工福利研究所的数据，在那些于 401(k)计划中提供了持有本公司股票这一投资选择的公司中，年龄在 40 岁或者以上的员工通常会将自己的 401(k)账户中大约 20%的资产用于投资本公司股票。这简直是疯了。

4. 过早支取社保金

如果你有能力晚点支取自己的社保养老金，那么就晚点吧。根据美国社会安全局的数据，年薪五万美元的员工若在自己年满 62 岁这一支取社保金的规定年龄后即开始使用社保，则通常每月可以得到大约 1000 美元。如果他们能够等到 70 岁，那么这个数字将会翻倍。

过早支取社保金，毫不考虑后果，这是美国人可能犯下的最大的理财错误之一——其不明智的程度堪比在 2000 年买入科技股，或是在 2006 年买下拉斯维加斯的一套公寓。早点拿到钱的诱惑可能会让人们对未来即将付出的巨大代价视而不见。(许多退休者可能没有太多选择。一辈子拿着低薪从事着艰苦的工作，是很折磨人的。而且，许多公司几乎是在强迫高龄员工早点退休。)

无论如何，多等上些时候去享受更高的福利，这样积累下来的数额用不了几年就能超过在退休年龄初期即开始提取的全部社保金额。

不过，这样说会让人们忽视一个更大的问题。社保金是一种保险。对于许多退休者而言，最大的风险不在于他们会在 70 岁之前没钱了，而是在 85 岁之后。根据美国疾病控制与预防中心的数据，在目前年龄为 65 岁的女性中，超过半数的人将活到 85 岁甚至更久，男性中的这个比例为八分之三。

晨星公司负责退休问题研究的主管戴维·布兰切特说，对于女性、已婚夫妇和那些身体状况良好者而言，应该多等些时间以便得到更高的福利，因为这样做更为合理。

5. 购买长期债券

令人吃惊的是，仍有很多人接受这样的观点：包括长期政府债券在内的债券是"安全的"。实际上，债券——特别是长期政府债券——是少有的一种已经被明确宣告的泡沫。

美联储在毫不掩饰地大肆印着钞票，并用这些印出来的钞票买国债，从而抬高这类债券的价格，压低利率，以便能够帮助提振美国经济。这一点毫无争议。这是公开的政策。30 年期美国国债目前的收益率仅为 3.1%。这比长期通货膨胀预期仅高出半个百分点。如果以过往的标准来衡量，30 年期国债的收益率应该至少达到 4.5%，比通货膨胀率高出两个百分点。

30 年期通胀挂钩国债的"实际"年收益率，即扣除通货膨胀因素后的收益率，为 0.6%。而以过往的标准来衡量，这一收益率应当是 2%。

购买这类债券的唯一理由只能是押注经济会重现 20 世纪 30 年代那样的大萧条，而且会出现全球性的通货紧缩。投资这类债券是在赌博，不是避险。

拓展阅读

第 1 篇

企业投资计划

在过去的 20 年中，企业投资经历了三股浪潮。第一次是 1997—2001 年的互联网投资热，大量资金注入手机网络和互联网主干的建设。接着是 2003—2010 年间的新兴市场狂潮。西方企业在中国、印度等地砸入 2 万亿美元开设工厂和建造其他设施。2005—2013 年又成了大宗商品疯狂年代，大宗商品走俏的部分原因是中国对此类商品的需求大。全球能源和金属材料企业斥资 6 万亿美金，不仅在澳洲大陆开采矿石，还在北达科他地区甚至是巴西海岸深海区域钻井采油。

如今，互联网泡沫破裂、新兴市场后继乏力、大宗商品价格也在过去一年中大幅跳水(砸了好几个企业老总的饭碗)。那么企业现如今的投资方向在哪里？最近，高盛银行的雨果·斯考特发布了一份研究报告，报告仔细分析了全球 2500 多家企业的资本投资数据，并预测了 2017 年投资形势相比 2014 年会发生怎样的变化。报告发现，不同行业间投资额差异巨大。

能源、矿业和化工企业预计会大幅削减资本投资预算，降幅可达 20～50%。房产公司也会采取同样的措施，这也从一定程度上反映了中国房地产热的终结。削减投资的举措会连带影响为这些产业提供设备的资本商品企业。以卡特彼勒公司为例，它专为矿业及建筑公司生产挖掘机，预计其 2016 年度的资本投资额会削减至 2012 年的一半。

与上述产业相反，互联网、软件和其他科技公司的资本投资额则将处于高位，预计投资预算会提高 25%或更多。尽管一些科技企业走轻资产化路线，将公司的数据处理及存储都交给网络"云"，但其他科技企业，包括云服务提供商本身却在大量购进硬件设施。2016 年，谷歌和苹果公司投资额总和将达到 240 亿美元，几乎等同于埃克森公司 280 亿美元的投资预算。

以美元计算，到 2017 年，全球企业资本支出将下降 15%。考虑到美元自 2014 年起已大幅增值，因此对地方货币来说，降幅应该只有 5%左右。这个数字还不包括研发支出。而研发成本增长迅速。如美国国民账户显示，整个经济体中研发和软件支出的增长，可抵消对实体工厂投资的减少。

不论从哪个方面分析这些数据，资本投资增长都呈现出不同寻常的集中化。在高盛此次调查涉及的产业中，以美元投资计算，预计会有 22 个产业的预算缩水，只有 12 个会呈现增长。据彭博社的数据显示，研发支出最多的前 20 家公司，如三星、罗氏、诺华和微软，就占到了全球所有上市公司总研发费用的 25%。企业界出现萧条似乎在所难免，投资和增长热点屈指可数。

所以投资者可能会希望有一个资本密集型的科技企业群体，可以占领全新市场，并率先获得利润增长。这正是硅谷那些企业助推者们认为必然发生的场景。每一次科技公司公布一个新的拓展领域，如智能手表、无人驾驶汽车、虚拟现实眼镜、无人机快递等，都会引来他们的一片喝彩声。

但是，历史经验告诉我们，每当人们对亟待投资的领域基本达成共识时，灾难也就不远了，因为处于该行业的公司会丧失原则，毫无节制地进行大量投资。正如此前那些大量投资能源及新兴市场的西方企业，在过去两年中股价落后于标普 500 指数五十多个百分点。到 2016 年，形势应该会变得明朗一些，让我们看看究竟如今一窝蜂地投资科技企业是经济运行方式的巨变呢，还是经济不景气的表现，把零星的机会鼓吹得天花乱坠、言过其实。

第 2 篇

学生理财：学生省钱十大妙招

无论这是你步入大学的第一年或第三年，花钱的诱惑总是无处不在——不仅仅在优年酒吧。问题是如果你想参加学校组织的滑雪旅行，你需要在学期末的时候留点钱给自己。本文将和各位新老生一起分享十大省钱妙招。

新学期第一周做好预算

生活费刚打到账户的时候，你觉得自己"坐拥资产"，总是蠢蠢欲动地想要花钱。请注意，你已进入危险地带。有人组织化妆舞会，你就下血本去买很贵的服装；想有个新的爱好，你就马上买来一个尤克里里(夏威夷弦拨乐器)。一心总想着娱乐是很难做好预算的，但是在早期克制自己的购买欲是值得的。学期末想要出去庆祝，先在相关学生预算应用上查查自己的账户，确保你还负担得起外出花费。

提前计划每餐

下课走在路上，你免不了会想和朋友一起买午餐，喝咖啡。注意这些小处的花费——一旦养成这样的习惯，你的资金会深受影响。在家准备好食物是很好的省钱方式。只要你合理预算，买食材的时候完全可以放心买自己爱吃的。

享受学生折扣

恭喜！作为学生，现在的你可以享受超多折扣。这并不是说你应该为了享受折扣多消费，而是在你真正需要购物的时候用折扣节省花费。切记在购买相关打折卡之前查看折扣清单，确保这张会员卡对你有用再买。

精打细算旅行

无论是要回家还是去找其他大学的朋友玩，都会是一件花钱的事情，但这些不应该阻挡你出行。记得买票时用火车票优惠卡能打五折。或者这样说，你的朋友们都只有一次 21 岁，所以你可以通过拼车服务去参加他们的生日庆祝会。如果你有车，可以捎上愿意付钱的人，毕竟多一个人可以帮你节省三分之一的油费。

大卖特卖

教科书总是贵得出奇，所以当你确定一本书以后会终老书架，不被问津的时候，用它在亚马逊换张礼品卡。你的衣服也可以这样处理。如果你觉得它们仍有所值，可以在易趣网卖掉时髦的奇装异服，或者去跳蚤市场。

在网上搜寻省钱妙招

一旦进入大学,你泡在网络上的时间很有可能已经超过健康范围——普遍在凌晨一点以后。既然你已经在网上了,好好利用你的时间去浏览某些网站,寻找特价产品、折扣和预算小贴士。

不买名牌

大家都知道平民品牌没有名牌那么炫。不要被这种说法影响——它的质量通常和名牌没有多大区别。不买知名品牌能帮你大省一笔再去买吃的补给冰箱,所以不被品牌迷住双眼是很明智的。下次宿醉之后再头痛,记得买药也是一样的道理。知名品牌的止痛药会比超市卖的普通品牌贵很多,超市的品牌一般只卖不到一英镑。

远离烤肉店

通宵唱歌后走在回家路上,试着回避震耳的音乐交谈,正是该来点油腻小吃的时候,而且你已经透过早晨清冷的空气闻到了来自烤肉店的诱人味道。停!在每个外出玩耍的夜晚都买快餐要付出代价的,不仅仅是你的腰围,还有你的钱包。你可以偶尔享受芝士薯片,但要真的想存钱,试着回家去吃碗麦片或者烤面包吧。

打工赚钱

不是应该叫"找工作"么?有点像吧。但是我们都知道,不是每个大学都有时间让你一边上学,一边在酒吧打工。如果你觉得自己有能力平衡二者,放手去找工作吧。如果你做不到,试着在网上完成一些有偿的调查问卷或者针对特定群体的市场调研。毕竟,大家都会默默爱上好的调研!益普索会奖励完成网上调研的用户,提供在如亚马逊或者约翰·路易斯购物的代金券。如果你有再多点时间,在像萨罗斯等每星期做两个小时的特定群体调研会给你30~100英镑的报酬,这会大大充盈你的钱包。

"去酒吧前,在家喝酒"

此处不是提倡喝酒,但你已经是大学生了,所以你总会有机会喝酒的。尽管如此,请采纳我们的建议——外出前先喝酒会帮你省钱。当地超市的酒几乎总是比学生酒吧卖得便宜,所以适时去超市买酒,和朋友们在家里开始晚上的娱乐。这样做的额外奖励:没了酒吧的喧闹,你还可以听到他们在讲什么。

第七章 银 行 业

课文

中国的银行业

在过去的二十年里,中国的银行业已经发生了重大变化,比起以前,如今的银行运转得更像西方的银行。然而，即使各银行已经获得了更多的自主权，但中国的银行业仍然掌控在政府手里。

从目前的情况看，中国的银行系统有明确的分级并具有各自的特性。它可以分为四个层次：第一层是领头银行——中国人民银行；第二层是五大国有银行——中国农业银行、中国银行、中国工商银行、中国建设银行和中国交通银行；第三层是其他中小型银行，包括地方银行、私人银行、外国银行、农村信用社和邮政储蓄银行。这三个层次的所有银行都是受中国人民银行调控的。

监督机构

中国人民银行是中国的中央银行，依法独立制定与执行国家货币政策。维护国家银行业金融机构的支付、清算及结算系统，并管理官方外汇和黄金储备。它监督国家外汇管理局制定外汇管理政策。中国人民银行的主要任务是调控货币政策、通过调整利率与准备金率来宏观调控我国经济，减少整体风险及促进金融体系稳定。

国内主要参与者

中国的四大主要银行包括中国银行、中国农业银行、中国工商银行和中国建设银行。1983年，中国人民银行分设这四家专业银行(或重新建立)，它们从中国人民银行手里承接了部分银行业务，使中国人民银行集中于银行监管(实施调控)和货币政策上。

1. 中国银行

中国银行专业从事外汇交易和贸易融资。它不仅是中国的主要银行之一，而且在国际贸易中起主要作用。中国银行的业务范围覆盖很多领域，例如金融银行、投资银行和保险业。它在全球范围内为个人和公司客户提供全面、优质的金融服务。旗下有中银香港、中银国际、中银保险等控股金融机构。2002年，中银香港(控股)在香港证券交易所成功挂牌上市，这在中国的银行业改革上是一个重大举措。

2. 中国农业银行

中国农业银行专门为中国农业提供贷款，向农民、乡镇企业及其他农村企业提供零售银行服务。

3. 中国工商银行

中国工商银行是中国的跨国银行公司，就资产而言，它是中国规模最大的商业银行，总资产和市值居全球上市银行之首。它一直位于世界五百强企业之列，在《银行家》杂志的"全球1000家大银行"排名中位居全球首位。中国工商银行因在外汇业务中排名第二及在人民币结算业务中排名第一区别于其他国有商业银行。它曾是中国城市和制造业资金的主要供应商。截至2016年8月19日，中国工商银行市值超过2 350亿美元。

4. 中国建设银行

中国建设银行是中国第四大银行，提供全方位的商业银行产品与服务，比如，基础设施贷款、住宅抵押贷款和银行信用卡。它还拥有广泛的客户基础，与多个大型企业集团及中国经济战略性行业的主导企业有银行业务联系，营销网络覆盖全国的主要地区。2015年，中国建设银行其市值位居世界上第二大银行。它在中国内地有大约14 917个分支机构以及68个海外机构，覆盖14个国家和地区。在香港、新加坡、东京、纽约、法兰克福、首尔、悉尼、约翰内斯堡、墨尔本、奥克兰和胡志明市都设有海外分行。此外,在莫斯科和台北设有代表处,在伦敦设有全资子公司。

除了以上提到的四个主要银行外,中国交通银行是中国第五大商业银行。如今它已是中国银行系统中具有悠久历史的龙头企业之一。

政策性银行

中国银行、中国农业银行、中国建设银行和中国工商银行一直是承担国家的政策性业务的专业银行。直到 1994 年,三大政策性银行组建起来,接替四大国有商业银行承担政府主导的政策性借贷职能。它们是中国农业发展银行、中国发展银行和中国进出口银行。

中国银行业监督管理委员会和银联

中国银行体系中存在两大组织——中国银行业监督管理委员会和银联。中国银行业监督管理委员会是一个政府机构,监督管理金融机构,比如银行和金融资产管理公司,维护银行业的合法、稳健运行,与中央银行共享一些监管职能,与中央政府分担工作以及配合国家金融监督部门工作,一起负责监督管理中国银行业金融机构。

中国银联是经国务院同意中国人民银行批准的,由八十多家国内金融机构共同发起设立的中国银行卡联合组织,成立于 2002 年 3 月。目前,总部设于上海的中国银联已拥有近 400 家境内外成员机构。它是中国唯一连接全国各地所有银行自动取款机的跨行网络,也是一项销售点电子自动转账购物系统。它通过银行卡实现全国性货币,促进银行卡的快速发展。如今,银联在中国的银行业系统中起着举足轻重的作用,在行业发展中起着至关重要的作用。为了响应中国经济社会发展,履行产业使命和社会责任,银联已经联手国内商业银行创造独立的银行卡品牌——银联卡。带有银联标志的标准卡已在全国范围内普遍使用,给人们的日常生活和现金流动带来了很大的方便。迄今为止,在全世界 160 个国家和地区可以顺畅地使用银联卡,以其交易值成为维萨卡和万事达卡之后的第三大网络支付系统。银联卡不仅被国内持卡者广泛接受,而且受到越来越多国家和地区的持卡人的高度赞赏。

拓展阅读

第 1 篇

手机银行——交易的一种平台

手机银行作为移动商务的一个重要应用方式,是银行业务的重要扩展和延伸。它是由银行或者其他金融机构提供的,允许其客户使用移动设备,比如手机或者平板电脑进行金融交易的一种服务。移动银行通常 24 小时都可使用。手机银行用户可以通过手机银行查询账户、转账、付账以及管理公司账户或者处理指令。

2015 年 12 月,印度手机银行的交易额达到最高。印度手机银行用户的交易额从 2014 年 12 月起超过 4 倍,达到 490000 卢比。印度银行家表示,大量用户采用手机银行登录账户而不通过网上银行来登录。

在一个移动互联网盛行的国家里,手机银行业务受到越来越多消费者的青睐,其中不仅包括年轻一代消费者。重要的是，正如手机不再只是手机，移动银行不仅仅是银行的另一个服务渠道，它是服务于数字化客户的一个平台。

印度有先进移动技术的银行利用移动银行业务的便利性从三个重要方面吸引客户，即银行交易效率、用户体验质量以及交易强度。首先，通过在手机上启动交易，银行帮客户更好、更快更便捷地把钱存入银行。一个简单的例子就是进行资金转账，只要在手机银行应用程序上轻点几下就能完成。

第二，手机银行非常适合提供丰富的、直观的体验。智能手机的自带功能使其提供基于地理位置的服务、理财建议、基于生物特征等的银行业务成为可能。例如，手机银行可以通过密码进行烦琐的身份验证和附加因素促进生物识别与认证。我们在 Infosys Finacle 平台上称它为"死亡密码"——深受我们所有客户赞赏的一个理念。

第三，银行客户通过手机与银行进行交易较于通过银行网点或者网络更为频繁。一份来自英国的研究称，2015 年英国活期存款客户通过营业网点访问银行 4 亿 2700 万次，而通过手机移动应用程序登录银行达到 8 亿 9500 万次。这种差距预计在 2020 年将大幅增长，访问营业网点大概只有 2 亿 68 万次，而移动应用程序使用情况将达到 23 亿。印度银行的相关数据很可能会更倾向于移动式交易，因为其国家的人口优势和各细分市场消费者对网点的影响力不足。显然，这对于银行来说，是将频繁来访的客户转变成更深度的客户参与的极好机会。

摆在印度银行面前的关键问题是，他们是否采取足够措施利用这个机会吸引客户。大多数银行仍然只有在客户与他们建立业务关系时才为客户提供服务。银行需要改变这种应对客户方法的结构，使得银行服务不张扬但随处可见，以至于当客户需要银行服务时，就能得到。其中一个例子来自于印孚瑟斯和 Finacle 的年度"Finacle 全球银行业创新奖"得主是波兰的 Alior 银行，它设计了一个在几分钟内就能获得批准的贷款产品，甚至是在某些情况中实时地确保其业务来往的客户在需要贷款时当场就能获取。事实上，参与是在业务中建立如此普及的差异化的唯一途径。其中一种方式是提高客户体验质量；另一种方式是通过向客户显示该银行把自己的财务状况放在第一位来激发客户对该银行的信任和信心。手机银行业务完美地实现了这一点，银行可以在实时交易时，与客户共享远见，达成一致，从而做出更明智、更可靠的金融决策。

第 2 篇

应对互联网金融 中国传统银行发起反击

据路透社报道，为了应对来自阿里巴巴及其他互联网巨头对中国传统银行业务的影响，中国传统银行正发起反击，旨在阻止银行存款外流到高收益率的互联网投资产品。

还不到八个月，阿里巴巴集团旗下的货币市场基金产品——余额宝总共吸收了 4000 亿元 (约 660 亿美元)，超过了 5 家中国最小规模上市银行的客户存款总和。

百度公司以及腾讯控股有限公司旗下类似的互联网产品也是一月份中国传统银行存款流失一万亿元的原因。

如今，措手不及的传统银行正开始反击。

最近几周，中国工商银行、中国银行、交通银行及平安银行全都推出了新产品对抗余额宝。银行还在游说监管部门采取措施，控制互联网产品的发展。

然而，最终各类产品对存款的竞争将会提高银行今年的融资成本，降低其利润空间。

随着中国存款利率不断地自由化，中国传统银行将会被迫进行内部竞争，提供更高回报率的产品来吸引客户。旨在与互联网产品对抗的新型类存款资金市场产品将会进一步加速融资成本的增大。

现钱交易

近年来，中国储户热捧银行所谓高回报率的理财产品(WMPs)，并从传统年利率上线为3.3%的储户存款中解放出来。

去年6月，阿里巴巴与天弘资产管理有限公司携手发行余额宝，完全主导着银行传统存款的外流。阿里巴巴持有天弘资产管理有限公司51%的股份，该产品目前的年收益率为6.2%。

余额宝及其他互联网货币市场基金之所以能够从传统的银行存款及线下理财产品中吸收资金，除了诱人的高回报外，还得益于其几项创新改革。与大多数银行理财产品不同的是，余额宝允许投资者随时赎回资金，而不是一次就锁定他们的资金好几月。而且余额宝没有设置最低投资门槛。

余额宝与支付宝(阿里巴巴旗下被广泛使用的第三方支付平台)的完美结合，也使得购入该产品更为简单方便。

现在，各银行都行动起来，推出各自现钱交易的资金市场产品。

世界资产总量最大的银行——中国工商银行，发行了资金市场理财产品——"天天益"。目前只有浙江地区的储户才能购买天天益,但是中国工商银行将有可能很快地扩大其试点范围。

中国工商银行希望赢得与阿里巴巴的竞争，借"天天益"吸收存款达3000万元。另外，中国工商银行还规定，储户每月向支付宝转账的金额不得超过5万元。

中国的第五大商业银行——交通银行，推出了"快溢通"，平安银行则推出了"平安盈"。

周三，中等规模的北京银行宣布与智能手机生产商小米科技建立合作伙伴关系，合作范围涉及移动支付及销售理财产品和保险产品。

银行也正对各自理财产品作调整，使其更具竞争力。

上海一家中等规模银行的理财产品经理表示："我们正试图增加我们理财产品的便利性，比如，在非工作时段让客户购买我们的产品。我们也在要求监管部门放宽某些产品5万元的投资门槛。"

要求监管

瑞士联合银行预计，如果银行总存款的10%流入互联网产品，那么银行的净利差可能减少0.1个百分点，同时手续费收入将会损失高达2014年预计净利润的4%。

上周，中国证监会表示，他们正与其他部门就互联网融资制定相关规则。业内观察家们表示，各银行正在游说监管部门，从第三方支付服务方面阻止互联网产品的扩张。

严表示："监管部门正试图找出一个折中的办法。他们不想扼杀一切有利于消费者的改革创新，但是他们也不想融资活动处于完全不被监管的状态。"分析师表示，即使银行有能力吸引资金投资它们的货币市场产品，融资的成本增加的趋势还会继续，因为银行产品将不得不与由互联网竞争对手提供的高回报产品进行抵抗。

的确，投资在余额宝以及其他类似产品的资金最终会流向银行。天弘主要是把余额宝资金投入到同业存款及回购上。因此，不管银行是向天弘借贷，还是从自己的产品中融资，成本仍旧比普通存款高。

第八章　保　　险

课文

保　　险

中国的人口正在迅速老龄化。独生子女政策和人民生活水平的显著改善加速了老龄化进程，使中国的老龄化问题比世界上其他国家更加严峻。根据世界银行的一份报告，中国老龄人口到2030年将达到顶峰(世界银行，1994)，将有3亿人超过60岁，占总人口的22%。到2030年，老年抚养比率预期从现在的六个工人养一个退休人员到2030年变成只有两个工人抚养一个退休人员。为了赡养巨大的老龄人口，中国面临着极大的挑战。因此，建立社会保障体系是必须的，能使公民共享发展成果，促进社会和谐稳定。

社会保险是社会进步的重要体现，也是人们所关注的。现今，中国政府正努力地通过立法形式以确保人们退休后能享有幸福生活。国家多渠道筹集社会保险资金，通过税收优惠政策支持社会保险事业。县级及县级以上人民政府把社会保险列入经济和社会发展计划中，并对其给予必要的基金支持。

中国社会保险体制包含五种不同的保险和强制性住房公积金。用人单位如何为他们职工登记和注销社会保险通常取决于该城市及其员工所在地。下面，我们来学习下这些保险的作用。

养老金

与许多国家一样，中国政府已实施这一体制，确保公民退休后能有一定收入，收入主要从每月职工和用人单位双方的缴款获得。职工所缴比例进入个人基金(缴款直接归于个人)，退休后可直接从中提取基金。不同的是，用人单位所缴款进入社会基金。这个基金中的资金将分配给所有在工作年份内缴纳养老保险费的公民。就每月职工和用人单位所缴款的总额而言，养老金可说在社会保险中是最大的组成部分。

医疗保险

中国公民在生病或受伤时可用缴纳的医疗保险基金支付部分医疗花费的费用。职工和用人单位需共同缴纳此基金。

在一些国家，医疗是免费提供的。与其不一样的是，在中国大多数城市，病人需要承担一定比例的医疗费用。此外，每个月个人可在他们的医疗保险卡得到一小部分的钱。这些钱可用来买药或到药店买其他物品，或在医院支付小额的医药费用。

失业保险

所有大城市的用人单位需要缴纳失业保险,大多数城市要求职工缴纳。如果个人失业,他们可以申请补偿以领取失业金,前提是失业险缴费至少要一年以上。然而,所领取的数额是当地政府规定的一定数额,与个人之前领取的工资或所缴费用的总额无关系。救济金最多可领取 24 个月。

生育保险

生育保险由用人单位缴纳。假如职工怀孕,她可获得一笔钱以支付部分的生产费用。在生育离岗期间,生育基金包含薪水的支付。

工伤保险

工伤保险由用人单位缴纳,其缴费数额依据职工工作性质而决定。其工作被认定越危险,所缴款比例就越高(通常是薪水总额的 0.4%到 2%)。保险费所缴比例的具体总额由当地社保局根据该公司被认定隶属于的行业类别决定。如果员工在工作中受伤,公司要收集有关受伤的证据和相关费用,向职业保险基金申请补偿。在职工工伤恢复期间,用人单位仍需支付薪水。

住房公积金

住房公积金与以上保险在这两方面有根本区别。首先,由职工和用人单位缴纳的费用直接增加给职工。其次,该基金管理是由住房公积金中心运作,与社会保险分开。

住房公积金管理在各城镇有较大不同。在深圳,职工不需要缴纳费用,而是要求用人单位支付 13%的固定比率。相比在大连,用人单位可要求支付高达 25%的费用(虽然可运用一些特殊手段降低利率),而职工最多可交 15%。住房公积金对用人单位而言是一笔可观的额外花费。

社会保险和住房公积金普遍被认为是"强制性福利"。用人单位通常要求代表他们的职工办理强制性福利管理工作。这意味着,首先职工要进入用人单位的"账",然后用人单位按月根据用人单位和职工比例计算和缴纳费用。

拓展阅读

第 1 篇

人 寿 保 险

对于大多数人来说,一听到人寿保险这个词,第一印象就是一对老年人正跟他们的孙子玩耍。我们经常被这样的想法误导,人寿保险是给老人买的,也许 30 年后我们会投资它。事实上,人们在二十几岁时不会把人寿保险作为在现阶段生活需要投资的东西来考虑。然而,你在二十几岁时投资人寿保险会比在五十几岁时更受益。

人寿保险并不是具有保险利益的个人可以决定放弃的。它听起来是那样可怕,可事实上它是确定死亡的遗物,人寿保险产业才得以生存发展。同时,也使每个人都意识到人寿保险的重要性，特别是有家眷的人，比如他们的配偶和孩子。因此，它绝对不是任何人可以避免投资的。然而，可以肯定的是，在年轻时投资人寿保险比在年老时更有益。下面是当你在二十几岁时购买一份人寿保单的一些重要且有用的好处。

健康就是财富

最大的原因之一就是人在二十几岁时会比在五十几岁时健康得多，因而保险公司会对相对较健康的个人收取相对较低的保费。当他或她年老后，会有越来越多的健康问题，保险公司就不会降低保费。因此，这就直接影响到个人购买人寿保险的花费。不管怎样，这是一个不争的事实，你的保费一旦锁定在一个特定的数额(在年轻时相对较低)，它就会一直保持不变且不会上涨。

忠实的回报

从长远来看，人寿保险会省钱的另一个原因是大多数保险商通过给顾客提供许多忠实的回报以保持竞争力，比如，降低保费或给具有特定保险人的忠实顾客修改保单条款。因此，如果在二十岁投保，到五十岁时，他将得到的比他在五十岁时投的新保单好处更多。

储蓄可以拯救你

在年轻时选择人寿保险的另一个好处就是当他或她刚开始挣钱时会每月或定期留出一笔钱，根据要求支付保单费用，这有助于我们每月或定期存一笔钱。简而言之，定期从他们工作初期相对微薄的工资中支付一笔费用，这有助于养成在年轻时储蓄的习惯。如果你可以从如此微薄的收入中存些钱，那么你肯定能为生活中更大的事情做好准备。

可以肯定地说，人寿保险是人生中绝对有必要的。不管怎样，你的生活方式要健康。当然，死亡是必然的，而且没有什么能使人复活。给已故者的爱人留下一笔有保障的保险也是某种安慰。更重要的是，有一份人寿保险单就是你开始投资这个政策，也就是说在二十几岁时你的生活就有了些稳定性。你开始投资得越早，你的基金就会越多。

第 2 篇

汽车保险市场

据毕马威会计事务所报道，在 25 年内私家车保险产业将缩减 60%。好消息是由于有了更安全的交通工具，汽车事故和死亡率将越来越少。

毕马威会计事务所指出，按需汽车服务业的上升和自动驾驶的采用也将会减少对汽车保险的需求，到 2040 年，即当新一代这些人到了 44 至 58 岁时，意外事故发生频率会下降 80%。事故发生频率的急剧下降将导致损失成本和保费的极大减少，但每次事故产生的费用可能会大大增加，因为这些新车和其部件会更贵。每年超过 90%的事故都是由驾驶员错误造成的。结合事故发生频率和责任的严重性，到 2040 年，个人汽车行业在损失成本上将会减少 500 亿美元。

随着事故预防功能的日益普及，个人汽车保险业已受到安全汽车技术的影响，比如交通堵塞援救、车道偏离警告，这些部分地使驾驶摆脱了人为因素，引自美国公路安全保险协会主要研究人员,执行副总裁大卫·祖比。他在研究中指出,带有预防正面碰撞技术的汽车会比没有此技术的汽车在财产损失责任险索赔率会低7%到15%。他说:"如果能成功,未来的自动驾驶会使保险索赔进一步减少。"

毕马威会计事务所预计,每次事故发生的严重性可能会相对增加,因为天气、道路条件、与动物碰撞仍会导致汽车意外事故发生。此外,技术故障也会产生问题。权威人士也指出,司机可能有时会选择关闭安全技术,选择手动驾驶。其他专家和顾问们也在衡量安全汽车的效果、汽车共享和无人驾驶汽车的保险业务。

据毕马威会计事务所报道,这些变化对汽车保险业的影响是巨大的。权威人士预测,汽车保险公司会进行扩展整合与全面变化。

毕马威会计事务所公司财务常务董事乔·施耐德认为,自动化汽车的持续增长会给运输公司带来相当大的压力。他说:"在快速变化的环境下,许多保险公司还没有削减其盈利,缺少结构灵活性策略去削减成本。一旦出现大规模的市场混乱,传统保险业务模式会被推倒。我们预计将有明显的动荡。"

毕马威会计事务所通过调查保险经理来评估他们对有关自动驾驶产业的意识,得出的结论是产业还没为即将到来的事情做好准备。超过一半的调查对象说,他们认为监管者应阻止采用自动驾驶。毕马威会计事务所指出保险公司寻求解决变化的四种可能经营策略如下:

合并:对于那些有一定规模的现有运营商,可考虑寻求机会,通过借贷的方式收购大型现有平台。

多样化:转向其他有关个人和商业汽车生产业务的产品,规避其潜在的挑战。

革新:随着新领域风险的出现,确定新领域目标以提供保险保障并开发新产品以满足需求。

合作与联盟: 考虑新的业务模式,这些可能需要与其他公司合作,可将保险嵌入车辆成本中或部分的使用费用中。

第九章 市 场 营 销

课文

市 场 营 销

导言

"市场营销"一词是什么意思?许多人认为市场营销仅仅是销售与广告。这种想法不足为奇,因为每天我们受到电视广告、报纸广告、直接邮寄广告、互联网广告和销售电话轰击。虽然它们很重要,但是它只是市场营销众多功能中的其中两种,而且通常不是最重要的功能。现在,我们不能再用"销售"这种旧观念来理解市场营销,而应该用"满足顾客的需求"这种新观念来理解它。销售只发生在产品被生产之后。相反地,市场营销早在一家企业生产产品之前就开始了。我们可以如下这样定义"市场营销":

市场营销是为了组织自身和利益相关者的利益而发现、预见以及满足顾客需求的管理过程。

这个定义是由英国特许营销协会提出的。从这个定义当中可以得到以下要点：

1. 市场营销是一个管理过程

市场营销与任何其他的企业职能具有同样的合理性，涉及同样多的管理技能。它同样需要计划与分析、资源分配、控制以及在资金、有适当技能的员工和物质资源方面的投资。当然，它也需要执行、监控以及评估。市场营销活动贯穿于产品的整个生命周期，它包括两方面的活动，一是设法寻找新顾客，二是通过提高产品的吸引力与性能，从产品的销售结果中获取信息以及管理重复的业绩等方式留住现有的顾客。就如其他管理活动一样，它可以被有效率地、成功地实施，也可能实施效果很差，进而导致失败。

2. 市场营销的主要内容是满足顾客的需要

市场营销是管理人员负责从事的工作，包括评估消费者需求、衡量需求的范围和强度，以及确定是否存在利润空间。所有的市场营销活动都应该以此为导向进行调整。这意味着市场营销的焦点是购买产品或服务的顾客或者最终消费者。

如果顾客的需求没有得到很好的满足，或者顾客没有获得他们想要或需要的东西，那么市场营销则辜负了顾客和组织。

营销组合

市场营销的管理决策主要分为四种类别：①产品②价格③地点④促销。

这些可变因素被称为营销组合或市场营销的"4P"。市场营销经理们通过控制这些可变因素，最大限度地满足目标市场中的顾客。

企业力图以最佳的方式融合营销组合中的四种可变因素，目的是为了引发目标市场的积极回应。

1. 产品

产品是指提供给消费者的实际产品或服务。实际产品也涉及其中所包含的任何服务或便利。产品决策包括诸如功能、外观、包装、服务、保修证书等方面。

2. 价格

在做出定价决策时，应当考虑两方面的因素，即利润率和竞争对手的定价回应。定价的项目不仅包括价目单上所列的价格，还包括折扣、赊货以及其他的项目，如租赁。

3. 地点

地点(或分销)决策与分销渠道相关，分销渠道就是商品顺利到达消费者手中的途径和方式。分销体系具有交易、物流以及提供便利等功能。分销决策包括市场覆盖率、分销商的选择、物流和服务标准。

4. 促销

促销决策与如何与潜在消费者沟通并向他们销售产品有关。由于这些花费可能在产品价格中占有相当大的比例，因此在做促销决策时，应当进行收支平衡分析。了解一个顾客的价值是有益处的，这样做的目的是确定增加顾客所获得的利润是否能抵消他们带来的成本。促销决策包括广告、公共关系、媒体类型等内容。

营销传播

营销传播是一个广泛的主题，涉及广告、公共关系、销售和促销等一系列内容。人们经常混淆销售和市场营销，实际上它们是有很大差别的。前者是关于将产品或服务引入市场、促进产品的销售、影响消费行为和提高销售量。营销传播理论将有关营销信息的策略分成几种基于信息目标的类型。使陌生人转变为顾客的过程可分为几个不同的阶段，我们需要在不同的阶段应用不同的传播媒体。

1. 广告

广告有许多种形式，这就使得我们很难概括它的所有特性，但是，可以归纳出它的几种特性：

(1) 广告可以通过一定形式的媒体，以较低的成本向散布于各地的消费者传递信息。例如，电视广告可以向大量的观众传递信息。

(2) 广告的特点除了传播范围广外，还有另一特点就是大规模广告也对销售商的规模、受欢迎程度以及成就做了正面的宣传。

(3) 由于广告具有公众性，消费者往往认为广告中的产品是符合标准及合法的——顾客们知道购买这种产品会被公众所理解和接受。

(4) 广告使得销售商可以多次重复某种信息，也使得购买者可以接收和比较各个竞争者的信息。

(5) 广告也富有表现力，使得企业可以通过对影像资料、图片、声音、颜色的巧妙应用，生动地展现它的产品。

(6) 一方面，广告可以用来建立一个产品的长期形象(例如，梅赛德斯-奔驰的汽车广告)。另一方面，广告可以快速地促进销售量的增长。(如德本汉姆和塞尔弗里奇这样的百货公司为它们的周末销售活动所做的广告。)

2. 人员销售

在购买过程中的特定阶段，人员销售是最有效的营销手段，特别在培养顾客的消费偏好、建立他们对产品的信心和促使他们采取购买行动等方面是非常有效的。与广告相比，人员销售有以下几种特性：

(1) 它与两个或更多的人之间的交流有关，因此每个人都可以观察别人的需求和特点，并做出快速的调整。

(2) 人员销售活动也使得各种各样的关系得以产生，包括从一般的销售关系到深入的个人友谊等一系列关系。

(3) 最后，在人员销售过程中，购买者通常意识到更有必要去倾听和回应，即使这个回应只是礼貌地说声"不，谢谢"。

3. 促销

促销有许多种手段——优惠券、比赛、降价、提供赠品、免费商品等，所有这些都有许多特性：

(1) 它们吸引消费者的注意力并提供可能引导消费者购买产品的信息。

(2) 它们提供刺激物，从而使得消费者产生强烈的购买动机，因为这些刺激物能给予消费者额外的价值。

(3) 促销能引起并对快速的反应给予回报。广告上说的只是"买我们的产品吧",而促销却能提供动机使消费者"现在就买"。

公共关系有几种特性。它是指组织与不直接支付费用的目标公众进行交流的一切活动。

(1) 公共关系是非常可信的,新闻故事、专题节目、赞助活动及公开活动对于读者来说比广告更真实也更可信。

(2) 公共关系营销活动可以影响许多回避销售人员和广告的顾客,因为它所传递的信息对于顾客来说是一种新闻而非以销售为导向的信息。

(3) 像广告一样,公共关系可以生动地表现一个企业或产品。美体小铺是少数选择公共关系而非大规模电视广告作为更有效的宣传手段的企业之一。

市场营销的重要性

市场营销在经济中担任着重要的角色,因为它促进了竞争。在一个充满竞争的市场中,企业会设法以比竞争者更低的价格生产新产品或经过改良的产品。在当今的商业世界中,没有营销意识的企业是处于不利地位的。那些仍然以他们的产品而非消费者为中心的企业注定会失败。

拓展阅读

第1篇

数字时代的市场营销

——全新游戏

随着人们将更多的时间用于社会化媒体上,广告主也转向于此。

今年早些时候,宝马在一款中国非常流行的应用程序——微信上发布广告,微信月用户约为 5.5 亿。宝马广告只定向发送给豪华车的潜在客户。其他人收到的则是诸如智能手机之类买得起的商品广告。这个案例戳到一些人的痛点。那些没有收到宝马广告的人称自己为"屌丝","失败者"。

现在,不满意的消费者非常容易发声,汽车制造商的经历显示了广告发布的复杂性。但是这也使市场营销主管能够找到如何通过新媒体平台将广告推送给消费者的好方法,在新媒体上消费者会花费更多的时间。

不久之前,品牌经理会让暑期实习生来处理社会化媒体的市场推广。现在社会化媒体却转而成为广告行业的支柱。调查公司 e 市场指出,全世界有 20 亿人在使用脸书、推特及领英等社交网络。各种线上广告持续增长,其中社交媒体广告在几年之内从零增长到 200 亿美元。

广告主喜爱社交媒体平台是因为它能搜集用户的各种数据,包括用户年龄、消费习惯、兴趣等。这意味着广告能精准到达用户,这在其他媒体是无法想象的。例如,美国汽车品牌雪佛兰通过脸书网页及推特回复将广告发送给关注或申请竞品汽车试驾的用户。

如此精细的定位意味着广告和电子商务的区别正在消失。脸书、推特、照片墙和其他平台在广告中加入"立即购买"按钮,使用户能立刻购买广告商品。现在就断定有多少消费者愿意使用这样的方便消费还为时过早,但未来可预见的是,社交平台将通过提供持续消费服务中获得更多广告收入,这些持续消费服务为用户提供更多的服务,并且提高用户的平台使用时间。

为了尽可能通过社交媒体精准定位目标受众,广告公司放手改变策略。取消通过电视、广播、平面及户外传播的单一粗放的信息,广告公司制作同一主题下不同变体的创意形式,来适应各种消费群体,这种定制推送使消费者更愿意做出回应。上个月,美国家装零售商洛斯在脸书上发布广告,根据用户在社交媒体上提到房子的不同部分来推送不同形式的广告创意。

数字营销的迭代性质意味着广告公司和公关公司要做大量工作。然而,食品制造商雀巢的皮特·布莱克肖说到,雇用他们的品牌必须衡量社交媒体个性化带来的"成本产出平衡,可以进行大量定位。"

市场主管也要尽力给出品牌的"线上个性"。在推特上,品牌宣扬正宗和聪明。2013年,苹果推出金色 iPhone,一家名为丹尼的连锁餐厅略带嘲讽地推出煎饼照片,他们的煎饼"一直是金色的",消费者接受度很好。

然而,试图跟进社会化媒体潮流,公司也很容易失败。冷冻披萨狄吉诺注意,到很多人在推特上使用"为何停留"的标签,并在他们为披萨停留时发出滑稽的鸣叫。结果却是该评论主题是关于家庭暴力以及为什么妇女仍然留在虐待关系中。狄吉诺这次因道歉又上了社交媒体。

即便有如此的陷阱,社交平台仍倾向于获得更多的营销预算。但是数字媒体公司仍很年轻且不稳定,很难预测哪个社交网络能与美国四大广播电视网络抗衡。目前看来,推特是广告主的选择;最近推特收到管理营业额及用户增长放缓的困扰。现在脸书在营销界受到追捧:宣称用户数是推特的近 5 倍,收入是推特的 9 倍。脸书并购了几个初创的社交媒体服务商,如照片墙,这是一款照片分享和消息应用程序;WhatsApp,这几个社交媒体都可能成长为脸书的对手。照片墙谨慎推出广告来看用户的反应,WhatsApp 还没开始推广告。

一些传统媒体还没感受到广告费流向新媒体所带来的痛苦。到目前为止,电视广告仍保持增长。但是随着时间的推移,电视观众减少,转到像网飞公司之类的广告服务商,竞争将更加激烈。电视广告主倾向于转投社交媒体,但社交媒体还没找出能替代视频广告的形式。2012 年,推特推出"Vine",它可以让大家录制 6 秒视频;几个月前,推特的一款叫潜望镜的直播视频应用程序风靡一时。广告主尝试这两种服务平台,但还没有决定最终采用哪个营销媒介。

因为在数字广告中有先发优势,对营销人员来说,尝试新的服务仍至关重要。通用电气公司市场主管琳达·鲍夫解释说,由于用户还未对营销信息产生抗体,率先使用新平台的品牌获益更多。

最新受到营销关注的社交平台是一种消息应用,如色拉布(Snapchat)、微信和基克(Kik),年轻的用户可以通过这些应用将信息、照片和视频直接发送给朋友。品牌也开始与品趣志(Pinterest)合作,在品趣志上,用户可以锁定他们感兴趣的图片。用户愿意购买他们锁定图片的产品似乎是个合理的假设,尽管这个拥有 7000 万用户的平台或许永远也达不到推特的量级(3 亿),更不用说脸书(1.5 亿)

即使营销人员可以精明且无误的运用社会化媒体,将多少广告转投社会化媒体平台仍需有个限制。电视广告将简单信息传递给大众的作用仍然非常大。平面广告增加品牌的可信度(我们这样说,对吧?)就像基金经理一样,广告主总是寻求平衡的投资组合。

第 2 篇

SWOT 分析法经典案例

案例一:沃尔玛(Wal-Mart)SWOT 分析

优势
- 沃尔玛是著名的零售商品牌,它以物美价廉、货物繁多和一站式购物而闻名。
- 沃尔玛的销售额在近年内有明显增长,并且在全球化的范围内进行扩张。(例如,它收购了英国的零售商 ASDA)
- 沃尔玛的一个核心竞争力是由先进的信息技术所支持的国际化物流系统。例如,在该系统支持下,可以清晰地看到每一件商品在全国范围内的每一间卖场的运输、销售、储存等物流信息。信息技术同时也加强了沃尔玛高效的采购过程。
- 沃尔玛的一个焦点战略是人力资源的开发和管理。优秀的人才是沃尔玛在商业上成功的关键因素,为此,沃尔玛投入时间和金钱对优秀员工进行培训并建立忠诚度。

劣势
- 沃尔玛建立了世界上最大的零售帝国。尽管它在信息技术上拥有优势,但因为其巨大的业务领域,这可能导致对某些领域的控制力不够强。
- 因为沃尔玛的商品涵盖了服装、食品等多个部门,它可能在适应性上比起更加专注于某一领域的竞争对手存在劣势。
- 该公司是全球化的,但是目前只开拓了少数几个国家的市场。

机遇
- 采取收购、合并或者战略联盟的方式与其他国际零售商合作,专注于欧洲或者中国等特定市场。
- 沃尔玛的卖场当前只开设在少数几个国家内。因此,拓展市场(如中国、印度)可以带来大量的机会。
- 沃尔玛可以通过新的商场地点和商场形式来获得市场开发的机会。更接近消费者的商场和建立在购物中心内部的商店可以使过去仅仅是大型超市的经营方式变得多样化。
- 沃尔玛的机会存在于对现有大型超市战略的坚持。

威胁
- 沃尔玛在零售业的领头羊地位使其成为所有竞争对手的赶超目标。
- 沃尔玛的全球化战略使其可能在其业务国家遇到政治上的问题。
- 多种消费品的成本趋向下降,原因是制造成本的降低。造成制造成本降低的主要原因是生产外包向了世界上的低成本地区。这导致了价格竞争,并在一些领域内造成了通货紧缩。恶性价格竞争是一个威胁。

案例二: 星巴克(Starbucks) SWOT 分析

优势

- 星巴克公司是一个盈利能力很强的组织,它在 2004 年的盈利超过六亿美元。同年该公司所产生的收入超过 50 亿美元。
- 通过提供声誉良好的产品和服务,它已经成长为一个全球性的咖啡品牌。它在全世界的 40 个主要国家已经有了大约 9000 个咖啡店。
- 2005 年,星巴克被评为《财富》最佳雇主 100 强公司之一。星巴克重视员工,被认为是一个值得尊敬的雇主。
- 该组织具有很强的道德价值观念和道德使命,"星巴克致力于做行业的佼佼者"。

劣势

- 星巴克在新产品开发和创造享有盛誉。然而,随着时间的推移,其创新仍有容易受到动摇可能。
- 它对于美国市场的依存度过高,超过四分之三的咖啡店都开在自己的老家。 有人认为它需要寻求一个投资组合的国家,用来分散经营风险。
- 该组织依赖于一个主要的竞争优势,即零售咖啡。 这可能使它在进入其他相关领域的时候行动缓慢。

机遇

- 星巴克非常善于利用机遇。
- 2004 年,公司和惠普共同创建了 CD 刻录服务,在美国加州圣莫尼卡咖啡馆,顾客可以制作他们自己的音乐 CD 。
- 在它的咖啡店里提供新的产品和服务,如平价产品。
- 该公司有机会扩大其全球业务。新的咖啡市场在如印度和太平洋地区的国家都开始出现。
- 在打造与其他厂商的食物和饮料的共同品牌,品牌特许经营权的制造商的其他商品和服务都具有潜力。

威胁

- 谁知道未来咖啡市场会增长并且保有客户,还是新品种饮料或休闲活动会出现从而取代咖啡?
- 星巴克面对着咖啡原料和乳制品成本上升的局面。
- 由于其概念被市场认可,在 1971 年西雅图,星巴克的成功吸引许多竞争对手纷纷进入市场或复制品牌,从而构成潜在威胁。

"星巴克的使命是使星巴克成为世界上最优秀的咖啡,在增长的同时继续我们不妥协的原则。"

第十章 新经济和新业务

课文

电子商务技术和电子商务介绍

电子商务技术的好处

互联网已经改变了世界的运作方式,你的公司可以利用此技术优势,为其自身谋取利益。电子商务是通过网上交换数据或信息接收订单、订货或与自己的员工进行互动,根据网上电子商务业务实现资源优化。通过了解电子商务技术的好处,你的公司可以更好地利用互联网作为一个商业工具。

每个人都是平等的

当你用电子商务与客户或供应商互动,一般很难向他们描述你的业务到底有多大。只要有一个专业开发和维护网站,任何小企业在网上也会像那些大公司一样令人印象深刻。这个公平竞争的环境会为小型企业创造机会。

订单录入

一个网上订单的界面直接连接进入你的实时库存软件,能让客户每周 7 天,一天 24 小时从你的公司订购产品。通过开放网站订单输入部分,客户可以下小额订单,有些客户一年只下几次单。这样你可以省去雇用销售人员的费用。这使销售人员有时间出去寻找新业务。

客户服务

电子商务可以在客户服务方面为你省钱。通过互联网你的提供的信息,客户可以查看自己的账户。通过创建网站客服部,客户可以要求退货授权,你可以在增加客户服务水平的同时降低经营成本。

营销

2010 年第一季度,根据安东·贡萨尔维斯在 informationweek.com 网站所写,消费者在网上购买了价值 340 亿美元的产品和服务,同时产生了 1 兆 1000 亿的在线广告。越来越多的消费者使用互联网获取产品信息、寻找供应商和购买产品。电子商务的出现可以帮助贵公司与正在增加的零售部门的联系。

电子商务的优点

互联网已经为无数新的商业机会开启了一扇大门。电子商务企业和他们的客户发现与实体店不同的网上交易的优势。如果你正想启动电子商务或在你现有的业务中加入一个网上组件,你会发现一些电子商务提供的好处。

成本有效的营销

有了电子商务，你所有的营销努力都是为了驱动目标流量流向您的网站。在一个集中的地方向客户发送你的电子商务网站。它允许你使用许多在线营销策略包括电子邮件营销、文章营销、社交媒体网络和电子通讯。大多数在线营销成本很低或免费，所以电子商务可以是极具成本效益的营销策略。

灵活的工作时间

根据电子商务教育，基于地理位置的业务打破了时间上的障碍。因为互联网是可以一周7天，一天24小时在线，你的企业永远不会关闭。电子商务在你熟睡时也可以赚钱。

消除了地域的界限

电子商务还可以拓展你的范围。电子商务可以到达地球各个角落的客户。只要有互联网连接，你可以接触到客户并向他们推销你的产品或服务。

降低交易成本

运行一个在线业务降低了每次交易的成本，因为它需要较少的人力完成在线交易。一旦你建立和运行网站，客户在线下订单，从而不需要销售人员。客户通过在线支付处理软件或系统付款，这又不再需要店员。有人下载订单和装运，这个人也许是你，但一个电子商务交易成本对企业负担少，使每个交易比实体店更符合成本效益。

低间接成本

经营电子商务会削减或消除大部分店面成本。电子商务比实体店在手机花费上更少，租金和水电费更低。电子商务也减少支付给员工的成本，因为网站在营业时间不需要别人。一些电子商务企业不需要任何额外的空间，可以在已经支付租金或抵押贷款支付的房子里。库存可能不是问题，因为可以建立一个代销直供模式，批发商可以代表你发货。

电子商务或电子商业模式

- 企业对企业(B2B)
- 企业对消费者(B2C)
- 消费者对消费者(C2C)
- 消费者对企业(C2B)
- 企业对政府(B2G)
- 政府对企业(G2B)
- 政府对公民(G2C)

拓展阅读

第1篇

阿里巴巴加快支付游戏，支付宝在欧洲推出

支付宝是由阿里巴巴附属蚂蚁金融公司经营的支付应用，继其在亚洲广泛地推出之后，

将在欧洲推出。中国游客今后可以在国外进行支付。

该应用程序将识别中国的支付宝用户在欧洲的地址，将发送就餐、优惠购物和景点通知。该应用上也有用户评论。用户想要支付单的话，只要让商家扫描用户手机上的条形码就可以了。

支付宝是中国最大的支付服务，与腾讯的微信支付竞争。支付宝已经深入中国消费者的生活。人们不管是乘车还是在餐馆就餐，购物都用它来支付。

公司称，阿里巴巴希望其活跃的支付宝用户，现在总人数为4亿5000万，将继续在国外使用这个应用程序，公司就能争取到越来越多在国外消费的中国游客。

"在未来的五到十年，不仅在中国，其他国家也一样，预计目标是二十亿人使用支付宝。"支付宝国际主席塞布丽娜·彭，在星期二哥本哈根的 Money2020 会议上告诉美国全国广播公司财经频道记者。

合作伙伴关系的关键

根据世界旅游业理事会提供的数据，中国游客去年出国花费 2150 亿美元，2014 年以来上升了 53%。支付宝希望这些大部分的支出都通过使用其应用程序。

蚂蚁金融向全国广播公司财经频道表示，去年有1亿2000万用户在国外全球范围里使用支付宝，现在每天处理1亿7000万笔交易。

支付宝最近这些年一直在中国之外发展。阿里巴巴和蚂蚁金融去年加大了在印度支付公司 Paytm 的投资，希望能够打入印度市场。彭透露给全国广播公司财经频道记者，公司积极在亚洲寻找更多的合作伙伴以开拓更广阔的市场。

但该公司不计划对欧洲的支付公司投入巨资。蚂蚁金融正在和一些合作伙伴谈，从欧洲各地的金融机构到餐馆和剧院，让它们都能接受支付宝。商家通过支付宝界面将能够查看中国消费者在他们商店的购物习惯。

去年，它与德国银行软件公司 Wirecard 达成协议，让商家通过使用 Wirecard 销售点终端接受中国游客使用支付宝。

为了让商家通过支付宝报价和交易，伙伴关系对平台来说将是关键。支付宝并没有直接与三星支付和苹果支付等这类软件竞争。因为这两种只允许人们用自己的手机购买物品。相反，关注商家使用支付宝有助于市场了解客户并学习客户行为，蚂蚁金融把它作为推动收入的一个工具。

"商家不会着急寻找另一个支付方案。他们想要的是更多的业务。我们不是支付服务，我们要的更多。支付是圈中非常关键的部分，它不只是这个圈的一部分，"彭告诉全国广播公司财经频道。"对商人来讲，都是同样的故事，他们想了解中国的消费者，亚洲的消费者，日本的，韩国的，印度的，但是他们对海外客户一无所知，因为他们缺乏一个平台。这就是我们正在做的事情：把消费者和商家联系在一起，让他们更好地联系。"

彭承认，考虑到公司想要的客户规模，寻找当地的合作伙伴是"有挑战性"。中国消费者从夏天开始，将能够在英国、德国、法国和意大利使用支付宝。

第 2 篇

印度现金紧缺电商开卖"现金"

数百万印度人为了取现金而大排长龙,为此,一家电子商务公司开始提供现金快递上门服务。

出现这一现象是因为六周前,印度政府突然取缔了 500 和 1000 卢比纸币,使该国 86%的现金消失,人们因此很难获取现金来满足日常开销。

Snapdeal 是印度最大的在线零售商之一,该公司出售的商品已有数百种,如今又新增了卢比纸币。用户可在 Snapdeal 送货员携带的机器上刷借记卡来购买最多 2000 卢比(30 美元)现金,并支付 1 卢比佣金。

这一试点计划已于周四在古尔冈和班加罗尔推行。Snapdeal 使用的现金是该公司通过货到付款方式收到的,这种网购商品支付方式在印度非常流行。

该公司一位发言人告诉有线电视新闻网财经频道,他们已经收到了"金额巨大"的现金购买请求,但他拒绝透露确切的数字。

许多印度人已经转而使用电子支付方式,但有些人却别无选择,只能花上数小时在银行或自动取款机前排队等候。据估计,印度 90%的日常交易都是用现金进行。对于这样一个国家来说,远离纸币的转变是一项艰巨的任务。

Snapdeal 的计划是为解决现金短缺问题而发明最新变通方案。一些银行已经推出了自助取款机公交车,人们甚至可以在一家公司雇用帮手为自己排队。

Snapdeal 联合创始人罗希特•班萨尔在一份声明中说:"推出现金快递服务旨在进一步帮助我们的消费者克服他们目前可能面临的现金紧缺问题,满足消费者的日常生活需求。"

该公司表示,他们计划在未来几周内将现金快递服务扩展至印度其他城市。

第十一章 跨国企业

课文

总部位于美国的跨国公司——沃尔玛

沃尔玛的简介

跨国企业是指在本国以外的至少一个国家拥有设施和其他资产。这样的企业在不同的国家设有办公地点或工厂,通常都有一个中央集权的总部,用以协调全球管理。几乎所有主要的跨国企业不是美国、日本的,就是西欧国家的,例如耐克、可口可乐、沃尔玛、美国在线、东芝、本田和宝马。

沃尔玛是总部位于美国的跨国零售企业,经营连锁的特大型超市、折扣百货商店和杂货店。山姆·沃尔顿于1962年创建这家企业，总部设于阿肯色州的本顿维尔。截至2016年9月30日，沃尔玛在28个国家的63个品牌下拥有11573家分店和会员商店。

根据2016年《财富》世界500强排行榜，沃尔玛是全球最大的盈利性公司，也是拥有220万员工的世界最大的私营雇主。沃尔玛是一个家族企业，因为这家公司被沃尔顿家族所控制。山姆·沃尔顿的继承人通过他们的持股公司(沃尔顿企业有限公司)和个人股份，拥有超过50%的沃尔玛股份。沃尔玛还是全世界市场价值最高的公司和全美国最大的食品零售商。2016年，沃尔玛销售收入(共计4786.14亿美元)中的62.3%来自其在美国本土的经营。

沃尔玛在北美以外的投资喜忧参半，其在英国、南美和中国的经营获得了极大的成功，而在德国和韩国的投资则失败了。

就我们所知，沃尔玛今日的成就源于山姆·沃尔顿追求最大价值和最好客户服务的目标。被大家所熟知的"山姆先生"坚信服务领导力。这种"真正的领导力依赖于自愿服务"的信念是沃尔玛的创建原则，也是过去50年公司的决策原则。因此，沃尔玛大部分的历史都与山姆·沃尔顿本人紧密联系在一起，公司的未来也是植根于山姆先生的管理理念之上的。

通往沃尔玛之路

1918年，山姆·沃尔顿出生于俄克拉荷马州的金菲舍。1924年，在他24岁那年，他参军了。1943年，他与海伦·罗伯森结婚。1945年，从军队退役后，山姆和海伦搬到爱荷华州，然后又到了阿肯色州的纽波特。在这段时间里，山姆获得早期的零售经验，最终开起了他自己的食品杂货店。

1950年，沃尔顿一家离开纽波特前往本顿维尔，在那里，山姆在市中心的广场开了沃尔顿的五元十元店。他们之所以选择本顿维尔，是因为海伦想过小镇生活，而这个小镇又处于四个州交界处，山姆可以在不同的打猎季狩猎。

1962年，受到早期廉价商店成功经验的启发，山姆在44岁时于阿肯色州的罗杰斯开办了第一家沃尔玛，为他的客户带来更多的机会和价值。

改变零售业的"样子"

山姆的竞争者认为，"一个成功的企业可以建立在提供低价产品和优质服务的基础上"这种理念是不会奏效的。结果出人意料，这家公司的成功甚至超出了山姆的预期。1970年，这家公司公开上市，所获得的收益为其稳定的扩张提供了资金。山姆认为，沃尔玛的快速发展不仅仅是低价格吸引了顾客，主要还是归功于他的同事们。他依赖他们为顾客提供优质的购物体验，这种体验使得顾客不断地回来购物。山姆以一种行业里前所未闻的方式与同事们分享他对企业发展的远见。他让他们成为企业成功发展的合伙人，并坚信这种合伙关系是沃尔玛成功的秘诀。

商店数量持续增加，山姆的期望也随之增加。除了给零售带来新的方式和技术以外，他还尝试新的商店模式——包括山姆会员商店和沃尔玛超级购物中心，甚至决定将沃尔玛引入墨西哥。山姆无惧提供低价格并让利于美国的顾客，除此之外，他还为公司设定了一个使之存活至今的标准。他对服务的强有力承诺和帮助人们、企业和国家成功的价值观，为他赢得了1992年布什总统颁发的总统自由勋章。今天，"为顾客省钱，从而让他们生活得更好"是我们做的每一件事背后的驱动力。

天天低价策略

天天低价是我们的基本策略，我们最关注的就是价格。现今的顾客都寻求我们提供的一站式购物所带来的便利。从食品、娱乐到体育用品，我们提供顾客们喜欢的各种产品，不管他们是在 Walmart.com 上购物，通过我们的手机 APP 购物，还是在我们的商店里购物。我们现在在美国有三种主要的商店模式，每一种都是根据附近社区的特点量身定制的。

我们的商店

沃尔玛在 50 个州和波多黎各，以低价格提供最广泛种类的产品，经营模式多样，包括超级购物中心、折扣商店和社区超市。

沃尔玛超级购物中心

沃尔玛于 1988 年开始创建超级购物中心，大约 182000 平方英尺，雇用 300 名员工。沃尔玛超级购物中心通过将食品和生鲜产品、烘焙食品、熟食、乳制品、电子产品、服装、玩具、家具陈设等商品结合起来，为顾客提供一站式的购物体验。大多数的超级购物中心是 24 小时营业的，还可能设有一些特殊的商店，比如，银行、理发店、美甲沙龙、餐厅或影视中心。

拓展阅读

第 1 篇

美国汉堡快餐连锁企业——麦当劳

麦当劳是美国汉堡快餐连锁集团。今天，麦当劳是世界最大的餐厅连锁企业之一，每天在 119 个国家的 36615 家门店为大约 6800 万顾客服务。麦当劳主要销售汉堡、芝士堡、鸡肉产品、炸薯条、肉卷、早餐、软饮料、奶昔还有甜品。为了迎合消费者的口味，公司扩展了菜单，还提供沙拉、鱼、冰沙和水果。一家麦当劳餐厅是由加盟商、分公司经营或由公司自主经营的。麦当劳公司的收入来源于租赁、品牌使用费和加盟商支付的费用，以及公司自主经营餐厅的销售收入。根据 2012 年英国广播公司的报道，麦当劳是世界上第二大私营雇主，有 150 万员工为其连锁餐厅工作(仅次于沃尔玛的 190 万员工)。

麦当劳的历史

1917 年，15 岁的雷·克洛克谎报年龄，加入红十字会，当了一名救护车司机，但是战争在他完成培训之前就结束了。之后，他从事了钢琴演奏师、纸杯销售员和多功能奶昔搅拌器销售员等工作。1954 年，他参观了加州圣博娜迪诺一个购买过多功能奶昔搅拌器的餐厅。在那里，他发现了一家规模小却很成功的餐厅，这家餐厅是由迪克·麦当劳和麦克·麦当劳兄弟经营的，他们的操作效率使他震惊。他们提供的菜单范围有限，只有几种菜品——汉堡、薯条和饮料——这样他们才能专注于质量和快速的服务。

当时他们在寻找一个新的代理商，克洛克看到了一个机会。1955 年，他成立了麦当劳系统公司，这是麦当劳公司的前身，六年后他买下了麦当劳这个名字的专利权。到 1958 年，麦当劳已卖出了它的第一百万个汉堡。

雷·克洛克想建立一个餐厅系统——以始终如一地提供高质量食品和采用标准烹饪方法而闻名的系统。他希望其所提供的汉堡、圆形小面包、薯条和饮料在阿拉斯加和阿拉巴马的味道是一样的。为了实现此目标，他选择了一条独特的道路：说服加盟商和供货商相信他的愿景，不是为麦当劳而工作，而是与麦当劳一起，为他们自己工作。他提出了一个口号："为你自己做生意，而不是独自做生意。"他的经营哲学是建立在简单的"三腿凳"原则上的，一条腿是麦当劳的加盟商；第二条腿是麦当劳的供货商；第三条腿是麦当劳的员工。只有这三条腿形成支柱，这张凳子才能牢固。

质量的根基

麦当劳对质量的热切追求意味着每一种原料都是经过测试、品尝、完善以适应操作系统的。克洛克分享他对麦当劳未来的愿景，向早期的供货商推销企业的未来。他们信任他，餐厅就迅速发展起来了。

雷·克洛克再次寻找合伙人，他设法创造食品服务业最有融合性、最有效率、最有创新力的供应系统。与供应商的这些关系几十年以来都非常融洽。实际上，今天麦当劳的许多供应商是自从与雷·克洛克合作后，才开始创业的。

麦当劳的国际连锁

麦当劳是全球领先的食品服务业零售商，在100个国家拥有超过36000家门店。全世界超过80%的麦当劳餐厅由当地的独立商人所拥有和经营。

公司中的这种强大联盟，即它的加盟商和供应商(统称为系统)，是麦当劳长期繁荣发展的关键。利用我们的系统，我们可以识别、实现和衡量那些满足顾客多变的需求和偏好的想法。另外，我们的商业模式使得麦当劳能够持续不断地向顾客传递与当地相关的餐厅经营经验，并成为我们所服务社区不可或缺的一部分。

麦当劳的商业模式

我们的加盟商、供应商和员工精诚合作，实现共同的目标，就是这种力量使麦当劳成为世界领先快餐品牌。

- 加盟商将企业精神和承诺带给社区。
- 供应商致力于提供最高级别的质量和安全保障。
- 公司促进超过36000家餐厅的学习与分享。

麦当劳的企业管理

麦当劳的成功是建立在诚信基础上的。全世界数亿人信任麦当劳。我们每天提供安全的食物，尊重我们的顾客和雇员，提供优质的质量、服务、清洁与价值，从而获得了信任。

麦当劳董事会受委托以一种诚实、公平、勤勉、道德的方式监管公司。董事会一直以来相信，好的公司管理对于实现公司股东所赋予的责任来说至关重要。我们将继续做这一领域的领导者。

麦当劳董事会相信，好的管理是一场长途旅行，而不是一个终点。因此，我们坚持至少每年检验一次我们的管理原则，以维持长期的发展。但是，有一件事不会变，那就是我们承诺，在与麦当劳系统中的利益相关者进行交易时，保证诚信。

第 2 篇

丰田和铃木的联盟标志着汽车工业为生存而战

丰田汽车公司预见到技术革命会震撼汽车工业,严重威胁它的生存,因此,这个世界上最有价值的汽车制造商将考虑与其在日本的一个最强有力的对手合作。

尽管历史上曾经有过失败的联盟,为了拓展丰田和铃木之间的合作,丰田公司的领头人丰田章男和铃木公司的领头人铃木修,希望两个公司能紧密联系在一起。两家公司会忽略丰田与特斯拉汽车公司之间的短暂合作,以及铃木与德国大众汽车公司由于在电气化和自动驾驶领域的技术革新需要巨大的资金支持而导致的合作关系破裂。

60 岁的丰田章男周三在东京的新闻发布会上说:"丰田真的并不擅长创建联盟,而且在过去,一直一门心思扑在满足我们自己的基本生产需要上。但是,周边的环境正在发生剧烈的变化,为了生存,我们必须有能力去应对这些变化。"

丰田章男和 80 岁的铃木修说,他们上周开始相互沟通,慢慢地考虑可能的资本联盟。尽管两位还没有决定联合研究和开发的具体领域,但是很明确的是,哪家公司会在这一点上获利最多。总部位于日本丰田市的丰田已经在这一财年做出 10700 亿日元(103 亿美元)的预算,超过铃木计划的研发支出的七倍。

占据印度市场

铃木提到台面上的是在印度市场的领先地位。马鲁蒂-铃木印度有限公司已经以廉价车型 Alto 和 Swift 长期占据市场。尽管丰田已经引入预算车型(如紧凑型 Etios),在上一财年,其市场份额仍然低于马鲁蒂-铃木所达到的 47%。

"在汽车工业中发生着巨大的变化,在那种情况下,我们必须分享资源,否则我们将无法生存。"铃木修说,"那是促成这个提议的主要原因。"

丰田今年早些时候完成了对大发汽车有限公司的收购,其主要责任更多是为母公司在新兴市场开发紧凑车型。大发公司在日本小型车市场的首要竞争者是总部位于滨松的铃木。

在日本的合作

与铃木的联盟会促进丰田与日本的轿车和货车制造商的大量合作。丰田方面称,去年其扩大了与马自达汽车公司的技术共享。丰田是日野汽车有限公司的第一大股东,斯巴鲁富士重工业公司的最大股东,并在五十铃汽车有限公司拥有股份。另外,丰田还在许多汽车配件供应商中拥有股份,这些供应商生产从发动机到汽车座椅等一系列汽车配件。

迫于压力,汽车制造商们正在建立产业合作关系,努力减少自己造成的污染丑闻带来的影响。三菱汽车公司在几十年前做的燃料燃烧效率的不恰当测试,导致其向日产汽车公司求救,而大众公司已经划拨了 180 亿欧元(199 亿美元)来处理因使用软件操纵柴油发动机在排放测试中作弊而带来的不良后果。

日产公司计划购买三菱公司的股份,两家公司原先已经是日本小型车的合作伙伴,计划的目的是在东南亚获得更稳固的市场地位。在东南亚市场,丰田公司占据着统治性的地位。

就在大众公司的排放丑闻爆出之前,这家德国汽车制造商结束了与铃木长达几年的合作,原因是无法开展一个单一的联合项目。同时，近两年，丰田已经逐渐减少与特斯拉合作开发的 RAV4 EV(一种电动运动型多用途车)的销售。

SBI 证券有限公司的汽车分析师远藤浩二说："在研发领域的竞争是非常，非常激烈的。"他说，在电气化、自动驾驶和其他领域，铃木落后于其同行。"如果不与大型汽车制造商合作，他们想继续待在竞争队伍中是比较困难的。"

第十二章 会 计

课文

什么是会计？

什么是会计？

会计是对与企业相关的财务往来进行系统、全面的记录，它还涉及向监管机构和税务部门总结、分析和报告这些财务往来。会计是几乎任何一个企业的关键功能之一；在小型公司，它可能由一位记账员兼会计处理，在大型公司，它可能由相当大的财务部门来处理。会计，被称为"企业的语言"，衡量一个组织经济活动的结果，向一系列使用者传递这一信息，这些使用者包括投资者、债权人、管理层和监管者。会计从业人员被称为"会计师"。会计可以分为几个领域，包括财务会计、管理会计、外部审计和税务会计等。会计信息系统是用以支持会计功能和相关活动的。

细分"会计"

会计报告是由各种会计核算汇集而来的，例如成本会计和管理会计，这对于帮助管理层做出明智的商业决策来说，是非常宝贵的。尽管记账员可以行使基本的会计职能，但是高等级的会计业务通常由具有以下资质的会计处理，如美国的注册会计师、加拿大的特许会计师、注册会计师或注册管理会计师。

创建会计报表

财务报表总结一定时期内，一家大公司的运营、财务状况和现金流，是建立在成千上万的财务往来基础上的简要报表。因此，所有会计专业资质都是经过多年的学习和严格的考试，并且拥有最低年限的会计实践经验才能获得的。

公认会计原则

会计工作由会计组织(如标准制定者、会计事务所和专业机构)完成。财务报表通常由会计事务所进行审计，并且根据公认会计原则进行编制。在大多数情况下，会计师使用公认会计原则(GAAP)编制财务报表。公认会计原则是一系列与资产负债表的确定、已发行股票的计算以及其他会计事宜相关的标准。此标准基于复式记账法制定，复式记账法是指公司的每一项费用或收入都以相等金额记入资产负债表中的两个相关账户中，做等额双重记录。

复式记账法的例子

为了说明复式记账法，请设想一家公司向一个客户开具一张发票。会计师使用复式记账法在应收账款项目中记入贷方，在资产负债表的收入项目中记入借方。如果是客户支付发票款项，会计师在应收账款中记入借方，在收入项目中记入贷方。复式记账也被称为平衡账簿，因为所有的会计科目都必须相互平衡。如果会计科目不平衡，会计师就会知道总账肯定有哪里出错了。

财务会计与管理会计

财务会计是指会计师编制公司年度会计报表的过程。财务会计的工作重点是向外部使用者(如投资者、监管者和供应商)报告组织的财务信息。管理会计也是进行类似的工作程序，但利用信息的方式则有所不同。管理会计的工作重点是评估、分析和报告信息，帮助管理层做出决策，实现组织目标。也就是说，在管理会计中，会计师每月或每季度编制报告，以便企业管理层做出经营管理决策。

财务会计与成本会计

就如管理会计帮助企业做出管理决策一样，成本会计帮助企业做出成本决策。基本上，成本会计考虑的是与生产产品有关的一切成本。分析师、管理人员、企业业主和会计师利用这些信息来决定他们的产品成本。在成本会计中，钱款是生产中的经济因素，而在财务会计中，钱款用以衡量一个企业的经济业绩。

税务会计

美国的税务会计重点在于对税务支出和税务申报的准备、分析和说明。美国的税务系统要求使用特定的税收会计原则，这些原则可以与财务会计中运用的公认会计原则不同。美国税收法规定了四种基本的企业所有方式：独资企业、合伙企业、股份有限公司和责任有限公司。企业和个人的收入按不同的税率征收，税率因收入水平的不同而变化，且都包括边际税率(每增加一美元收入增加的税)和平均税率(按总收入的一定比例设置)。

会计信息系统

在计算机会计软件的帮助下，许多会计实务已经被简化。企业资源计划系统(ERP)通常被运用于大型组织，它提供了广泛的、集中化的、完整的信息来源，企业可以使用这些信息来管理从采购、生产到人力资源等的所有主要业务流程。会计信息系统减少了累积、储存、报告管理会计信息的成本，实现了将所有系统的数据都存入一个更详细的账户。

拓展阅读

第 1 篇

管理会计信息

管理会计是一系列实践操作与技术，其目的在于为管理人员提供财务信息，帮助他们做出决策，保持对公司资源的有效控制。组织中履行管理会计职责的专业人员主要实现两大目标。首先，他们编制有关成本控制以及企业运营计划与控制的常规信息报告。其次，管理会计师为管理人员编制用于做出战略和战术决策的特殊报告，例如产品或服务的定价、主打产品或非主打产品的选择、机器设备的投资、总体政策的制定和长期计划等决策。

管理会计信息针对的是内部管理人员和决策者。它的预期用途是提供与管理运营有关的财务数据，以帮助管理管理人员做出合理的经营决策。管理会计信息的主要形式有财务比率、预算预测、差异分析和成本会计。没有管理会计，管理层所做出的决策风险大且缺乏科学性。

预测

所有企业都必须做出战略性计划以保持竞争力。这种对未来运营的计划过程则需要用到预测。预测的目的是通过趋势分析预测未来运营的结果。趋势分析计入过去的收益、销售和增长等数据，并将这些运算计到未来周期中。如果每年的平均收益增长达到了10%，那么预测模型将使用每年10%的增长率。

预算

预测过程会为企业建立一个有关预期收益数据的模型。一旦这个预测模型建立了，预算程序就启动了。预算程序分配资本——也就是钱——给未来的运营，估算未来成本和负债。这些以美元计价的数额源于对过去债务和成本趋势的分析。如果材料的成本每年增长都达到20%的平均值，那么这相同的20%将被用于创建下一年的预算。这个预算模型将考虑到现有的资金和预计的销售收入。

差异分析和成本会计

差异分析是比较实际费用和预算费用的过程。如果纠正是有必要的话，任何差异都要经过检验和纠正。这可能包括人工时长、机器使用时长、原材料消耗和生产时间，其中还有其他的输入因素。所有这些因素可能影响公司的预算，并最终影响公司的盈利能力。例如，如果一个产品的生产要比预算多花20%的人工时长，那么劳动力成本就会超过预算。这个例子对于以上提到的许多不同的输入因素都适用。超过预算公差的差异，必须立即纠正。但是，如果一个正面的差异出现，那么就可以用于抵消负面差异或提高生产力，从而提高运营的边际利润。正面差异的例子有：当生产一个产品的人工时长少于预算20%时，结果便是减少了20%的劳动力成本。

比率分析

比率分析是在每个会计周期结束时完成的——每月、每季度、每年——以决定公司偿还长期和短期债务的能力。这些比率说明了一个企业的偿还能力和资产折现力。这种比率分析工具用于确定企业库存和原材料是否得到有效利用，并告诉管理团队，公司是否在提高盈利能力的总体方针下运营。其他比率分析可以确定应收账款收账期是多长，以及是否维持适当的库存水平。

为决策而进行的会计工作

管理会计是利用所有可获得的会计数据进行更好的经营决策的过程——根据趋势、事实、计划做出的可靠决策。这些决策对于任何公司的未来都是至关重要的。有效的管理会计排除了决策过程中的很多风险，使决策更多地建立在事实基础上。当然，经营过程中的财务风险总是存在的。分析过去的趋势可以使未来更加清晰。

第2篇

一项会计规则的变化会破坏就业吗？

美国和国际会计委员会提出改变企业经营性租赁的记账方式。经营性租赁类似于长期租赁，但不改变财产或设备的所有权。尽管这项改变何时生效尚未确定，国会议员们(包括共和党和民主党)、商会和全国的房地产专业人士都积极地开展活动抵制这项提案。反对者声称，改变企业使用的会计规则可能会"破坏"高达330万的就业机会，并且会致使年平均家庭收入每年减少超过1000美元。

会计规则的改变对经济会产生实质性的影响，也进一步提醒投资者他们是否需要企业报告更具有实质性的信息或以一种更清晰的形式呈现现有的信息。实际上，经营性租赁记账方式的改变是要求公开那些目前没有记入资产负债表的项目，将它们更清楚地呈现出来。

两种类型的租赁

在现有规则下，企业必须把资本租赁(承租的主体于支付租金后可获取厂房或设备的所有权)和经营性租赁(只是为了短期使用，不取得所有权)区别开来。

资本租赁目前在企业的资产负债表中有体现，既作为一项资产——其价值是产生收益——又作为一项负债——一项持续支付给资产所有者的债务。另一方面，经营性租赁目前并没有体现在资产负债表中。在支付租金时，它们作为租赁费用呈现在企业的收益表中。但是，关于使用者的经营性租赁合同的其他重要细节仅在财务报表的附注中有记录。

提出的这项会计规则要求，超过一年以上的经营性租赁像资本租赁一样呈现出来，就像资产负债表中的资产和负债一样。因此，租赁的资产会增加，但它们负债也会增加。

这项新的会计规则受到投资者和美国证券交易委员会的支持，其目的是促使资产负债表更全面、信息量更大。企业中有着各种经营性租赁和资本租赁的组合，这项新规则也会提高财务报表的可比较性，使得出租人、投资者和监管者能更容易地评估企业相关的财务实力。

批评家们的看法

他们的争论源于一项预测，这项新的会计原则将引起美国公开上市公司的资产负债表增加15 000亿美元的负债。也就是这些公司现有负债增加1.2%。

负债的增加会减少受影响公司的流动资产与负债的比率。反对者们声称，负债率是银行和其他信贷提供者衡量企业财务实力的关键指标。流动资产或现金流量与债务的比率的减少会被借贷者视为信用质量的下降，即便企业真实的财务状况并未改变——因为租赁一直存在，只是记账方式不同而已。

为了使负债率恢复从前的水平(明显令人满意的水平)，企业会被迫减少支出，那很有可能意味着裁员。同时，降低的信用质量会增加借贷成本，进一步减少开展经营活动的能力。最终，为了应对会计规则的改变，企业的运营反应就会是减少雇用员工，许多人的收入会减少，商业地产的租赁价格也会下降。

258

不会那么快

这种说法并不完全有说服力，因为它假设的是对现有会计制度的未知影响，以及人们会如何应对这种改变。实际上，这项提案的预计影响是非常不确定的，也取决于其是建立在何种假设上的。到底有多么不确定？根据所选的假设，预计的就业损失范围从 190 000 美元到 3 300 000 美元不等，年家庭收入的减少量可能低至 68 美元，高至 1180 美元。这种范围包含了极其高的数字，也包含几乎接近 0 的数字。

参 考 文 献

1. Lehman, Lee & Xu. Insurance Law of the People's Republic of China, 1995.
2. Thomas JE. (2002).The role and powers of the Chinese insurance regulatory commission in the administration of insurance law in China.Geneva Papers on Risk and Insurance.
3. Insurance Information Institute. "Business insurance information. What does a businessowners policy cover?". Retrieved 2007-05-09.
4. Federal Trade Credit-Based Insurance Scores: Impacts on Consumers of Automobile Insurance. , 2007).
5. 刘胜军. 现代会计与财务管理专业英语. [M]. 哈尔滨：哈尔滨工程大学出版社. 2007.
6. 李昌麒. 经济法学. [M]. 北京：中国政法大学出版社，2011.
7. 张昌宋. 英语阅读技巧与训练[M] . 北京：机械工业出版社，2005.
8. 温倩，贺欣. 会计审计专业英语[M]. 北京：机械工业出版社，2008.
9. https://en.wikipedia.org/.
10. http://www.chinadaily.com.cn/business/2017-03/17/content_28596217.htm.
11. http://www.insurancejournal.com/news/national/2015/10/23/385779.htm.
12. http://corporate.walmart.com/.
13. https://en.wikipedia.org/wiki/Walmart#Chile.
14. https://www.mcdonalds.com/us/en-us.html.
15. http://www.japantimes.co.jp/news/2016/10/13/business/corporate-business/toyota-suzuki-allia.
16. http://www.investopedia.com/terms/a/accounting.asp.
17. https://en.wikipedia.org/wiki/Accounting.
18. http://www.ehow.com/about_5452762_management-accounting-information.html.
19. http://www.referenceforbusiness.com/encyclopedia/Man-Mix/Managerial-Accounting.html.
20. https://www.weforum.org/agenda/2015/01/could-an-accounting-change-destroy-jobs/.
21. http://www.24en.com.
22. http://www.hjenglish.com.
23. https://www.thedevco.com/free-resources/twelve-tips-for-becoming-a-successful-manager/
24. http://www.docin.com/p-497329677.html
25. http://www.360doc.com/content/16/0307/22/31364794_540336589.shtml
26. http://www.insurancejournal.com/news/national/2015/10/23/385779.htm
27. www. Chinadaily.com.cn
28. http://www.answers.com/Q/Explain_the_Importance_of_international_financial_management
29. http://www.cnbc.com/2016/04/05/alipay-to-launch-in-europe-as-alibaba-steps-up-payments-game.html
30. https://en.wikipedia.org/wiki/Financial_market
31. http://www.investopedia.com/articles/basics/11/how-to-pick-a-stock.asp
32. http://www.kekenet.com/read/201507/385251.shtml
33. http://www.financialexpress.com/industry/banking-finance/mobile-banking-a-platform-for-engagement
34. https://en.wikipedia.org/wiki/Banking_in_China
35. https://wenku.baidu.com/view/2be3c4a70029bd64783e2c33.html
36. http://www.linkedin.com/pulse/mobile-banking-platform-customer-engagement-puneet-chhahira?trk=pulse-det-nav_art
37. http://m.kekenet.com/read/201403/278218.shtml

北京大学出版社第六事业部高职高专经管系列教材目录

书　名	书　号	主　编	定　价
财经法规与会计职业道德	978-7-301-26948-0	胡玲玲，等	35.00
财经英语阅读（第2版）	978-7-301-28943-3	朱　琳	42.00
公共关系实务（第2版）	978-7-301-25190-4	李　东，等	32.00
管理心理学	978-7-301-23314-6	蒋爱先，等	31.00
管理学实务教程（第2版）	978-7-301-28657-9	杨清华	35.00
管理学原理与应用（第2版）	978-7-301-27349-4	秦　虹	33.00
经济法原理与实务（第2版）	978-7-301-26098-2	柳国华	38.00
经济学基础	978-7-301-22536-3	王　平	32.00
经济学基础	978-7-301-21034-5	陈守强	34.00
人力资源管理实务（第2版）	978-7-301-25680-0	赵国忻，等	31.00
Excel在财务和管理中的应用（第2版）	978-7-301-28433-9	陈跃安，等	35.00
财务管理（第2版）	978-7-301-25725-8	翟其红	35.00
财务管理	978-7-301-17843-0	林　琳，等	35.00
财务管理实务教程	978-7-301-21945-4	包忠明，等	30.00
财务会计	978-7-301-20951-6	张严心，等	32.00
财务会计实务	978-7-301-22005-4	管玲芳	36.00
成本会计	978-7-301-21561-6	潘素琼	27.00
成本会计（第2版）	978-7-301-26207-8	平　音，等	30.00
成本会计实务	978-7-301-19308-2	王书果，等	36.00
初级会计实务	978-7-301-23586-7	史新浩，等	40.00
初级会计实务学习指南	978-7-301-23511-9	史新浩，等	30.00
管理会计	978-7-301-22822-7	王红珠，等	34.00
会计电算化技能实训	978-7-301-23966-7	李　焱	40.00
会计电算化项目教程（即将第2版）	978-7-301-22104-4	亓文会，等	34.00
会计基本技能	978-7-5655-0067-1	高东升，等	26.00
会计基础实务	978-7-301-21145-8	刘素菊，等	27.00
会计基础实训（第2版）	978-7-301-28318-9	刘春才	30.00
基础会计教程与实训（第3版）	978-7-301-27309-8	李　洁，等	34.00
基础会计实务	978-7-301-23843-1	郭武燕	30.00
基础会计实训教程	978-7-301-27730-0	张同法，边建文	33.00
企业会计基础	978-7-301-20460-3	徐炳炎	33.00
税务会计实用教程	978-7-301-26295-5	周常青，等	37.00
商务统计实务（即将第2版）	978-7-301-21293-6	陈晔武	29.00
审计实务	978-7-301-25971-9	涂申清	37.00
审计业务实训教程	978-7-301-18480-6	涂申清	35.00
实用统计基础与案例（第2版）	978-7-301-27286-2	黄彬红	38.00
统计基础理论与实务	978-7-301-22862-3	康燕燕，等	34.00
统计学原理	978-7-301-21924-9	吴思莹，等	36.00
预算会计	978-7-301-20440-5	冯　萍	39.00

书　名	书　号	主　编	定　价
中小企业财务管理教程	978-7-301-19936-7	周　兵	28.00
个人理财规划实务	978-7-301-26669-4	王建花，等	33.00
保险实务（即将第2版）	978-7-301-20952-3	朱丽莎	30.00
货币银行学	978-7-301-21181-6	王　菲，等	37.00
纳税申报与筹划（即将第2版）	978-7-301-20921-9	李英艳，等	38.00
企业纳税计算与申报	978-7-301-21327-8	傅凤阳	30.00
企业纳税与筹划实务	978-7-301-20193-0	郭武燕	38.00
商业银行会计实务	978-7-301-21132-8	王启姣	35.00
商业银行经营管理	978-7-301-21294-3	胡良琼，等	27.00
商业银行综合柜台业务（即将第2版）	978-7-301-23146-3	曹俊勇，等	30.00
税务代理实务	978-7-301-22848-7	侯荣新，等	34.00
新编纳税筹划	978-7-301-22770-1	李　丹	30.00
报关实务（第2版）	978-7-301-28785-9	橐云婷，等	35.00
报关与报检实务（即将第2版）	978-7-301-16612-3	农晓丹	37.00
报检报关业务	978-7-301-28281-6	姜　维	38.00
国际海上货运代理实务	978-7-301-22629-2	肖　旭	27.00
国际金融	978-7-301-21097-0	张艳清	26.00
国际金融实务（即将第2版）	978-7-301-21813-6	付玉丹	36.00
国际贸易结算	978-7-301-20980-6	罗俊勤	31.00
国际贸易实务	978-7-301-22739-8	刘笑诵	33.00
国际贸易实务	978-7-301-20929-5	夏新燕	30.00
国际贸易实务（第2版）	978-7-301-26328-0	刘　慧，等	30.00
国际贸易实务	978-7-301-19393-8	李湘滇，等	34.00
国际贸易实务	978-7-301-16838-7	尚　洁，等	26.00
国际贸易实务操作	978-7-301-19962-6	王言炉，等	37.00
国际贸易与国际金融教程（即将第2版）	978-7-301-22738-1	蒋　晶，等	31.00
国际商务单证	978-7-301-20974-5	刘　慧，等	29.00
国际商务谈判（第2版）	978-7-301-19705-9	刘金波，等	35.00
国际市场营销项目教程	978-7-301-21724-5	李湘滇	38.00
国际投资	978-7-301-21041-3	高田歌	33.00
互联网贸易实务	978-7-301-23297-2	符静波	37.00
商务谈判	978-7-301-23296-5	吴湘频	35.00
商务谈判（第2版）	978-7-301-28734-7	祝拥军	30.00
商务谈判实训	978-7-301-22628-5	夏美英，等	23.00
商务英语学习情境教程	978-7-301-18626-8	孙晓娟	27.00
外贸英语函电	978-7-301-21847-1	倪　华	28.00
外贸综合业务项目教程	978-7-301-24070-0	李浩妍	38.00
新编外贸单证实务	978-7-301-21048-2	柳国华	30.00
ERP沙盘模拟实训教程	978-7-301-22697-1	钮立新	25.00
连锁经营与管理（第2版）	978-7-301-26213-9	宋之苓	39.00
连锁门店管理实务	978-7-301-23347-4	姜义平，等	36.00

书　名	书　号	主　编	定　价
连锁门店开发与设计	978-7-301-23770-0	马凤棋	34.00
连锁门店主管岗位操作实务	978-7-301-26640-3	吴　哲	35.00
连锁企业促销技巧	978-7-301-27350-0	李　英，等	25.00
秘书与人力资源管理	978-7-301-21298-1	肖云林，等	25.00
企业管理实务	978-7-301-20657-7	关善勇	28.00
企业经营 ERP 沙盘实训教程	978-7-301-21723-8	葛颖波，等	29.00
企业经营管理模拟训练（含记录手册）	978-7-301-21033-8	叶　萍，等	29.00
企业行政工作实训	978-7-301-23105-0	楼淑君	32.00
企业行政管理（第2版）	978-7-301-27962-5	张秋垫	31.00
商务沟通实务（第2版）	978-7-301-25684-8	郑兰先，等	36.00
商务礼仪	978-7-5655-0176-0	金丽娟	29.00
推销与洽谈	978-7-301-21278-3	岳贤平	25.00
现代企业管理（第2版）	978-7-301-24054-0	刘　磊	35.00
职场沟通实务（第2版）	978-7-301-27307-4	吕宏程，等	32.00
中小企业管理（第3版）	978-7-301-25016-7	吕宏程，等	38.00
采购管理实务（第2版）	978-7-301-17917-8	李方峻	30.00
采购实务（第2版）	978-7-301-27931-1	罗振华，等	36.00
采购与仓储管理实务（第2版）	978-7-301-28697-5	耿　波	37.00
采购与供应管理实务（即将第2版）	978-7-301-19968-8	熊　伟，等	36.00
采购作业与管理实务	978-7-301-22035-1	李陶然	30.00
仓储管理实务（第2版）	978-7-301-25328-1	李怀湘	37.00
仓储配送技术与实务	978-7-301-22673-5	张建奇	38.00
仓储与配送管理（第2版）	978-7-301-24598-9	吉　亮	36.00
仓储与配送管理实务（第2版）	978-7-301-24597-2	李陶然	37.00
仓储与配送管理实训教程（第2版）	978-7-301-24283-4	杨叶勇，等	35.00
仓储与配送管理项目式教程	978-7-301-20656-0	王　瑜	38.00
第三方物流综合运营（第2版）	978-7-301-27150-6	施学良，高晓英	33.00
电子商务物流基础与实训（第2版）	978-7-301-24034-2	邓之宏	33.00
供应链管理（第2版）	978-7-301-26290-0	李陶然	33.00
进出口商品通关	978-7-301-23079-4	王　巾，等	25.00
企业物流管理（第2版）	978-7-301-28569-5	傅莉萍	39.00
物流案例与实训（第2版）	978-7-301-24372-5	申纲领	35.00
物流成本管理	978-7-301-20880-9	傅莉萍，等	28.00
物流成本实务	978-7-301-27487-3	吉　亮	34.00
物流经济地理（即将第2版）	978-7-301-21963-8	葛颖波，等	29.00
物流商品养护技术（第2版）	978-7-301-27961-8	李燕东	30.00
物流设施与设备	978-7-301-22823-4	傅莉萍，等	28.00
物流市场营销	978-7-301-21249-3	张　勤	36.00
物流信息技术与应用（第2版）	978-7-301-24080-9	谢金龙，等	34.00
物流信息系统	978-7-81117-827-2	傅莉萍	40.00
物流营销管理	978-7-81117-949-1	李小叶	36.00

书　名	书　号	主　编	定　价
物流运输管理（第2版）	978-7-301-24971-0	申纲领	35.00
物流运输实务（第2版）	978-7-301-26165-1	黄　河	38.00
物流专业英语（第2版）	978-7-301-27881-9	仲　颖，等	34.00
现代生产运作管理实务	978-7-301-17980-2	李陶然	39.00
现代物流管理（第2版）	978-7-301-26482-9	申纲领	38.00
现代物流概论（即将第2版）	978-7-301-20922-6	钮立新	39.00
现代物流基础	978-7-301-23501-0	张建奇	32.00
物流基础理论与技能	978-7-301-25697-8	周晓利	33.00
新编仓储与配送实务	978-7-301-23594-2	傅莉萍	32.00
药品物流基础	978-7-301-22863-0	钟秀英	30.00
运输管理项目式教程（第2版）	978-7-301-24241-4	钮立新	32.00
运输组织与管理项目式教程（即将第2版）	978-7-301-21946-1	苏玲利	26.00
运输管理实务	978-7-301-22824-1	黄友文	32.00
国际货运代理实务	978-7-301-21968-3	张建奇	38.00
生产型企业物流运营实务	978-7-301-24159-2	陈鸿雁	38.00
电子商务实用教程	978-7-301-18513-1	卢忠敏，等	33.00
电子商务项目式教程	978-7-301-20976-9	胡　雷	25.00
电子商务英语（第2版）	978-7-301-24585-9	陈晓鸣，等	27.00
广告实务	978-7-301-21207-3	夏美英	29.00
市场调查与统计（第2版）	978-7-301-28116-1	陈惠源	30.00
市场调查与预测	978-7-301-23505-8	王水清	34.00
市场调查与预测	978-7-301-19904-6	熊衍红	31.00
市场营销策划（即将第2版）	978-7-301-22384-0	冯志强	36.00
市场营销项目驱动教程（即将第2版）	978-7-301-20750-5	肖　飞	34.00
市场营销学	978-7-301-22046-7	饶国霞，等	33.00
网络营销理论与实务	978-7-301-26257-3	纪幼玲	35.00
现代推销技术	978-7-301-20088-9	尤凤翔，等	32.00
消费心理与行为分析（第2版）	978-7-301-27781-2	王水清，等	36.00
营销策划（第2版）	978-7-301-25682-4	许建民	36.00
营销渠道开发与管理（第2版）	978-7-301-26403-4	王水清	38.00
创业实务	978-7-301-27293-0	施让龙	30.00

　　如您需要更多教学资源如电子课件、电子样章、习题答案等，请登录北京大学出版社第六事业部官网www.pup6.cn 搜索下载。

　　如您需要浏览更多专业教材，请扫下面的二维码，关注北京大学出版社第六事业部官方微信（微信号：pup6book），随时查询专业教材、浏览教材目录、内容简介等信息，并可在线申请纸质样书用于教学。

　　感谢您使用我们的教材，欢迎您随时与我们联系，我们将及时做好全方位的服务。联系方式：010-62750667，sywat716@126.com，pup_6@163.com，lihu80@163.com，欢迎来电来信。客户服务QQ号：1292552107，欢迎随时咨询。